Ecocomposition

*Theoretical and
Pedagogical Approaches*

Edited by

Christian R. Weisser
and
Sidney I. Dobrin

State University of New York Press

Published by
State University of New York Press, Albany

© 2001 State University of New York

For information, address State University of New York Press,
90 State Street, Suite 700, Albany, N.Y. 12207

Production by Michael Haggett
Marketing by Michael Campochiaro

Library of Congress Cataloging-in-Publication Data

Ecocomposition : theoretical and pedagogical approaches / edited by Christian
Weisser and Sidney I. Dobrin.
    p. cm.
    Includes index.
    ISBN 0-7914-4939-4 (alk. paper)—ISBN 0-7914-4940-8 (pbk. : alk. paper)
    1. English language—Rhetoric—Study and teaching. 2. Environmental litera-
ture—Authorship—Study and teaching. 3. Ecology—Authorship—Study and
teaching. 4. Interdisciplinary approach in education. 5. Academic writing—
Study and teaching. 6. Nature—Study and teaching. I. Weisser, Christian, 1970-
II. Dobrin, Sidney I., 1967-

PE1404 .E27 2001
808 ' .042 ' 071—dc21
                                                            00-055621

10 9 8 7 6 5 4 3 2 1

Ecocomposition

To Traci, who has been there through it all.

———————

This one's for Adam, Ben, and Sara.

Contents

Acknowledgments

We would like to thank the contributors for their efforts in putting this book together. We are also grateful to the reviewers who offered suggestions for revisions during early drafts of this book. We are especially grateful to our friend Sofie for her patience. We would like to offer special gratitude to Priscilla Ross, Jennie Doling, Michael Haggett, Michael Campochiaro and State University of New York Press for their help and continued support of this project.

The cover artwork is taken from a drawing by student artist Tiffany Fisher of Ephrata High School in Lancaster County, Pennsylvania. It is particularly appropriate that this collection's cover should bear the image of a frog as frogs are regarded as indicator species of most ecosystems. That is to say, if change is beginning to occur in a particular place, frogs are the first organism to show indication of those changes. Ecocomposition offers potential change in composition studies. This collection is an indication of that change. Ribbet.

Foreword: The Truth Is Out There

Marilyn M. Cooper
Michigan Technological University
Houghton, Michigan

I have to confess that I feel a certain ambivalence about the notion of eco-composition. Perusing the essays in this collection, it dawned on me that it is the same ambivalence I feel toward "The X-Files." In both cases, much in sympathy with what I see as the underlying worldview—the centrality of systems thinking in ecocomposition; an Heideggerian *unheimlichkeit* in "The X-Files"—but nervous about appropriations of both that seek to reject rather than embrace that worldview, which reduces ecocomposition to a matter of teaching nature writing and *unheimlichkeit* to a paranoia focused on government conspiracies. My doubts about whether or not I should re-ally like "The X-Files," however, are more serious (and more unresolved) than my feelings about ecocomposition, especially as represented in this col-lection of diverse and creative works. For the most part, the authors of these essays strive to articulate a systems approach to teaching writing, only occa-sionally slipping into the binary language of nature versus culture. My desire in this foreword is to support this emphasis by suggesting that it is through an ecological understanding of writing that the field of composition studies aligns itself with the dominant paradigm shift of the last century.

As Christian R. Weisser and Sidney I. Dobrin say in the introduction, "ecocomposition is about relationships," (9), and it is the understanding of relationships, rather than the analysis of properties of entities, which underlies the cultural transformation that can be traced to the physics and philosophy of the 1920s. Fritjof Capra identifies systems thinking as beginning in physics, developing through the life sciences, and spreading to "the larger social arena" (5); he explains:

> The great shock of twentieth-century science has been that systems cannot be understood by analysis. The properties of the parts are not intrinsic properties but can be understood only within the context of the larger whole. . . . What we call a part is merely a pattern in an inseparable web of relationships. Therefore the shift from the parts to the whole can also be seen as a shift from objects to relationships. . . . In the mechanistic view the world is a collection of objects. These, of course, interact with one another, and hence there are relationships among them. But the relationships are secondary. . . . In the systems view we realize that the objects themselves are networks of relationships, embedded in larger networks. For the systems thinker the relationships are primary. (29, 37)

Capra rejects analysis because of its implications of division into parts, with the parts then being broken down into further parts, each part characterized by its inherent properties. Analysis destroys relationships, which must be understood as wholes, and even more so as dynamic, changing patterns, rather than as discrete objects (or subjects and objects) acting on each other.

This shift from analyzing objects and their relations to understanding relationships as dynamic patterns is pervasive throughout academic disciplines and in the culture at large: we recognize it in such diverse sites as the shift in biology from the study of the characteristics of the individual organism to the functioning of a biome; the shift from a Daltonian chemistry of matter to the geochemical study of cycles of carbon or calcium; Martin Heidegger's attempt to shift the basis of knowledge from subjects acting on objects to a preontological being-in-the-world; the shift from a modernist unitary code of ethics to a postmodern morality realized in the responsibility for others; the shift in writing pedagogy from a focus on the characteristics of good writing (product) to the interrelated processes that constitute writing; and even, in the world of figure skating, Michelle Kwan's oft-repeated interview comment that the process is more important than the result.

But despite the seeming breadth of this cultural transformation, the paradigm shift, at least in composition studies, is still struggling to happen. Thomas Kent's call for a "postprocess" pedagogy, like Sharon Crowley's observation that the process movement was a continuation of current-traditional pedagogy, is a recognition which, in large measure, that composition studies still clings to a mechanistic rather than a systems view of writing. Fifteen years ago, I wrote about the ecology of writing:

> all the characteristics of any individual writer or piece of writing both determine and are determined by the characteristics of all the other writers and writings in the systems. An important characteristic of ecological systems is that they are inherently dynamic; though their structures and contents can be specified at a given moment, in real time they are constantly changing, limited only by parameters that are themselves subject to change over longer spans of time. (7)

From my perspective now, I only dimly understood what I was saying then. I had read Wittgenstein, so I understood that meaning was generated in use, but I hadn't read Heidegger, and I didn't fully understand that that meant that meaning was mostly not conscious, not intentional, not under our individual or collective control, but grew out of our ways of life. Hubert L. Dreyfus explains that Heidegger rejects both intention and convention as the basis of meaning in favor of our situatedness in the world:

> For Heidegger, like Wittgenstein, meaning is grounded neither in some mental reality nor in an arbitrary decision, but is based upon a form of life in which we necessarily dwell, and which, therefore, is neither immediately given nor merely a matter of choice. (201)

Similarly, I thought I understood that relationships were primary in biomes, but in biomes it is easy to see organisms interrelating rather than focusing on the relationships themselves. When I read Bill Green's book on Antarctic lakes I understood better how relationships could be primary. Commenting that "only the pattern remains, only the name. . . . Even the pattern changes" (45), he traces the cycle of calcium through the world:

> Water works into stone like a plant's root hair, pries and etches and corrodes, beckons what ions will come to come. And calcium, more often than not, does, leaving the rock to its own devices, pitted and honeycombed and collapsing to soil, turning to clay. This is happening every second of every day, on every ridge, in every swale and farm field, this silent, unnoticed release by

which the world is undone and remade, undone and remade, in the same breath. (68)

He continues:

> Even more important in the marine chapter of calcium is the coccolithophore, the single-celled photosynthetic plant that is believed to be the most prolific of the calcite-producing organisms. Armored in plates and ovals, which are themselves nuanced arrays of calcite and trace organics, coccolithophores bob like buoys in the bottle green of the sea and fix at their protoplasmic center wind-mixed molecules of carbon dioxide. Then, in the hidden exchange of green plants, they transform those molecules in a pierced instant to living matter and to molecular oxygen. In this way, over the vastness of the sea, dissolved calcium becomes calcite, and oxygen is set free. Water turns to stone and the atmosphere is renewed. (73)

Had I read this story of unceasing transformation, I might have written more about the changing patterns in the systems of writing and less about the structures and contents of the systems; had I read Green's musings over "these cycles of matter we cannot control, which pass through us, which link us irretrievably to all that is" (204), I would not have seen writing as so different from breathing. I know that when I wrote that essay I did, as Christian Weisser (and Killingsworth and Krajicek) says, see an ecology of writing as a metaphor: at least, I remember very clearly reading it over some years after it was published and realizing that the systems that constitute writing and writers are not just *like* ecological systems but are precisely ecological systems, and that there are no boundaries between writing and the other interlocked, cycling systems of our world.

In *Ecocomposition* the ecology of writing is envisioned more clearly than I saw it in 1986, but it is still a struggle to see relationships as primary, rather than focusing on—especially on—the human actors relating to human and nonhuman others, and even harder to see writing as part of a whole, interrelated, ceaselessly changing environment rather than as a social system through which humans act on and make conscious choices about the nonsocial other system, the natural environment. The editors boldly claim that "all of the many projects housed within rhetoric and composition are already ecological" (Dobrin, 20), and that our identities are "always already ecological; we are who we are as a result of the people, places, things, animals, and plants that have touched our lives" (Weisser,

131). Many of the essays in this collection expand on this vision. Anis Bawarshi sees genres as environments, and although he argues that as rhetorical beings we are different from animals, it is a distinction without a difference, for rhetoric/writing is simply one way we deal with the world, as he later explains:

> Writing is not only about learning to adapt, socially and rhetorically, to various situations via genres; it is also about reproducing these various situations via genres. Writing is not simply something we do somewhere; it is something that we are—not a tool, really, but a way of being in the world in a particular time and place in relation to others" (78).

Bradley John Monsma, engaging his students in the genre of university naturalist web writing, envisions how the genre could reproduce itself across successive classes and, as it gains enough critical mass to be noticed, could reproduce the situation in which paying attention to the natural history of a campus becomes part of normal discourse and decision making (281). Monsma also explains how language, rather than setting us apart from other animals, links us to the rest of the world: "If we understand the body not as a protective shell but as the means by which we meet that which is other than human, then we can also understand embodied language as one of our links to the environment in which we breathe, speak, and write" (288).

Many of the writers here emphasize that the natural environment is not separate from human culture. Sidney I. Dobrin notes how in Florida the wild and development, and the real and the spectacle, are so enmeshed that "Boundaries blend here; separating the place from the writing, from the teaching, from the living is impossible." (16). Arlene Plevin uses the concept of place to expand the notion of environment:

> To move place forward in our studies, to add it to race, gender, and class, is to recognize more fully that place is not just about environmental destruction, but is, in part, how we live in relation to other cultures, discourses, and species. In many respects, this move releases the environment from the background and expands it: it is no longer merely setting. (150)

Paul Lindholdt also offers *locophilia* (place-relatedness) as an antidote to the cognitive barriers that humanism has erected between us and the natural world, and Edward Lotto ascribes the notion "that nature is

somehow outside human intellectual constructs" (358) to natural realism. Mark C. Long explains quite precisely the pedagogical problem with
seeing nature as separate in an ecocomposition course:

> the working definition of environment guiding the field of envi-
> ronmental education conflates the inclusive term environment
> with the exclusive term "nature." Working within the limited
> conceptual framework of this definition, the environmental edu-
> cator understands human beings and their culture as apart from
> the natural world. In practice, this reductive definition leads envi-
> ronmental educators to lead the ritual pilgrimage of students
> from the "isolated indoor practices" of the traditional classroom
> with the intent of reconnecting students to the natural world. . . .
> However with notable exceptions, the ritual of retreat to nature in
> the writing course simply leads most students nowhere. (133)

In his course, he hopes for his students to "take responsibility for their
place in the environment of the college or the university," and he argues
that "it is only by expanding the term environment to encompass more
than discerned landscapes . . . that more students will begin to find reasons
to take their relation to their environment seriously." (135).

Indeed, as two of the essays in this collection vividly demonstrate, the
most valorized forms of ecological writing—the narrative of retreat into
unspoiled nature and the preservationist arguments of deep ecology—may
be the least effective readings in an ecocomposition course, for they are
both grounded in a mechanistic view in which nature is seen as separate
from human culture and as an object to be contemplated or saved by a
controlling, dominating subject. Observing that none of the African-
American students in his class chose to write retreat narratives, Christopher J. Keller notes that "Cultural, social, and discursive constructions of
nature tend to exclude African Americans and other peoples of color"
(195), that "hegemonic structures present nature as a place where white
people leisure away happily and black people toil away grimly" (195).
Though he argues that retreat narratives are not simply playful and
leisurely, he notes that it is "a genre that is often not taken seriously" and
thus not likely to be attractive to African-American students who quite
reasonably strive "to prove their texts' legitimacy as well as their own
voices' worth" in their writing (195).

In one of the most fascinating essays in this collection, M. Jimmie
Killingsworth and John Krajicek explain how "nature writing as it has become canonized, largely in the woodsy and wordy tradition of Thoreau"

(43) excludes not only people of color, and they suggest that the rhetoric of deep ecology tends toward an ironic contemplation of the ignorance of most of the population: "You and I can see how stupid and misguided they are. It's up to us to save the world" (45). This is not only an essentially conservative rhetoric that "suggests elitism and projects a 'Mandarin-like disdain' for the mass of humanity" (46, quoting Aune), but also one that rejects an ecological (i.e., systems view) approach in which human culture is recognized as ineluctably part of the environment and questions of environmental racism and justice cannot be avoided. I agree with Killingsworth and Krajicek in applauding deep ecologists for arguing against an androcentric notion of ecology, but deep ecologists' vision of saving the wilderness is often simply a reverse image of the technological mind-set that sees all of nature (including humans) as a "standing reserve" (Heidegger); both mechanistically oppose nature to culture and see the human actor or human culture as the controlling force.

Too often, for nature writers and for deep ecologists, the truth is out there in nature (cf. Lotto, 253), but I would argue that, as Oscar Wilde said of Wordsworth, they "only discover in [nature] what they bring to her"; the sermons they find in the stones are the ones they have already hidden there. Instead of learning from nature how all things are tied together in the web of life, they seek to impose their own private and preferred vision of pristine wilderness, attributing an intrinsic meaning and value to nature untrammeled by human culture. Ecological balance has nothing to do with ideals, but refers to the inexorable patterns that form in response to changes in the web of life. The paradigm shift Capra traces through physics and the life sciences can also be traced to Heidegger's phenomenology, and in this foreword I have been drawing on both strands to argue that an ecological approach demands that we give up working on the world and instead understand how we work with it. Working with the world does not mean relinquishing responsibility, as Dreyfus explains: for Heidegger, "giving up the hope for ultimate or intrinsic meaning lets [one] see and appreciate relative meaning"; rather than paralyzing one into inactivity, it instead enables authentic action, action located in the immediate situation. Dreyfus notes how "our authentic athlete"—I think again of Kwan—

> can therefore pursue sports without worry, enjoy success without fear of being crushed by defeat, accept a broken leg without grief, and indifferent to what one would normally do, [s]he can find convalescing, if that is the immediate task the Situation imposes, as meaningful (i.e., meaningless) as winning a world championship.

Indifferent to [her] desires and to making sense of convalescing as one normally does, e.g. as a reason to feel sorry for oneself or as an obstacle to getting back to pursuing one's life-goal, [s]he can take up [her] new facticity in a nonnormal way as an exciting new opportunity. [According to Heidegger] "The genuine individuation of the individual, determined by the moment . . . does not mean clinging obstinately to one's own private wishes but being free for the factical possibilities of current existence." Once one stops demanding meaning and imposing stereotypes, one's facticity will always provide a Situation in which there are unique possibilities for action. (323)

The truth is out there. It is out there in all of the systems, social and natural, we participate in, in our attempts to make ourselves at home in the world. It responds to our intentions and our actions, but we cannot control or construct it fully. In seeing writing as one of the ways in which we participate in the web of life, ecocomposition provides a vision of how to achieve rhetorical and political efficacy not only in environmental discourse, as Killingsworth and Krajicek call for (39), but in all discourse.

WORKS CITED

Capra, Fritjof. *The Web of Life: A New Scientific Understanding of Living Systems.* New York: Anchor Books, 1996.

Cooper, Marilyn M. "The Ecology of Writing." *Writing as Social Action,* Marilyn M. Cooper and Michael Holzman. Portsmouth, NH: Heinemann-Boynton/Cook, 1989. 1–13.

Crowley, Sharon. *Composition in the University: Historical and Polemical Essays.* Pittsburgh: University of Pittsburgh Press, 1998.

Dreyfus, Hubert L. *Being-in-the-World: A Commentary on Heidegger's* Being and Time, *Division I.* Cambridge: MIT P, 1991.

Green, Bill. *Water, Ice & Stone: Science and Memory on the Antarctic Lakes.* New York: Harmony Books, 1995.

Heidegger, Martin. "The Question Concerning Technology." *Basic Writings.* Ed. David Farrell Krell. New York: Harper, 1977. 287–317.

Kent, Thomas, ed. *Post-process Theory: New Directions for Composition Research.* Urbana: Southern Illinois University Press, 1999.

Wilde, Oscar. "The Decay of Lying: An Observation." *Literary Criticism of Oscar Wilde.* Ed. Stanley Weintraub. Lincoln: University of Nebraska Press, 1968. 165–96.

Breaking New Ground in Ecocomposition: An Introduction

Christian R. Weisser
University of Hawaii (Hilo)
Hilo, Hawaii

Sidney I. Dobrin
University of Florida
Gainesville, Florida

All thinking worthy of the name must now be ecological.
—Lewis Mumford, *The Myth of the Machine*

Recently, scholarship, research, and knowledge-making in composition studies began to redefine the discipline's boundaries in order to provide more contextual, holistic, and useful ways of examining the world of discourse. At the same time, one of the slowly developing, though crucial, trends in American universities has been toward the integration of ecological and environmental studies in academic disciplines across the spectrum. While theoretical and pedagogical studies in disciplines throughout academia have made significant inroads toward linking knowledge between the sciences and humanities, composition and rhetoric's inclusion of the "hard sciences" in its interdisciplinary agenda has been limited for the most part to cognitive psychology. True, some of the most influential and important works in composition have drawn upon works in history, philosophy, sociology, anthropology, literary criticism, and other areas of study within the humanities, but only recently have compositionists begun to significantly inquire into scientific scholarship to inform work in their own discipline. *Ecocomposition: Theoretical and Pedagogical Approaches* seeks to explore the connections between interdisciplinary inquiries of composition research and ecological studies and forwards the potential for theoretical and pedagogical work in ecocomposition. That is, this collection examines composition studies through an ecological lens to bring to the classroom, to scholarship, and to larger public audiences a critical position through which to engage the world.

Ecocomposition: Theoretical and Pedagogical Approaches examines current trends in universities toward more environmentally sound work,

1

explores the intersections between composition research—that is, discourse studies—and ecostudies, and offers possible pedagogies for the composition classroom. As the essays in this collection demonstrate, the intersections between ecotheory and composition studies in theory and pedagogy have never before been addressed in a scholarly collection in depth or in detail. This volume brings together a diverse array of prominent voices to discuss ecocomposition.

Though it may be our urge in this introduction to provide a concrete definition of *ecocomposition,* we are going to resist doing so to some degree, since the eighteen essays gathered in this collection stand as that very definition. Or, to be more accurate, they stand as the initiation of that definition; that is, we hope that these essays contribute to a larger conversation about ecocomposition. Having said that however, let us offer the premise that ecocomposition is an area of study which, at its core, places ecological thinking and composition in dialogue with one another in order to both consider the ecological properties of written discourse and the ways in which ecologies, environments, locations, places, and natures are discursively affected. That is to say, ecocomposition is about relationships; it is about the coconstitutive existence of writing and environment; it is about physical environment and constructed environment; it is about the production of written discourse and the relationship of that discourse to the places it encounters.

It seems to us that in a collection about ecocomposition, the locations from which these contributions emerge are inseparable from the very ideas that they report. These essays come from a diverse array of locations, both theoretical and physical, and these perspectives provide a variety of approaches to understanding and practicing ecocomposition. In the spirit of biodiversity, hearing from a range of scholars from a range of places is crucial to ecocomposition scholarship. Ecocomposition must be a bio-diverse discipline. The essays in this collection move toward such a diversity.

In the opening essay of the collection, "Writing Takes Place," Sid contends that composition is an ecological pursuit. He provides an initial definition of ecocomposition in light of traditional definitions of ecology and claims that ecocomposition "is the investigation of the total relations of discourse both to its organic and inorganic environment and the study of all of the complex interrelationships between the human activity of writing and all of the conditions of the struggle for existence." He then provides a rationale for why ecocomposition is critical to composition studies and extends the notion that composition is already ecological and "that writing and rhetoric cannot be separated from place, from environment, from nature, from location."

Providing more initial definitions, Derek Owens examines the concept of sustainability. He writes, "I hope it will suffice to equate sustainability with living more simply, buying less stuff, conserving and preserving limited resources, and resisting the addictions fostered within our current consumer culture." This, and his more detailed definitions are necessary as Owens claims that "Such definitions present a holistic interpretation of sustainability useful to educators who agree that we've a responsibility to invent a locally based, pedagogical ethic informed and inspired by an awareness of the need to think and act sustainably." He writes that "Given composition's access to incoming college students and its cross-disciplinary makeup, few fields might play as important a role as composition could in promoting a sustainable ethic. Those of us who teach composition and design writing programs have perhaps more responsibility than other faculty to promote sustainable thinking throughout the curriculum."

M. Jimmie Killingsworth, whose work in environmental rhetoric stands as fundamental to the evolution of ecocomposition, collaborates with John Krajicek in "Ecology, Alienation, and Literacy: Constraints and Possibilities in Ecocomposition." The authors begin by exploring some of the rhetorical stances that environmental writers might assume, and they examine the tradition in American nature writing toward alienated, individualistic perspectives as an example of the connectedness and disconnectedness that written discourse offers. Through an interesting narrative of their lives as writing teachers, both inside and outside of the classroom, Killingsworth and Krajicek make the point that writing—particularly that which locates itself within the natural world—often involves both alienation and communion. They write, "Like literacy, environmentalism could not be sustained without both alienated individuals and mass identification, indeed without a degree of alienation and identification within each individual." The movement from solitude to society and back again, they argue, "is the very motion of literacy."

Like Killingsworth and Krajicek's contribution, many of the essays in this collection focus on thinking and writing about "Natural" places; however, Julie Drew's essay focuses on the primary "place" of writing instruction—the composition classroom. She argues that compositionists might reimagine students as travelers, and by extension, we might construct a "politics of place that is more likely to include students in the academic work of composition, and less likely to continue to identify and manage students as discursive novices." Drew's innovative approach seeks to engage students in a form of discursive map-making, in which students become more responsible for identifying the various locations they inhabit, the power relations indicated by language use that reside in those locations, and the discursive conventions familiar to insiders. Drew argues that rather than envisioning students as novices in the environment of academic discourse, they might more accurately be viewed "as travelers who, to varying degrees, have arrived in a place where power relations are obscured, the discourse is unfamiliar, and the conventions are as yet unmastered."

Like Drew's notion of inhabiting discursive locations, Anis Bawarshi suggests an ecological conception of genres, arguing that they are the sites in which communicants reproduce both the habits and habitats of discourse. In other words, he contends that writers use language to construct rhetorical environments or situations in which they exist, interact with one another, and enact social actions. Bawarshi states that "genres are the rhetorical ecosystems that allow communicants to enact and reproduce various situations, social practices, relations, and identities." To emphasize the ecological nature of genres, he examines several sites of discourse— most notably, a physician's office—and highlights the ways in which this genre-constituted habitat shapes and mediates the discursive relationships therein. Bawarshi rightly urges compositionists to pay more attention to the rhetorical ecosystems within which communication and communicators take place and are made possible.

Following Drew's and Bawarshi's initial exploration of discursive sites, Christian's essay suggests that composition's conceptions of identity do not account for the degree to which various ecosystems and their inhabitants affect the discourse that individual human beings produce. He begins by tracing the recent history of composition theory to show how it has expanded to account for a greater number of influences on a writer's identity, and he goes on to argue that our conceptions of identity will remain *pre-ecological* until we begin to account for the "degree to which we orient ourselves to nonhuman others as well as to human reference groups." This move toward a more expansive conception of identity, Christian posits, allows us to envision writers and their discourse as "socially constructed and sustained in community with an enormous number of interconnected others along with their ecologies and habitats." He rightly urges us as compositionists to expand our field, and our field of vision, to include the nonhuman world in our investigations of the production of discourse and identity.

Randall Roorda, whose work in ecological literacy and nature writing has been crucial to the development of ecocomposition, begins his essay, "Great Divides: Rhetorics of Literacy and Orality," by noting the parallel development between composition and literacy studies and the "great divide" between perceptions of literacy and orality. He explores the various camps of thought regarding literacy and sketches "grounds upon which these disparate camps might agree to disagree, cognizant of points of departure in premises and argumentative procedures." Roorda couches this discussion in "claims made about literacy by environmentally oriented commentators" and indicates " respects in which those claims might be found wanting from the standpoint of many literacy professionals." Rhetorics of literacy and orality, Roorda contends, "can serve as instruments for thinking about instrumentation in thinking—one element in a more generalized critique of technology and culture from which educators cannot be excepted."

Stephen G. Brown, then, offers the Alaskan environment as "a master trope not only for indigenous identity, but for native resistance as well—resistance to neocolonial imperialism in general, and to its particular manifestation in borderland signifying practices." Brown explores the "tension between signification and a native landscape, between the colonizer's tendency to take possession through naming and the Alaskan environment's ability to elude linguistic containment" and develops "the implications of foregrounding the environment as a category of critical inquiry in Composition Studies," a category he sees as significant as the "categories of race, class, and gender that have driven so much of the discourse in the field." Brown's inquiry develops "the usefulness of the environment as a topos of inquiry for actualizing the second, and oft-neglected aspect of Freirean praxis: for translating academic analysis of oppression in its various guises into meaningful social action" and analyzes "the manner in which signification functions as a vehicle of cultural domination, deploying as an analytical tool a postcolonial reading of representation in the borderlands across a spectrum of texts."

Mark C. Long begins his essay "Education and Environmental Literacy: Reflections on Teaching Ecocomposition in Keene State College's Environmental House" with the claim that "With academic writing and critical thinking understood as a function of cultural literacy, theorists and practitioners of writing have advocated the study of cultural production, introducing students to the ideological and material forces that reflect and shape their lives. Inviting students to draw upon their personal experiences with these cultural forces, and to sharpen their skills at identifying and interpreting cultural signs, composition theorists have definitively resituated the creative acts of reading, thinking, and writing in the ever-expanding domain of political and cultural practices." Like Brown's turn to Freirean praxis, Long goes on to explain that ecocomposition has defined itself with a goal similar to Paulo Freire's "critical consciousness" and to the latter's understanding of literacy in mind. Long posits that for ecocomposition "the ambitious goal of linking academic and ecological literacy hinges, in part, on redefining the term *literacy* and then using it to address the local and global dimensions of environment problems." Long offers the theory that "the shift in emphasis from cultural to ecological literacy generates a space for the conceptual category of the environment in the composition course." He then describes two types of ecocompositions that push toward the agendas of literacy he sees as critical to ecocomposition.

Like Brown and Long, Arlene Plevin sees ecocomposition as a means through which more liberating pedagogies can be theorized and practiced. She argues that the complexity of theorizing place as a critical category as important as race, class, gender, or culture "reinvigorates composition studies by offering the additional potential for political engagement—environmental activism—a kind of activism that can be, as Freire writes in *Pedagogy of the Oppressed,* 'not pseudo-participation, but committed involvement.'" Plevin grounds her position in both Freire's work and in the writing that her own students have produced.

Greta Gaard—one of the most influential ecofeminist scholars—explores the close relationships between the important new work in ecocomposition and its indebtedness to research and activism in ecofeminism. Gaard correctly suggests that "ecocomposition and ecofeminism share many features of both process and perspective, and that ecocomposition offers a new and valuable approach to teaching not only writing but environmental ethics and social justice as well." Through her exploration of the theoretical and pedagogical intersections between ecofeminism and ecocomposition, Gaard posits that composition courses organized around these intersections have the potential to "encourage a healthy diversity of environmentalisms in the classroom and to teach students an appreciation for diversity that can prepare educated citizens to shape and participate in a multicultural, democratic, and ecological society."

Similarly, Colleen Connolly's essay explores the notion of diversity— an important topic of discussion in composition studies—through the lens of feminism. She suggests that compositionists consider a writing curriculum that "examines how our relationship to the natural world, like our relationship to each other and to the social world, is based on the values, discourses, and institutional practices that shape and maintain our realities." Interestingly, Connolly's essay offers an ecofeminist pedagogy that aims to examine and think about the discursive and cultural practices that define the relations among individuals, society, and nature— providing students with opportunities to write environmentally conscious essays.

Christopher J. Keller's "The Ecology of Writerly Voice: Authorship, Ethos, and Persona," theorizes as to why African-American students in a composition course engage nature writing differently than their white classmates. Keller's essay considers an assignment made to two sections of a composition course that provided as an option for an assignment to have students "retreat" to a natural setting and to write about that experience. Keller writes that "my intention is never to force students to visit natural places that may evoke discomfort or fear (students always have an option *not* to write the retreat narrative), but personally and pedagogically I hoped and still hope that through their writing students come to *experience, engage,* and *feel* more intimately the larger ecological web of life, in addition to becoming more aware of the current destruction and devastation of the natural world." What Keller found, however, upon receiving the final written assignments was that none of his African-American students chose the retreat option. His essay asks; "Why had most of the white students in my courses decided to write narratives of retreat while *all* the African-American students chose the assignment that let them stay away from nature and write instead about contemporary politics and issues of the environment?"

One key component of ecocomposition, as we have noted, is that it extends the boundaries of the classroom. That is, ecocomposition must include a component of activism and participation that moves beyond the classroom space. In her contribution, Annie Merrill Ingram discusses service learning as a critical facet of ecocomposition, and visa versa. She suggests that incorporating service learning into environmental writing courses is one way to extend ecocomposition, since a "service learning component benefits not only students and teacher—in terms of greater motivation, productivity, and investment in the course—but also the wider community, while broadening the scope and contribution of the class in real, tangible ways." Ingram's essay juxtaposes some insightful theoretical and pedagogical investigations of service learning in ecocomposition with an interesting narrative of one particular activity (a volunteer cleanup of a nature preserve) she used in a first-year writing course.

Like Ingram, Paul Linholdt urges us to approach ecocomposition as a form of civic participation, what he calls "applied composition," in order to make our work more meaningful and consequential. He argues that we should refigure composition in ways that "validate personal experience in our own work and in our classrooms" in order to move toward praxis and away from abstract theorizing. Linholdt suggests that to gain "greater consequentiality, the principles of rhetoric and composition need to be applied," and ecocomposition is an important arena in which this application can occur.

In "Written In Its Own Season: Nature as Ground in the Postmodern World," Edward Lotto posits that "the postmodern world seems to delight in pulling the rug out from under us, in calling into question any ground we might try to stand on." He argues that the concept of nature can serve as the kind of nonfoundational authority that postmodern theorists such as Lester Faigley and Patricia Bizzell claim are needed in order to develop a national public discourse. Lotto claims that a careful use of nature "can indeed work as a ground for thought and action both in the classroom and in the world. It can serve as a powerful authority in a world that has at least the glimmerings of an ecological ethic, and it can be used in a nonfoundational way if we use if properly."

David Thomas Sumner's essay, "Don't Forget to Argue: Problems, Possibilities, and Ecocomposition," begins with a critique of the Association for the Study of Literature and the Environment's (ASLE) on-line publication of syllabi for courses that address environmental/ecological subject matter in English classrooms. Sumner was invited to assist with the portion of the publication that addressed composition classes in particular. Sumner's essay questions the ways in which composition is incorporated into these classes. He writes that "after editing these syllabi, it became clear to me that before embarking on a project we call "ecocomposition," we first need to discuss, argue about, and explore what we mean when we use the term *composition* and the role we see composition playing at the university." Sumner's experiences with the ASLE syllabi "makes it clear that as we begin to define the field of ecocomposition, we need to not only emphasize our commitment to the more-than-human world, but, if we expect to be taken seriously, we also need to be aware of how that commitment fits into contemporary rhetoric and composition theory and practice."

Finally, Bradley John Monsma examines the relationships between a number of environments—including the composition course, the campus, and the World Wide Web—and explores the problems and possibilities of incorporating these seemingly diverse spaces. His essay explains how he "put a whole class to work at compiling a natural history of our campus in a pursuit of wisdom appropriate to our place on the border between the Verdugo Hills and urban Los Angeles." Monsma suggest that while assignments done in webbed environments certainly do not insure that students will become better writers or more ecologically conscious, it might "encourage writers to respond more readily to other writing and to changes in the world."

What we hope readers will glean from this diverse collection of articles is the array of possibilities that ecocomposition holds for composition studies. However, we do also want to be cautious in offering this want from this collection that ecocomposition not become a master narrative that proselytizes ecological thinking as somehow better or more important thinking. During State University of New York Press' initial review of this collection, one reviewer noted concern that the essays gathered here failed to pay critical attention to the overriding positions that ecological thinking, activist pedagogies, and benevolent teaching of ecological discourses strive for a position of totalizing narrative. The reviewer wrote, "The activist pedagogy seems a given here, established without the kind of inquiry directed at every other aspect of the classroom dynamic: students (Brown, Long, and Lotto), texts (Roorda and Keller), genres (Bawarshi), even the classroom itself (Drew)." We are grateful to this reviewer for leveling this important critique. It is essential that any of us working in ecocomposition studies (or any field for that matter) be willing to problematize and self-reflexively critique these initial explorations into ecocomposition. The reviewer notes that ecocomposition must be willing to consider "counter-hegemonic" arguments within ecocomposition and notes specifically Long and also Sumner's contributions as moving in such directions. Sumner, for instance, exemplifies this sort of maneuver when he writes, "we do not do justice to our role as teachers if our composition classroom turns into a cheering section for pet causes, environmental or other. Such a class may generate converts, or even enemies, but it will not provide students with the necessary critical writing and thinking skills to address the complexity of issues they will face at the academy and in life." While we don't think that our enthusiasm—and the enthusiasm of the authors gathered here—should be abandoned, we certainly agree that ecocomposition must remain self-aware and open to critique. Perhaps the continual influence of ideas, insights, and epistemologies from other disciplines—an integral aspect of ecocomposition—will help to avoid close-minded thinking or proselytizing.

As we have mentioned, this is a book about relationships and communities; the authors who have contributed to this collection hope to promote the idea that the relationships between words, thoughts, communities, and locations are significant and worthy of study by scholars and teachers of writing. In a way, this book can be seen as a small ecosystem of ideas about this very subject, a conversation that occupies a place within the larger region of composition studies, which is situated within the larger ecospheres of English studies, academia, and the Earth, respectively. This book intends to make these locations more obvious while at the same time venturing into new disciplinary, epistemological, theoretical, and pedagogical territories.

Writing Takes Place

Sidney I. Dobrin
University of Florida
Gainesville, Florida

Writing is to living as grass is to soil.
— Scott Russell Sanders, "Letter to a Reader."

[T]here's always (no matter where) place and language.
— Gary Snyder, "Cultured or Crabbed"

Context . . . 1: the parts of a discourse that surround a word or passage and can throw light on its meaning 2: the interrelated conditions in which something exists or occurs: ENVIRON-MENT.
— Webster's New Collegiate Dictionary

DEFINING ECOCOMPOSITION

For many months now I've been pondering the definition of *ecocomposition* both for this collection and for Christian's and my book *Natural Discourse: Toward Ecocomposition.* I have been considering what it means to examine ecology and writing and thinking about the ways in which the massive cultural projects of ecology and writing inform one another. I have been contemplating what it means to say that there is a relationship between nature, place, environment, habitat, location, and discourse, that rhetoric and composition and ecology might somehow be bound in their historical constructions and might somehow be productively constructed for compositionists and ecologists alike. I have been intrigued by the host of spatial and place-oriented metaphors that rhetoric and composition studies uses such as "nature of writing," "writing environment," "cyberspace," and "classroom environment." As Nedra Reynolds writes of these metaphors, they "have long dominated our written discourse in this field because, first, writing is spatial itself, or we cannot very well conceive of writing in ways other than spatial" (14). I have been examining the relationships between discourse and nature, and between writing and environment, and through the work of scholars such as M. Jimmie Killingsworth and Jaqueline S. Palmer, Marilyn M. Cooper, Carl G. Herndl, Stuart C. Brown, and Gertta Gaard, I am drawn to the notion that rhetoric and composition—the study *and* teaching of writing—is ecological.

Ernst Haeckel first defined ecology as "the total relations of the animal both to its organic and to its inorganic environment" and as "the study of all the complex interrelationships referred to by Darwin as the conditions of the struggle for existence" (quoted in Ricklefs 1). Haeckel may as well have also offered these words as the definition for contemporary rhetoric and composition studies. After all, composition and rhetoric studies in its postcognitive, postprocess, postexpressivist incarnation is also a study of relationships: between individual writers and their surrounding environments, between writers and texts, between texts and culture, between ideology and discourse, and between language and the world. And, as we now discuss it, understanding these relationships is crucial to survival. Oppressive hegemonies manifest themselves in discourse; racial, cultural, sexist, classist oppression recurs through discourse. How we transgress those oppressive constructs, how we survive in them is both a matter of discursive maneuvering and a matter of physical, material positioning, and consequence. And in my thinking about such matters, I continue to wonder why composition and rhetoric has embraced the metaphors of space and place, but has been limited in its adoption of ecological methodologies. Does our postmodern mistrust of scientific inquiry keep us from turning to the science of relationships to develop our own methodologies? Does our concentration on the human activity of language encourage us to separate our studies from the natural world? I find that ecocomposition becomes the site from which we must ask these questions, the place in which ecology and rhetoric and composition can converge to better explore the relationships between language, writing, and discourse; and between nature, place, environment, and locations. Ecocomposition draws attention to the ideas of context and social construction of identity to include physical realities of place, and of natural and constructed space, both ideological constructs that often seem ignored in favor of more conceptual ideological structures such as gender or race. When we question the construction of identity, we must include a stronger sense of physical places when we contend that identity comes from other places, that we know ourselves through the surrounding world. Ecocomposition, to paraphrase Haeckel, then, is the investigation of the total relations of discourse both to its organic and inorganic environment and to the study of all of the complex interrelationships between the human activity of writing and all of the conditions of the struggle for existence. In the pages that follow, I hope to show that rhetoric and composition is an ecological endeavor in that writing and rhetoric cannot be separated from place, from environment, from nature, or from location, and I hope to show why ecocomposition is a critical part of rhetoric and composition studies.

Quite frequently, it seems that ecocomposition, because of its emphasis upon ecology, is often identified as an environmentalist approach to composition studies, just as "ecology" is often used synonymously with "environmentalism" by the popular press. It is often assumed that ecocomposition deals solely with nature writing and with environmental rhetoric and that it addresses environmentalism as a subject. Indeed, ecocomposition has its roots in ecological methodologies and environmental concerns, but ecocomposition is an area of inquiry influenced by an array of schools of thought. It is encouraged by not just ecology and composition, but by ecocriticism, cultural studies, ecofeminism, environmental justice, conservation, service learning, race and ecoracism, public intellectualism, and a host of other critical areas of study. Primarily, however, ecocomposition is informed by rhetoric and composition. Hence the agendas of ecocomposition mirror those of composition studies in its inquiry as to the function and role of written discourse. While much of ecocomposition is informed by environmental and ecological theory and focuses on the ways in which nature gets written and mapped, part of ecocomposition must also be the study of the sites and places of writing, of discourse, of scholarship, of pedagogy. That is, ecocomposition must examine not just "natural" environments, but other environments: classroom environments, electronic, environments, writing environments, and textual environments since, as Julie Drew so rightly explains in her contribution to this collection, these are some of the many locations in which the relationships between discourse and place are highly political and in which actual learning takes place. Ecocomposition, growing from rhetoric and composition and ecology, must inquire as to the relationships between writers, writing and all places, spaces, sites, and locations. If ecocriticism is a literary criticism that focuses on textual interpretation, ecocomposition is the flip side of the same coin, concentrating on textual production and the environments that affect and are affected by the production of discourse.

Having said that however, it may actually be more useful to leave ecocomposition relatively undefined. In fact, in this collection and in other discussions of ecocomposition, what is offered in ways of definitions are not definitions, but descriptions of what we already do in rhetoric and composition studies. What we do in ecocomposition is a series of things that are already in place: feminism, pedagogy, literary criticism, ecology, conservation, stewardship, environmentalism, deep ecology, philosophy, cultural studies, race theory, service learning, public intellectualism, and so on. Ecocomposition, however, can provide insights into the relational values of written discourse; what composition does is examine the ways in which these constructs get written. If we say that ecocomposition is the study of the relationship between discourse, nature, environment, location, place, and the ways in which these categories get mapped, written, codified, defined, and in turn, the way in which nature and environment affects discourse, that is not a definition but a description. *Ecocomposition* is not a term for definition, but an inquiry for action. Just as the term *ecofeminism* was first used by Francoise d'Eaubonne in 1974 as a political call to action, so too must ecocomposition be seen as a site for the kind of activism that resists the oppression not just of nonhuman organisms and environments, but of all oppressive structures. What I am learning is that we must resist defining ecocomposition because defining suggests codification and hegemony (despite the fact that this book is published by an academic press by and for academics for extended theoretical and pedagogical work). I'm afraid of defining ecocomposition because it is all of those things I've mentioned before; ecocomposition, like rhetoric and composition, is an integrative and interdisciplinary inquiry. Part of the benefit of an interdisciplinary approach to ecological composition is that ecocomposition opens doors to sciences, to philosophy, to literature, to ecology, and the likes. In particular, ecocomposition turns to the "hard sciences" in ways that composition has been resistant in the past. For the most part, composition has only embraced the sciences through cognitive psychology, whereas ecocomposition stands to turn to science as rhetoric and to engage natural sciences and "hard" sciences in the exploration of rhetoric and writing. That is, ecocomposition extends its interdisciplinarity beyond that of rhetoric and composition in its own search for disciplinary identity. Like rhetoric and composition, ecocomposition must face an identity crisis. It must question its own definition. It must disagree with itself; it must, as any discipline must, fracture within itself as those working within ecocomposition direct their attentions toward subspecialties and disagree with one another over theory, method, and teaching. It must, as this collection attempts to do, provide diverse approaches to theories and pedagogies. Ecocomposition must grow.

WHY ECOCOMPOSITION?

Many compositionists have asked me why I concentrate on ecocomposition these days, claiming that it's only a flash in the pan fad that won't have any real impact on what we do in rhetoric and composition studies. Part of my answer has to be because all of the many projects housed within rhetoric and composition are already ecological and ecocomposition has the potential to shed light on its implications. However, what is also critically important is the place from which I examine writing, the location where I teach writing, and the environment in which I live. I agree wholeheartedly with Kenneth Burke when in *Permanence and Change: An Anatomy of Purpose* he argues that intellectual life cannot be removed from "life," from biologic, natural existence, and I extend that to argue that our academic, professional lives, cannot be separated from our daily lives, from the places we live those lives, that is, ecocomposition asks that we consider our own roles and the roles of our environments in larger systems alongside all others rather than, for instance, simply continuing the age-old practice of identifying students as objects of study as well as objects of teaching.

I write from within my home state of Florida, a state riddled with environmental problems, a place dominated by conversations of location, of the intrusion of population, of growth, and of development. I teach at a location classified as a large state institution in which students come to classrooms—sites with their own environments, their own politics, and their own ecologies (see Drew)—in order or to learn how to survive in, and manipulate other, writing environments. These sites, both "natural" and pedagogical, ecological and institutional, and constructed and contested are dictated by the same legislative body in Florida. The state legislature, the same governing body that allocates environmental legislation, names habitats, lists endangered species, and passes water rights laws, also dictates what constitutes writing pedagogy in the Florida university system. In Florida, undergraduate writing requirements are mandated statewide through a legislative act known as the "Gordon Rule." As the Department of English Handbook for New Teaching Assistants at the University of Florida explains it;

> A Gordon Rule course is one that is in accord with a Florida law passed by the Florida legislature because of the efforts of Jack Gordon, who proposed the law when he was a member of the Florida Senate. According to this law, a course will be called a Gordon Rule course if each student enrolled in it is assigned a minimum of 6000 words that receive feedback for the purposes

of revision, are graded, and give experience in different kinds of discourse (narration; comparison-contrast; casual or classificatory analysis) or discourse for different purposes (thematic analysis; interpretation).

The Gordon Rule is a horrible intrusion of legislative power into composition pedagogy; it is a state law many, myself included, detest. Yet, it is mandated through the same legislative body that dictates "environmental" legislation and influences local writing environments. In Florida, it is difficult to separate writing pedagogy from the environment because they are regulated by the same legislative body, by the same individuals, and from the same physical location. Ecocomposition connects the political and material effects of the text of legislation because it identifies location, geography, and spacial situatedness of textual production as generative.

Hence, in Florida, composition pedagogy gets written into the lives of students and teachers in the same manner that a protected habitat is mapped into the land and water. Because of excessive population growth, Florida legislation has begun to dictate which areas of land are to remain wild, natural. The Florida State Park system, for instance, has adopted the motto "Real Florida" to identify natural Florida as opposed to developed Florida. The Real Florida is advertised on highway billboards and tourist brochures as the last bastions of natural Florida. The naming of certain, fenced-off areas as "real" stands directly in opposition to all areas outside those fences that are "man-made." Housing developments, too, advertise that you can "experience the wild" in your own backyard incorporating an enmeshed notion of "wild" and "development." This rhetorical demarcation of landscape stands in opposition to other billboards that advertise the overwhelming number of tourist attractions—highlighted by Disney's prominence in the state—which promise an escape from the real into a fantasyland. Disney's new Animal Kingdom—its crowning attraction, a giant, artificial tree—blurs the boundary between the wild and the simulacrum to excessive proportions. Advertisements for "Real Florida" and fantasy Florida compete openly for the tourist dollar. The "Real Florida" is as much a tourist attraction as are the constructed representations of different nations found within the walls of Epcot—the quintessence of market multiculturalism. People flock to Florida to see The Mouse or to see an alligator or to see a manatee or to catch a fish; which one doesn't matter; each are of equal spectacle. Each earns capital. The rhetorical construction of Florida affects what my students see when they see the environment, when they consider the geographies of the real and the simulated and the reality of the simulated. Boundaries blend here; separating the place from the writing, from the teaching, from the living is impossible.[1]

The site from which I write directly affects how I write and what I write, and how I teach and what I teach. My nonacademic writing (is there such a thing?) is deeply enmeshed in the very ecological-political issues that dominate our daily lives in Florida. Like most of the contributors to this collection, I am an outdoor enthusiast. My time is spent on or in the water, in the Everglades, in the swamps, on the beaches, in the back-country, in my office, or in a classroom. I am always someplace. To deny that the experiences in natural Florida affect what I do in my professional time, in academic locations, would be remiss, just as it would be remiss to deny that my time in academic terrains affects my time in wild places. To deny that relationships exist between my life as a teacher-scholar and my relationship with Florida environments would be to deny my role in the Florida university system, to deny, in fact, the role of the university in Florida.

And, let us not forget that for those who experience Florida not first-hand, but through textual images—and even those who live or visit here—Florida is constructed and represented textually. Florida is text. Florida is sunny beaches, flamingos, oranges, and *Miami Vice*. Florida is a mythical place where panthers once roamed and where Ponce De Leon found the fountain of youth. Florida is written in news stories of murdered tourists, in stories of big drug deals, and in stories of Cuban refugees. Florida is written by Disney, by Gatorland, and by Sea World. Florida is written by television shows like *The Golden Girls,* which depicts Florida as a grand retirement village; *The X-Files,* arguably the most popular television show in the past five years, which regularly mocks everything Floridian; and lesser-known shows like *Maximum Bob,* which presents its Floridian characters as hyper-quirky weirdos. Similarly books and movies show Florida as a place of insane levels of violence, a place populated by conmen, freaks, and escapees from the asylum. I note as examples the recent films *Striptease* and *Palmetto.* Florida is written everyday in America's mass media. Florida is also written about everyday by university students. As R. C. Lewontin et al. explains, "All organisms—but especially human being[s]—are not simply the results but are also the causes of their own environments" (quoted in Cooper 368). Marilyn M. Cooper is correct to note that "systems reflect the various ways writers connect with one another through writing: through systems of ideas, of purposes, of interpretational interactions, of cultural norms, of textual forms" (369). Writers, too, reflect and connect with systems. When students write, they write about their own environments; they participate in conversations that discursively construct the text of Florida, "natural" and "man-made." And, in turn, those places reinscribe Florida, writing, and ideology on those student writers. We write our places and in turn those places write us. That is, the relationship between discourse and the construction of environment, nature, and place is a deeply enmeshed, coconstitutive relationship. It is difficult, if not impossible, to separate the writing from the place and the place form the writing (see Bawarshi's essay in this collection for more on this relationship).

And so, if ecocomposition is to be a flash-in-the-pan fad in composition studies, then I believe we have lost sight of what rhetoric and composition studies is and should be: an inquiry into the ways in which discourse affects, and is affected by, our daily lives and environments and the ways in which the production of written discourse reflect those very effects. If we are to embrace Geertz's notion of local contexts, then we must look at all local context, all local environments. Interestingly, rhetoric and composition readily turns to anthropological and psychological theories, and to other human-oriented social science theories to understand context, but has been slow to embrace ecological theory to examine contextual relationships. Ecocomposition asks why rhetoric and composition has ignored environmental/ecological sciences, and, more importantly, offers the theory that places and environments are crucial to understanding context and contextual relationships. To follow, then, ecocomposition, with roots deeply reaching to service learning and critical pedagogy (see essays by Owens, Ingram, and Weisser in this collection), afford the opportunity for students and teachers to participate in, react with, and relate to their surrounding environments and to the organisms that they encounter in those environments. Ecocomposition is a participatory discipline; it requires hands-on living.

THE ECOLOGY OF RHETORIC AND COMPOSITION

Writing is an ecological pursuit. In order to be successful, it must situate itself in context; it must grow from location (contextual, historical, and ideological). As Nedra Reynolds has put it, "to control textual space well is to be a good writer" (15). And certainly the scholarship of rhetoric and composition has reflected the importance of place and more recently of space, in particular.[2] Writing does not begin in the self; rather, writers begin writing by situating themselves, by putting themselves in a place, by locating with in a space. Writing begins with *topoi,* quite literally with place. As Edward M. White points out, "The very word topic comes from the Greek word for 'Place,' suggesting that the thinking process is a kind of geographic quest, a hunt for a place where ideas lurk" (8). In their contribution to this collection, M. Jimmie Killingsworth and John Krajicek note that "Readers become part of the environment, held at a distance from the writer, ordered into a system, an ecology, controlled." But let us not forget as Robert Scholes puts it, "Reading comes after writing" (60). Killingsworth and Krajicek's claim holds true for writers, as well: writers are ecological beings. Writers become a part of an environment; they are a product of that environment. They write themselves into the order of a system, and they help define that system.[3] Just as the Disney movie *The Lion King* sings of "the circle of life," rhetoricians and compositionists study the circle of writing. Writers write from a place, a *topoi*. By writing, they write about that place and define that place. Writers engage in a circular reinscription of place and environment that in turn writes who they are as writers. If rhetoric and composition are to ask questions of identity, of social construction, of discursive construction, of ideology, of production and interpretation, then what composition is really asking is: From where does writing take place? From where does identity take place? As Mary Morris explains, "Goethe once wrote that all writers are homesick, that all writers are really searching for home. Being a writer is being on a constant search for where you belong" (29). Though, Morris's words echo a more sentimental, personal search, they also resonate a basic tenet of writing: writing takes place.

Writing begins in context. We teach our students about context and convention. Context is the situated place where writing happens. Not just the physical environment where a writer writes, but the environment of writing, the ideological environment, the cultural environment, the social environment, the economic environment, the historical environment. If writing takes place, it takes place in context. Context is, quite literally, as I have noted in my epigraph, the interrelationship between words that give meaning to text. Context is environment, not just the environment where writing takes place, but the environment where words are situated in relationship to other words, to other knowledges, to other texts, to other traditions in order to construct a system of words that have meaning. Much like organisms that may stand alone for short periods of time, words require relationships with other words, with their environments in order to function. Words are dependent upon each other for survival. Writing is Darwinistic; revision culls out the words that don't work well in relation to other words. Critics filter even more. Conventions of writing are nothing more than the ordering of words into relationships that provide for sufficient survival in particular contexts, particular environments. Context, as

all writing teachers know, dictates convention. The activity of writing is
the activity of creating an ecosystem of words. Sentences, paragraphs, and
texts are habitats for words and for knowledge. When we talk about continuity and coherence in a paragraph, we're talking about symbiotic relationships between inhabitants of a paragraph. Coherence is symbiosis.

Certainly, looking at context as an ecological metaphor can be of
benefit to understanding writing as an ecological pursuit. However, ecocomposition offers a more encompassing inquiry than this simple
metaphor. As Cooper notes in "The Ecology of Writing," "the term ecological is not, however, simply the newest way to say 'contextual'" (367).
Cooper is the first to propose an ecological model for writing, and her article serves as a precursor to ecocomposition. Her argument, that writing
involves dynamic relationships with other writers, can be seen as con-
tributing to the postprocess, social construction paradigm in composition, but it is also the first ecologically based inquiry that asks us to consider uniquely ecological relationships. She writes, "the ecological model
postulates dynamic interlocking systems which structure the social activity of writing" (368). This is the first step toward ecocomposition inquiry. Ecocomposition, however, asks that we extend this inquiry beyond
social relationships to examine all relationships not just those with other
writers and readers. Ecocomposition asks that we examine relationships
with other texts, discourses, other organisms, environments, and locations, that is, ecocomposition posits that writing is an activity that affects
not only other writers and readers, but the total relations of discourse
both to its organic and inorganic environment. Looking at context from
an ecological standpoint becomes helpful for compositionists, then, for
asking questions regarding situating writing in new environments, for instance, Writing Across the Curriculum (WAC) theories and programs
might benefit from looking at the relationships between varying writing
environments and conventions needed in those contexts. The first rule of
writing must be to know your terrain; identifying context as environment
promotes survival and allows writing to find its place in an environment
more effectively.

All affects all. Cooper notes, "The metaphor for writing suggested by
the ecological model is that of a web, in which anything that affects one
strand of the web vibrates throughout the whole" (370).[4] This is precisely
why ecocomposition inquiry is so critical. When we write, we write about
our environments. Those environments affect how and what we write.
When a student writes, he or she shakes the web of classroom environments, institutional environments, and state environments. In Florida,
for instance, the Gordon Rule was imposed following the dissatisfaction

of the writing skills of graduating college students. Their writing disturbed environmental webs until the legislature responded to the disrup-
tion in the web and altered the classroom environment: what gets taught,
and how it is assessed and measured. For every action there is a reaction,
my junior-high science teacher taught me. However, more often than
not, as Cooper notes, writers do not create enough motion to vibrate the
web. Often, the web doesn't shake, but it always accepts the new writer
into the web. Context seems passive at times, a backdrop to the writing.
Thinking of context from an ecological point of view, we are never separate from context: it reverberates within us and we reverberate in it. There
is no way to not affect the environment and be affected by it, though
such effects are not always evident. Writers become a part of the web; organisms become part of an ecosystem. This also leads to an ecological understanding of hegemony. It seems almost "natural" to become a part of
the web, for the web to accept or resist disturbances. Hegemony is an
ecological process.[5] The writing classroom, as we have come to know in
rhetoric and composition, is a highly political arena. The politics and ideologies of first-year writing classrooms, of all writing in all classrooms, reverberates through environmental systems with such force that all places
feel the effects. Of course, the Gordon Rule was but a reaction to other
movements and relationships along the web. Likewise, we can trace all of
composition studies to earlier movements, schools of thought, inquiries,
and research. Aristotle's movements in the web are still being felt. Just as
any bioregion is in a constant state of flux—rivers cut through many
bioregions; species migrate; droughts and floods occur; disease spreads—
so too does the writing habitat shift. Again, WAC programs reflect such
thinking.

Habitats are important to us in rhetoric and composition. Take for instance the value we assign to understanding the place of rhetoric and composition within the university. For decades, rhetoric and composition has
sought to locate its own niche within the academic systems, to find its relationship to English departments. The field itself can be looked at ecologically; we must ask as to the relationships rhetoric and composition has to
other departments, to their needs. What happens to those departments, to
students when those needs are not met? What, for instance, does a Writing
Across the Curriculum program say about the place of composition in a
particular institution, say, versus a program that has been relegated to a
service-course-providing entity in another? Composition and rhetoric's
role in the university affects all other parts of the university and are equally
affected by those other parts. Take for instance the way in which a com-
plaint from the Engineering Department that their students "can't write"

is registered in the dean's office, or in the English Department. Curriculum may be questioned, new courses offered. Or perhaps as a better example, think of the resounding vibrations felt throughout the University of Texas—throughout academia around the country—when Linda Brodkey introduced her new curriculum for first-year writing classes in the early 1990s. Rhetoric and composition is part of larger systems; its relationships with other parts of those systems, from other departments to individual undergraduates and graduate students, is affected by, and affects, those very relationships.

Cooper claims that "one always writes out of a group" (370). Certainly, one not only writes out of a group, but one writes for a group and to a group, that is, one writes in relation to others. This essay, this collection, for instance grows from a group of teachers-scholars we have named "compositionists" and is written for members of that group. Without that relationship, there would be no writing here. But, one also always writes out of a place. And, like the group from which one writes, the relationship a writer has with that place is of critical importance to the writer, to the writing. Again, without place, there could be no writing. Writing takes place.

In the introduction to *The Ecocriticism Reader: Landmarks in Literary Ecology,* Cheryll Glotfelty and Harold Fromm offer a simplified definition of ecocriticism: "Simply put, ecocriticism is the study of the relationship between literature and the physical environment. Just as feminist criticism examines language and literature from a gender-conscious perspective, and Marxist criticism brings an awareness of modes of production and economic class to its readings of text, ecocriticism takes an earth-centered approach to literary studies" (xvii). They continue to point out that one of the questions that guides ecocritical inquiry is that "In addition to race, class, and gender, should *place* become a new critical category?" (xix). One of the crucial points I want to make here is that while ecocomposition does draw heavily on the work of ecocriticism, unlike ecocriticism, it isn't looking to establish place as simply a critical category. Rather, ecocomposition looks to engage place as rhetoric, that is ecocomposition sees (or should see) composition as activity and rhetoric as environment. When we write, we create rhetorical environments that we inhabit and that we reinvent, reinscribe. Composition, then, is the activity of creating and reacting to environments, and rhetorics are those environments. Composition and rhetoric, of course, operate in a symbiotic relationship; one cannot be separated from the other. That is to say then, ecocomposition not only identifies the ecological aspects of rhetoric and composition as a discipline, but suggests metaphors and methodologies through which we can better understand the relationships between rhetoric and composition, for instance, when we use terms like *nature, wilderness, site, location, habitat,* and *environment,* we are identifying ideological labels; naming with such terms represents local ideology. That's what rhetoric is.

ECOCOMPOSITION'S PLACE

For as long as humans have produced writing, they have done so in order to articulate and define relationships within environments. Early writings, like the famous cave paintings of Altamira or Nile valley hieroglyphs, depict human relationships with food species, with agricultural cycles, and with other tribes. Writing grew from a need to express and record human relationships with places and with the organisms that inhabit places. Writing began with a need to represent, catalog, and manage "natural" environments and organisms, and though it—if the singular pronoun is appropriate for "writing"—has evolved into an intricately developed organism of its own, writing still operates with the basic agenda of managing the environment. Writing, like early incarnations of the science ecology, developed as a managerial tool. Early ecologists saw the study of relationships as a way to better understand the environment and nature in order to make better use of it for human consumption. Likewise, the study of writing has evolved so that we may better understand written discourse so that it may be better managed and consumed.

Craig Osenberg, an ecologist at the University of Florida writes that contemporary ecologists "seek to develop a theory that organizes and explains the diversity of life and the patterns that emerge across different biological systems" (7). This seems to me to parallel rhetoric and composition's desire to develop a theory (or theories) which organizes and explains the diversity of writing and the patterns that emerge across different discursive systems. Osenberg continues to point out that "because ecologists deal with heterogeneneous systems, whose dynamics operate at different scales, ecologists must rely on a suite of tools and approaches; we are jacks-of-many trades and seldom masters of a single technique" (7). So to is this a reflection of contemporary rhetoric and composition. Many of us are technical writers, film experts, classical rhetoricians, on-line specialists, writing center directors, and program administrators; we teach a host of classes addressing a variety of subjects all located within the umbrella terms *rhetoric* and *composition.* Many of us extend our expertise within the larger rubric of English studies.

Ultimately, then, ecocomposition's place within rhetoric and composition and within English departments must be defined by those local places and by the individuals who inhabit those places. Ecocomposition begins locally with concern for, and inquiry into, the relationships that affect local, student, and experienced writers. Ecocomposition may begin with concerns for "natural" environments and for discussions of how nature writing, environmental rhetoric, and political action affect those environments. But ecocomposition must move beyond its stereotyped role of just addressing "environmentalist" concerns—though these are critical not just to ecocomposition, but to sustaining ecosystems—to examining concepts of environment, location, space, and place as encompassing all of the spaces we inhabit. Ecocomposition must turn to the conversations that composition and rhetoric provide us with for understanding how discursive construction interacts with those places, builds those places, maps those places, defines those places, and ultimately controls those places.[6]

NOTES

1. See Dana Philips's essay "Is Nature Necessary" for another discussion of the postmodern simulation of nature in Florida.

2. See, for instance Nedra Reynolds, Jacques Derrida, Collin Gifford Brooke, or Jay David Bolter.

3. Here, the term *system* refers to an ecosystem in which all organisms are dependent upon their relationships with each other and their environment for survival. Marilyn N. Cooper uses the term *system* in "The Ecology of Writing," to express such dependent, interwoven relationships. I use it here with such a meaning in mind and to parallel M. Jimmie Killingsworth and John Krajicek's use of the term.

4. Certainly, the notion of connectedness that Cooper and ecocomposition forward seem akin to feminist theory. Ecocomposition draws heavily on both feminist and ecofeminist thinking. For a detailed look at the links between ecofeminism and ecocomposition, see Dobrin and Weisser, *Natural Discourse: Toward Ecocomposition*.

5. Often the terms *nature* and *natural* are understood to mean inherently good. Phrases such as "natural ingredients" are intended to evoke an understanding that the ingredients are good, or better than artificial ingredients, because they are "natural." Of course, nature and natural are neither good nor bad until we assign such a value to them. In the case of my statement "hegemony is an ecological process," I do not intend to invoke "ecology" as either "natural" or good. Rather, I mean to say that hegemony grows from relationships with others and environment; how it develops within its own context and how that context receives it will determine its value.

6. I want to thank Anis Bawarshi, Christian Weisser, and Julie Drew for their comments on early drafts of this essay.

WORKS CITED

Bolter, Jay David. *Writing Space: The Computer, Hypertext, and the History of Writing.* Hillsdale, NJ: Lawrence Earlbaum, 1991.

Bowler, Peter J. *The Norton History of The Environmental Sciences.* New York: Norton, 1992.

Brooke, Collin Gifford. "Making Room, Writing Hypertext. *JAC* 19 (1999): 253–68.

Burke, Kenneth. *Permanence and Change: An Anatomy of Purpose.* 2nd ed. Indianapolis: Bobbs, 1965.

Cooper, Marilyn M. "The Ecology of Writing." *College English* 48 (1986): 364–75.

Derrida, Jacques. *Of Grammatology.* 1st ed. Trans. Gayatri Chakravorty Soivak. Baltimore: Johns Hopkins University Press, 1976.

Dobrin Sidney I. and Christian Weisser. *Natural Discourse: Toward Ecocomposition.* Albany: State University of New York Press, 2001.

Glotfelty, Cheryll and Harold Fromm, eds. *The Ecocriticism Reader: Landmarks in Literary Ecology.* Athens: University of Georgia Press, 1996.

Morris, Mary. "Looking for Home." *A Place Called Home: Twenty Writing Women Remember.* Ed. Mickey Pearlman. New York: St. Martin's Griffin Press, 1996.

Philips, Dana. "Is Nature Necessary." In Glotfelty and Fromm. 204–22.

Reynolds, Nedra. "Composition's Imagined Geographies: The Politics of Space in the Frontier, City and, Cyberspace." *CCC* 50 (1998): 12–35.

Ricklefs, Robert E. The Economy of Nature. 4th ed. New York: Freeman, 1997.

Sanders, Scott Russell. "Letter to a Reader." *Writing from the Center.* 1995

Scholes, Robert. *Protocols of Reading.* New Haven, CT: Yale University Press, 1989.

Snyder, Gary. "Cultured or Crabbed." Deep Ecology for the Twenty-First Century. Ed. George Sessions. Boston: Shambhala, 1995. 47–49.

Osenberg, Craig. "The Nature of Ecology." *CLASnotes* 14. no. 5. University of Florida College of Liberal Arts and Sciences. May 1999. 7.

Webster's New Collegiate Dictionary. Springfield, MA: G & C Merriam Company, 1979.

White, Edward M. *Assigning, Responding, Evaluating: A Writing Teacher's Guide.* 3rd edition. New York: St. Martin's Press, 1995.

Sustainable Composition

Derek Owens
St. John's University
Queens, New York

The common definition of sustainability is meeting the needs of the present without jeopardizing the needs of future generations. The idea of sustainability has been compared to the Iroquois Indians' alleged practice of anticipating the impact of their major decisions seven generations into the future. To put this in contemporary terms, the production cycle of a sustainable business might entail not just conserving but replenishing resources used in the production and distribution of the product. This type of business would also most likely take into consideration the necessity of its product in relationship to its "ecological footprint": even if a new product was manufactured according to principles of sustainability, presumably the new product would have to be socially worthwhile in the first place, and not simply just another excuse to make more unnecessary stuff for profit.

While this example does not do justice to the complexity of sustainability—there are competing definitions of "strong" and "weak" sustainability for example (Harris)—here I hope it will suffice to equate *sustainability* with living more simply, buying less stuff, conserving and preserving limited resources, and resisting the addictions fostered within our current consumer culture: "existing in a way that does minimal harm to the planet or other people," as the term was recently defined in one newspaper (Flaherty C14). Richard Clugston and Thomas Rogers of the Center for Respect of Life and Environment advocate a view of sustainability characterized by personal and spiritual growth: a mixture of humility, recognition of limits, and an awareness of natural systems as "circuits of aliveness." We can add to this the six fundamental values that W. Edward and Jean Garher Stead locate within sustainability: wholeness, posterity, smallness, community, quality, and spiritual fulfillment (132–46). Such definitions present a holistic interpretation of sustainability useful to educators who agree that we have a responsibility to invent a locally based, pedagogical ethic informed and inspired by an awareness of the need to think and act sustainably.

The problem is that so far a sustainable culture remains a goal, not a reality. Although the number of green businesses has increased significantly in the last two decades, along with public awareness of the many environmental crises facing us, those of us in the consumer class are not living sustainably. We are characterized by insatiable consumer appetites that do daily damage to our communities, watersheds, and children's futures. We buy stuff we don't need; we support businesses that ruin ecosystems. The implications of our consumer practices become distressingly clear once we consider the resources used in making the (seemingly) simplest of products. At the end of his book *Gain* Richard Powers pauses to explain all of the natural resources expended in the making of a disposable camera, from start to finish:

> Camera in a pouch, the true multinational: trees from the Pacific Northwest and the southeastern coastal plain. Straw and recovered wood scrap from Canada. Synthetic adhesive from Korea. Bauxite from Australia, Jamaica, Guinea. Oil from the Gulf of Mexico or North Sea Brent Blend, turned to plastic in the Republic of China before being shipped to its mortal enemies on the Mainland for molding. Cinnabar from Spain. Nickel and titanium from South Africa. Flash elements stamped in Malaysia, electronics in Singapore. Design and color transfers drawn up in New York. Assembled and shipped from that address in California by a merchant fleet beyond description, completing the most heavily choreographed conference in existence. (348)

Academics, of course, are as guilty as anyone. While it takes Powers more than three pages to describe this amazingly complex conference, imagine how many volumes it would take to painstakingly delineate the ecological impact of a different kind of conference, like the Modern Language Association or the Conference on College Composition and Communication. Thousands of academics flying to cities and staying for several days in superhotels owned by multinationals with net worths surpassing those of Third World countries: all the fuel, food, water, labor, and resources consumed so that a person from Albany might fly to Phoenix to talk for fifteen minutes about whatever in front of a dozen people, then fly back home again. When I consider the fact that in my quest to get a job and get tenure I have in the last ten years at more than thirty conferences, I should hang my head in shame. There is no way I can justify the significance of my various papers and performances against the environmental toll of having gone to these places. The sustainable thing of course would not to have attended such spectacles, to boycott such irresponsible displays of excess while promoting alternative means of exchanging information and ideas. But academic culture demands that its employees—at least grad students and junior faculty—attend such monstrosities in order to get and hold onto their jobs. American academics, like all other Western consumers, are not living sustainable lives.

Institutions of higher education that ignore and work against the goal of building a sustainable culture are ethically indefensible. Disciplines can no longer afford to situate themselves "outside" the need to envision a sustainable culture; sustainability can no longer be a trope associated only with the "specialized" programs of environmental studies, planning, architecture, economics, and ecology. Educators, particularly those of us who like to view ourselves as promoters of critical pedagogy, need to imagine ways in which a sustainable pedagogy might surface within our classes. And because thinking sustainably requires a shift from compartmentalized to holistic thinking, and because the disciplinary permeability of the field of composition studies already implies a challenge to the culture of academic specialization, composition offers a logical working space for the promotion of sustainable pedagogies. Given composition's access to incoming college students and its cross-disciplinary makeup, few fields might play as important a role as composition in promoting a sustainable ethic. Those of us who teach composition and design writing programs have perhaps more responsibility than other faculty to promote sustainable thinking throughout the curriculum.

The composition classroom offers a unique intellectual space to experiment with sustainable pedagogies. Unless they are forced to adopt a specific reader or text by some *boss compositionist,* to use James Sledd's term, what students actually write, think, and talk about, and who it is precisely they write for, is determined locally by the teacher and by the students. The cross-disciplinary permeability of the composition classroom makes it a logical working space where students can further investigate the past and future of their local environments, their current jobs and future career goals, their cultures (a number of which are increasingly at risk, especially linguistically), and their futures—all of which are and will continue to be affected by our ability to live sustainably. Because of their extensive contact with first-year undergraduates, composition faculty can create environments that serve as filters through which students might apply a growing sense of sustainable awareness to the goals implicit within their chosen majors. Few courses and programs

within the curriculum provide this kind of workspace for addressing individual, disciplinary, and local needs and desires within a sustainable
context.

For the last three years I have divided my composition courses into
four phases, each approximately three or four weeks long. During these
phases students select from two or three writing sequences I have choreographed with the intention of emphasizing certain themes I consider necessary in developing an awareness of sustainability. So far I have been fairly
surreptitious in my approach to promote initial forays into sustainable
thinking. Not only am I conscientious about making my students feel that
they have been misled into taking a course in ecological economics more
than composition, but I also have little interest in lecturing about anything, sustainability included. Consequently, discussions about sustainability per se only surface in the final quarter of our course, when my students write future scenarios. And while I assign a good deal of reading in
my writing classroom, these introduced texts always take a backseat to the
students' prose. This often means that we never have time to discuss some
of the readings, since all of our class time has been devoted to talking
about student prose. Within the composition classroom, which of course
must preoccupy itself with student writing more than anything else, I am
content to downplay not only the assigned readings but my own interest
in sustainability in order to try and respond to my students' concerns
about what they are writing about.

Nevertheless, in giving students the chance to write about and investigate themes that matter to them, it is not hard to create a classroom environment where all of us can reflect on issues directly and indirectly related
to sustainability: what makes a neighborhood good or bad; what makes
jobs desirable or miserable; and what it means to preserve a culture,
whether or not our prospects for the short-term future look hopeful or
scary. Following is a synopsis of some of the writing sequences used in my
classes.[1] I offer these assignments—none of which are all that innovative,
except that they have been constructed in response to certain sustainable
imperatives—less as examples of what ought to happen in the composition classroom than as a testimony of how one teacher is experimenting
with the need to bring sustainability, directly and indirectly, into the classroom arena.

1. *Place Portraits.* Students research their immediate neighborhoods
and compose detailed written and visual portraits about where they live.
The goal is to vividly portray not only the buildings they live in but the
local community within, say, a radius of several blocks so that their class-

mates might visualize this area. Midway into this sequence students bring in photographs of their neighborhoods and share them with the rest of the class, and then discuss what the photographs reveal that could also be included within the written accounts, as well as what the written accounts can show that the photographs can't. Throughout this sequence students revise and expand their portraits, and ultimately draw conclusions about their places: what makes them good or bad, how they feel about them, and to what degree their daily surroundings influence their attitudes, goals, and personalities. When this sequence is over, and students have further revised their community portraits, I invite them to publish their written and photographic studies on a website I monitor, as a means of building a growing student-constructed map of the surrounding environs (I teach at a predominantly commuter campus, where the majority of our students come from the five boroughs of New York City and Long Island). Throughout this sequence students read and discuss other place portraits, particularly by those who have also written about the local area (Birkerts; Kunstler 9–15, 175–87, 189–216; Hiss 103–25; Sullivan; and Caro).

One of my goals for the future is to work with other faculty throughout the country interested in having their students create similar maps, and eventually to link all of these accounts on the World Wide Web. I fantasize about a future project where every year a percentage of all American college students use the World Wide Web as a place to show the rest of the world what their apartment buildings, suburban streets, and rural homes look and feel like. Such a growing network of written and visual information could be a tremendous pedagogical and social resource.

2. Designing Eutopia. Whereas utopia refers to the "perfect place" or a "noplace," eutopia instead implies "the good place." After writing their place portraits some of my students want to further their research into their local communities, and for them I have assembled a writing sequence where they move beyond their place portrait and write a speculative essay on what it would take to make their local neighborhood a eutopia. This sequence involves more reading by authors who have also sought to articulate the characteristics of good places (Kunstler 245–75, Calthorpe 15–38; and Rosel and 1–12), and students write responses to excerpts from these texts, using them as a vehicle for helping them figure out what they believe to be the necessary ingredients for transforming places from bad or average to good and desirable. This becomes their chance to design not only their ideal homes, but to create a portrait of what their ideal neighborhoods would be like. We close this sequence by comparing their eutopias to their current neighborhoods, discussing the viability of their finding, creating, and living in such eutopias, and reflecting upon what their eutopian ideals say about their own needs and values.

3. Neighborhood Histories. Some of my students choose a sequence in which they research their current neighborhood or some other community—perhaps where they grew up as a child, or where they'd like to eventually settle down—but from a more expansive historical perspective. Students write imagined descriptions of what their particular place must have been like 500, 200, 100, and 50 years ago, and then imagine what their place will be like 25 or 50 years into the future. Those who opt for this sequence have to conduct a fair amount of research in their local library, as well as read excerpts from texts by authors who have written similar texts (Metcalf, Mitchell, and Sullivan). The goal here is to give students a chance to recognize the fact that all environments are in continual states of flux, to see how their communities have evolved radically over several generations, and to begin contemplating the ways in which those places will continue to change, for better or worse. My intention here is also to create a context where students might realize that, while they are indeed shaped by the status of their communities, this flow of influence is not only one-directional; members of a community are always potential agents of change for that community.

4. Oral History Preservation Project. In this sequence students begin by reading a short text indicating that within the next century more than half of today's languages will become extinct (Kane), a statistic that matters to a number of my students, many of whom are first-generation college students from families where English is not the primary language spoken at home. Here I make it obvious that my goal in this sequence is to cultivate something like a preservational ethic, and to give them an opportunity to spend three weeks interviewing an older family member, neighbor, or friend of the family. After a quick introduction into the art of making oral histories (McMahan and Rogers; and Brown 34–47) and making available existing examples of oral histories (Cowan and Cowan, Davis, Dolci, Frommer and Frommer, Hurmence, Tenhula, and Terkel), students conduct three or four hour-long interviews with their subjects over the course of several weeks. When finished they compile the results in an interview format, or fashion a narrative based on those interviews. For a number of my students, this also becomes an exercise in translation, since many of the interviewees don't speak English. Unlike their place portraits, which I encourage them to publish on the World Wide Web, these oral histories are more private documents, intended to circulate within their families; consequently only a few of them find their way onto the website. Part of my motive in creating this assignment is to help students understand the value of preservation. It is the same motive one finds in various green readers, where students read about damaged ecosystems and the demise of the rain forests, but for my urban and suburban students it makes more sense to work locally, and to focus on what so many of them truly want to preserve: their family stories. Of all of the writing sequences I have designed so far, this one by far elicits some of the most captivating prose; the stories my students and their family members and friends tell are filled with joy and humor and sorrow. Their narratives make for some of the most compelling reading I've ever encountered as a teacher.

5. *Tribal Testimonies.* This is similar to the oral history sequence, only here the student observes, describes, and thus preserves a particular culture or subculture he or she is part of or has easy access to. In the past students have written on the significance (and gradual disappearance) of Sunday dim sum in Chinatown, traveling with the Grateful Dead, Goth culture, snowboarders, Botanicas, Carneval, the politics of clubbing, Sioux humor, Rrriot Grrrls, Santeria, Trekkies, Queer zines, and Guyanese values. Like the place portraits, these pieces sometimes find their way onto the website. During this phase students also read one or two examples of cultural reportage/construction (Geertz), not so much as an example of how one ought to write about culture, but to help illustrate the richness and complexity implicit within seemingly mundane cultural activities.

6. *Work Stories.* Work is the main reason why our students are in college in the first place. Their primary motivation for being in our classes is because those college credits will eventually bring them the degree they hope will eventually lead them to the kind of work they want. For most college students, work is not just a goal but a reality, as the majority of them work at least twenty hours a week. Because work plays such a central role in the lives of my students, and certainly in their working and middle-class families, many of them are interested in writing about what work means to them. This is similar to both the place portrait and the eutopia sequences because students get a chance to describe in detail not only what their jobs (or their parents' or siblings' jobs) are like, but what makes these jobs good or bad. Students conclude this sequence by designing what they would do if they owned a business, and wanted to make their employees regard work as synonymous with joy. Throughout

this sequence students also read various critiques of works (Black; Brandt; Greider; Mander; Hawken xi–xvi, 1–17; Rifkin 108–21; and Schor), a number of which I have chosen because they criticize unsustainable businesses, multinationalism, and the current trend toward longer work weeks and shorter wages.

   7. Future Scenarios. At the end of the semester, while having them read a series of works by both optimistic (Gates and Schwartz 31–46, 170–98) and pessimistic (Linden 200–212; Gordon and Suzuki 9–37; and Ehrenfeld) futurists, as well as those who advocate "fork-in-the-road" positions indicating that the near future could go either way (Yaro and Hiss 1–9, 239–43; and Hammond 22–61), students write their own speculative narratives about what the next twenty-five years will be like for them and their families. In this sequence I emphasize the fact that they are not to write about what they hope to see in the future, but rather what they feel will most likely happen in the future—what their best guess is about the quality of their life twenty-five years hence. To help them get a handle on the topic, students are encouraged to focus on issues or topics of particular interest to them—say, the media, education, their neighborhoods, technology, medicine, city life, transportation, and the environment. The goal here is to give students an opportunity to examine what they think they're currently in the process of inheriting, and to reflect upon whether or not they feel good about what they imagine to be the likely status of their futures.

   Will these writing sequences lead my students toward more sustainable habits of living? I have no idea. More importantly, since so many of my students come from poor families, they are inflicting a lot less damage than a middle-class consumer like myself who, even though he tries in a number of ways to live simply, nevertheless enjoys many of the trappings of a middle-class life-style. As conscientious as I think I am, and as hard as I try, I cannot claim to live a sustainable life-style. I can hardly expect anymore from my students.

   So why have I developed these writing sequences if there is no evidence that these kinds of conversations and writing projects lead to sustainable behavior? Partly out of fear—fear that if we don't consciously make sustainability part of our ongoing conversations, regardless of what disciplines we teach in, things are just going to get worse. Partly out of a need to cultivate a space for honest communication within a culture like ours that is so pervasively silent and ignorant about the implications of our consumer addictions. Partly out of a desire to make the classroom as cross-disciplinary as I can, and in ways that ultimately relate to my students' immediate, local lives.

But mostly because I've come to view the composition course as a microcosm of what higher education ought to be. The freedom that writing faculty enjoy implies an exciting if not daunting responsibility: if the teacher can make students read and write almost anything, what then are *the* most important things for them to read and write about? Of all the information out there in the world, what is absolutely crucial to their intellectual, spiritual, economic, and physical survival? From this perspective the classroom becomes a course in local, necessary knowledge—a thumbnail sketch revealing not only what that teacher deems important for students, but what is most important, period. Teachers who view their courses this way have something to contribute to conversations about the larger curriculum. Not because faculty presume to be authorities in ecological economics or regional planning or environmental studies, but because we supposedly know something about designing pedagogical environments where information from a variety of sources might be choreographed with student writing in ways that are, if we are doing our jobs, supremely relevant to those students' lives. Whether we call it "sustainable composition" or "ecocomposition," teachers who design their courses in response to our threatened local environments are doing something that needs to spill over into the rest of the curriculum. Whether we teach first-year writing courses, design writing across the curriculum initiatives, or run writing centers, compositionists need to acknowledge their fundamental roles in creating a sustainable curriculum that moves continually toward environmental stability and community revitalization.

NOTES

1. For a more detailed treatment of my assignments, as well as a more comprehensive discussion of sustainable pedagogy in English studies, see my book *Survival and Sustainability: Composition for a Threatened Generation,* NCTE Press, forthcoming Urbana.

WORKS CITED

Birkerts, Sven. "Place: A Fragment." *The Sacred Theory of the Earth.* Ed. Thomas Frick. Berkeley, CA: North Atlantic Books, 1986. 53–55.

Black, Bob. "The Abolition of Work." *Semiotext(e) USA.* Brooklyn: Autonomedia. 15–26.

Brandt, Barbara. "Less Is More: A Call for Shorter Work Hours." *Transitions: Lives in America.* Eds. Irina L. Raicu and Gregory Grewell. Mountain View, CA: Mayfield, 1997. 300–307.

Brown, Cynthia Stokes. *Like it Was: A Complete Guide to Writing Oral History.* New York: Teachers and Writers Collaborative, 1988.

Calthorpe, Peter. *The Next American Metropolis: Ecology, Community, and the American Dream.* New York: Princeton Architectural Press, 1993.

Caro, Robert A. "The City Shaper." *The New Yorker,* 5 January 1998. 38–50, 52–55.

Clugston, Richard M., and Thomas Rogers. "The Earth Charter." Tufts Environmental Literacy Institute. Fletcher School of Law and Diplomacy. Tufts University, Medford, MA. 11 June 1997.

Cowan, Neil M., and Ruth Schwartz Cowan. *Our Parent's Lives: Jewish Assimilation and Everyday Life.* New Brunswick, NJ: Rutgers University Press, 1996.

Davis, Marilyn P. *Mexican Voices/American Dreams: An Oral History of Mexican Immigration to the United States.* New York: Holt, 1990.

Dolci, Danilo. *Sicilian Lives.* Trans. Justin Vitiello. New York: Pantheon, 1981.

Ehrenfeld, David. "Life in the Next Millennium: Who Will Be Left in the Earth's Community?" *The Last Extinction.* Eds. Les Kaufman and Kenneth Mallory. Cambridge: MIT Press, 1987. 167–86.

Flaherty, Julie. "Living By the Books: Vermont Publisher Succeeds With Guides for a Simpler Life." *New York Times,* 19 June. 1995 C1, C14.

Frommer, Myrna, and Harvey Frommer. *Growing Up Jewish in America: An Oral History.* New York: Harcourt, 1995.

Geertz, Clifford. "Dep Play: Notes on the Balinese Cockfight." *The Interpretation of Cultures.* New York: Basic, 1973. 412–53.

Hiss, Tony. *The Experience of Place.* New York: Vintage, 1990.

Hurmence, Belinda, ed. *My Folks Don't Want Me to Talk about Slavery: Twenty-One Oral Histories of Former North Carolina Slaves.* Winston-Salem, NC: J. F. Blair, 1984.

Gates, Bill. *The Road Ahead.* With Nathan Myhrvold and Peter Rinearson. New York: Viking, 1995.

Gordon, Anita, and David Suzuki. *It's a Matter of Survival.* Cambridge; Harvard University Press, 1991.

Greider, William. "'Citizen' GE." In Mander and Goldsmith. 323–34.

Hammond, Allen. *Which World? Scenarios for the 21st Century.* Washington DC: Island Press, 1998.

Harris, Jonathan M. "Theoretical Frameworks and Techniques: Overview Essay." *A Survey of Ecological Economics.* Eds. Rajaram Krishnan, Jonathan M. Harris, and Neva R. Goodwin. Washington DC: Island Press, 1995. 97–105.

Hawken, Paul. "Preface." *The Ecology of Commerce: A Declaration of Sustainability.* New York: HarperBusiness, 1993.

Kane, Hal. "Half of Languages Becoming Extinct." *Vital Signs 1997: The Environmental Trends that Are Shaping Our Future.* Eds. Lester R. Brown et al. New York: Norton, 1997. 130–31.

Kunstler, James Howard. *The Geography of Nowhere: The Rise and Decline of America's Man-Made Landscape.* New York: Touchstone, 1993.

Linden, Eugene. *The Future in Plain Sight: Nine Clues to the Coming Instability.* New York: Simon & Schuster, 1998.

McMahan, Eva M., and Kim Lacy Rogers, eds. *Interactive Oral History Interviewing.* Hillsdale, NJ: Erlbaum Associates, 1994.

Mander, Jerry. "The Rules of Corporate Behavior." In Mander and Goldsmith. 309–22.

———, and Edward Goldsmith, eds. *The Case Against the Global Economy: And for a Turn Toward the Local.* San Francisco: Sierra Club, 1996.

Metcalf, Paul. "Waters of Potowmack." *Collected Works. Vol. 2, 1976–1986.* Minneapolis, MN: Coffee House Press, 1997. 361–598.

Mitchell, John Hanson. *Ceremonial Time: Fifteen Thousand Years on One Square Mile.* Garden City, NY: Anchor Press/Doubleday, 1984.

Powers, Richard. *Gain.* New York: Farrar, 1998.

Rifkin, Jeremy. "New Technology and the End of Jobs." In Mander and Goldsmith.

Roseland, Mark. "Dimensions of the Future: An Eco-city Overview." *Eco-City Dimensions: Healthy Communities, Healthy Planet.* Ed. Mark Roseland. Gabriola Island, British Colombia: New Society, 1997.

Schwartz, Peter. *The Art of the Long View.* New York: Currency, 1991.

Stead, W. Edward, and Jean Garner Stead. *Management for a Small Planet: Strategic Decision Making and the Environment.* 2nd ed. Thousand Oaks, CA: SAGE, 1996.

Sullivan, Robert. *The Meadowlands: Wilderness Adventures at the Edge of a City.* New York: Scribner, 1998.

Tenhula, John. *Voices from Southeast Asia: The Refugee Experience in the United States.* New York: Holmes and Meier, 1991.

Terkel, Studs. *Race: How Blacks and Whites Think and Feel about the American Obsession.* New York: New Press, 1992.

Yaro, Robert D., and Tony Hiss. *A Region at Risk: The Third Regional Plan for the New York-New Jersey-Connecticut Metropolitan Area.* Washington DC: Island Press, 1996.

Ecology, Alienation, and Literacy:

Constraints and Possibilities in Ecocomposition

M. Jimmie Killingsworth
Texas A&M University
College Station, Texas

John Krajicek
Texas A&M University
College Station, Texas

> I like it when the lines blur between students and teachers: when you're not sure who's doing the teaching.
> —Rick Bass, *The New Wolves*

The class—second-year composition and introduction to literature with a focus on nature writing—is discussing a cranky essay by Jim Dodge about bioregionalism. Early in the essay, the author strikes a pose of knowledge-able distance from the ordinary citizen. The perspective suggests ecologi-cally informed alienation, identification with the land certainly, and with the few hearties who take the time to know the land well, but who are alienated from the great mass of car-driving, mall-shopping, burger-grazing mortals in the Great Society. Bioregionalism, Dodge says, "means life terri-tory, place of life, or perhaps by reckless extension, government by life" (231). With what might be less than calculated rhetorical risk, he directly addresses his readers, practically urging a certain percentage to take a hike (in every sense of that phrase): "If you can't imagine that government by life would be at least 40 billion times better than government by the Reagan administration, or Mobil Oil, or any other distant powerful monolith, then your heart is probably no bigger than a prune pit and you won't have much sympathy for what follows" (231). To those who might continue reading after this audience-culling maneuver, he proclaims, "To understand natural systems is to begin an understanding of the self" (231) and then serves up a gumbo of scientific information (a brief exposition on "biotic shift," e.g., the concept that "if 15 to 25 percent of the species [of plants and animals] where I live are different from those where you live, we occupy different biological regions" [232]) spiced with an anarchic political philosophy: "The United States is simply too large and complex to be responsibly governed by a decision-making body of perhaps 1,000 people representing 220,000,000 Americans and a large chunk of biosphere" (234).

We're not really surprised by the class' initial response. A couple of front-rowers who bear the markings of Dallas Republican urbanites beg to differ with Dodge: "I love nature as much as anybody," says the first, "but I don't think I need to know everything he says to be really in touch." She pauses to see if the teacher is hunkering down for an argumentative counterstrike. When it seems safe, she resumes,

> In our social system, I buy my groceries from someone who has bought them from someone else and on down to the farmer. Even though I'm at a distance from where my food's grown or the oil for my car is produced, that doesn't mean I don't contribute something to the world. All those people have jobs and families to support and by buying the way I buy, I help support them. Dodge doesn't seem to think about how everybody's going to pay for everything.

The second chimes in, "It's like he cares more for trees and birds than for people." It seems very predictable, and several others join in, while in the back row, a few farm-and-ranch-raised readers demur. (We are teaching at a huge land-grant university, after all.)

What might be more surprising is that in the midst of the complaints about Dodge's failures in sociability, we hear more than once a lament against the length of the essay, even though it is only eight pages long and written in a style that appears to us as breezy and journalistic: "He could have made all his points in a page or two but he just rambles on for paragraph after paragraph." Most of the class agrees that the essay is too long. Many also feel that the science in the essay is pompous and pretentious: "He uses way too many big words and tries to make you feel stupid." The same points come out in the student's journals. One writes, "I thought Dodge was excessively wordy with long explanations that were for the most part hard to understand and tie all together. I thought it was pretty boring." The same journal-writer has a problem with a descriptive essay by John Muir, one of Dodge's spiritual predecessors: "It is a little too wordy and boring. He describes the wind and trees lively with action verbs, but it has no action; therefore it is boring. I would add some animals to his writing. I would also use shorter sentences." Wordiness and woodsiness begin to be linked in the minds of these respondents. The woodsy authors, purveyors of the wilderness ethic from Muir on down, seem distant to the current so-ciability of many student readers. Cranky prophets or kindly hermits, they appear more at home in nature than in human society. But somewhat iron-ically—since we don't normally associate Paul Bunyan and Davy Crockett and other mythical figures of woodsiness with heavy-duty linguistic pro-ductivity—these nature writers seem rather windy, garrulous, like some-body who's been alone too much and, once in company, can't quit talking.

Of course, they aren't "in company" exactly, and they aren't "talking": they are writing. Indeed the very condition of literacy supports their gar-rulousness. There's nobody to talk back or interrupt, so on they go. Liter-acy is perfect for the woodsy types in other senses, too. It offers a portable technology for communication. You can carry your books and notebooks out to the woods, read what you want, write everything that comes to mind, then send it all off to the printer and never have to deal with par-lors, nice clothes, tea cups, and polite listeners. Readers become part of the environment, held at a distance from the writer, ordered into a system, an ecology, controlled.

Our students are encountering a species of environmentalism unique to Western culture and central to the political ethos that has driven the en-vironmental protection movement in the United States for over one hun-dred years. This ethos forms links among a triad of intellectual conditions, two elements of which have been frequently recognized—ecological awareness and alienated consciousness—but the third of which, an intel-lectual commitment to literacy and dependency upon the written word, has been largely overlooked. But the elements of the triad have become tightly bound in communication practice. And they make a nice fit. Ecol-ogy positions the individual life-form within a system, or environment. The pressure to adjust to one such system—the sociopolitical lifeworld—yields the condition of alienation in human experience. Likewise literacy tends to decontextualize, to such an extent that the isolated reader alone with a book or the writer confronting a blank page rather than a present audience becomes the very figure of the alienated individual, according to literacy theorists like McLuhan and Ong. (For an excellent overview and critique of the cultural and cognitive issues in literacy studies, see Roorda's essay in this collection.)

Political environmentalism emerged from the intertwined strands of ecology, alienation, and literacy. The connection appears at the roots of American environmentalism, at least as early as Henry David Thoreau. Remember that the third chapter of his protoenvironmentalist manifesto *Walden,* entitled "Reading," celebrates a form of literacy as deep as the ecological and alienated sensibilities cultivated in the more famous first two chapters (entitled "Economy" and "Where I Lived and What I Lived For"). Thoreau writes,

> However much we may admire the orator's occasional bursts of eloquence, the noblest written words are commonly as far behind or above the fleeting spoken language as the firmament with its stars is behind the clouds. *There* are the stars, and they who can may read them. The astronomers forever comment on and observe them. They are not exhalations like our daily colloquies and vaporous breath. (69)

"A written word is the choicest of relics," he contends, "It is something at once more intimate with us and more universal than any other work of art" (69)—"more intimate" because, as Walt Whitman suggests, the reader is curiously alone with the author in a private space ("Is it night?" the poet whispers in "So Long," "are we here together alone? / It is I you hold and who holds you, / I spring from the pages into your arms" [611]), and "more universal" because of the printed word's range over time and space.

The first great environmentalists—Thoreau, Muir, Leopold, and Carson—were loners, writers, and naturalists. In this sense, environmentalism and modernism are coeval and mutually supporting. And, insofar as it is an equally modernist invention, the emerging discipline of composition keys into environmental concern through the connection with literacy. No wonder why Marilyn Cooper's metaphor of an "ecology of writing" resonates so strongly in the current generation of politically conscious composition teachers (see Weisser's essay in this collection) and why so many books and articles on environmental rhetoric have appeared in the last decade. (Just counting books, we have Cantrill and Oravec; Herndl and Brown; Killingsworth and Palmer, *Ecospeak;* Peterson; and Waddell.)

As teachers of composition, purveyors of literacy, and as environmentalists ourselves, our identification flows easily toward writers like Thoreau, Muir, and Dodge. We must be aware of the fact, however, that with ecology and literacy comes the third conceptual partner, alienation. And while the political alienation of a Muir or a Thoreau has represented a powerfully productive critical force in American culture at large, close identification with the form of environmentalism that depends upon the conceptual triad of ecology, alienation, and literacy, may alienate the teacher of ecocomposition from not only Mobil Oil and the Republican Party, but also from a large percentage of any contemporary class of students, and may thereby stand in the way of effective teaching. Moreover, the students who resist this perspective may well have something to teach us about the rhetorical shelf life of the old environmentalism with its woodsiness and wordiness. Their perspectives may point the way toward the need to find or create alternative forms. Let us not be too quick to go with our instincts and worry too much that, if we drop our guard, environmental literacy will be reduced to sound bytes on MTV; or that productive political alienation will give way to greenwashing in business ads and lines of argument like "I love nature but love my money better"; or that a deep understanding of ecological relations will yield to total ignorance of the issues. Let's wait, and go slowly into the terrain of ecocomposition, listening carefully to the inhabitants as we go.

In class on another day, we're discussing a novella by Rick Bass, "The Sky, the Stars, the Wilderness." John's teaching the class; Jimmie's observing (lurking, as the students say). John wants the students to discuss the chief character in the story, the narrator Anne. In reading the story we both have been impressed with the character; her close knowledge of her home in the Central Texas Hill Country; her insistence on following her grandfather's example of loving the land by knowing it closely; her resistance to treating the land abstractly, even after she goes off to college and graduate school to study science; her rejection of the scientistic approach even when it means alienating her lovers, the researchers whom she meets at school; and her refusal to compromise when she joins her father, a county agent, in resisting the local "Predator Club," the farmers and ranchers who see eagles, wolves, and coyotes as a grave danger to their economic well-being, as well as the Catfish Man, the resident of a local city who threatens the water table with the huge demands of a catfish farm. Anne's critique of the general society in which she finds herself, her very personal alienation from it, is solidly based in an equally personal knowledge of local ecology, which would make a bioregionalist like Dodge proud.

Along with ecology and alienation, we find in her character the other ingredient of our triad, literacy. She disdains the members of the Predator Club, for example, not just because of their ignorance of natural processes but also because of their general ignorance, represented to her as illiteracy, which she displays to the reader with sardonic humor in quotations from their letters to the local paper: "It is spring again," writes one, "and I have lost another babe lamb to the wolf of the sky, the feathered Adolf Hitler—the gold eagle come out of the sun and struck lamb and ewe and pulled there *[sic]* entrils out and flew away with entrils hanging like a joke, smiling. . . ." (Bass 151). The experience of deep literacy, a solid foundation for individuality beyond the more superficial pleasure of inserting a knowing *sic* into her quotation, sets Anne apart from her peers as well. She sees herself as a loner among loners even in grade school, and her bookishness supports her in this view. At recess, she tells us, "The other girls would wander off to play and I would wander off to stand under a tree and read" (153). Standing under a tree, reading apart from the others, Anne is the environmentalist par excellence.

But she is no Jim Dodge. She does not let her alienation lead beyond aloofness to preachiness and dismissive rhetoric. She draws us sympathetically to her. She seems to share her story with us, to trust us with it, and to call out to us in whatever pocket of alienation we may have inhabited ourselves. (We are readers at the very least and thus share that level of aloneness with the book—even if we are forced to read as part of an English class.) We grow to admire the affection and tolerance Anne shows her cranky old grandfather, the hired man Chubb, and her little brother Omar. She tugs at us with the story of her mother's dying just when the little girl needed her most, as she enters adolescence, and of the girl's consequent search for the mother's spirit in the beautiful spread of the ranch land.

So we are eager to hear how the class responds to our ecological, alienated, and literate heroine. We are nearing the end of the class when John gets around to discussing the novella for the first time: "Well, tell me," he says, "what did you think of Anne's connection to the land?" We have been talking about being connected to the land, how some writers argue that we are only half alive if we don't pursue connection. But John's question falls surprisingly flat. We exchange looks. Maybe the students haven't read the novella yet. But no, one of them pops up, back row Farm and Ranch: "Uhh, she certainly knows the land. And her grandfather reminded me of my grandfather. They know all about the birds and the animals and plants." "Well," John probes, "How does this affect them as people?" Nothing. Time is running out: "Think about this some more," John finally says, "and we'll get back to this story next time." Papers and books fly into backpacks and they're gone.

John's frustrated as we walk back to our offices. A thought strikes Jimmie: "Maybe we're asking them to move too quickly to agree with us about Anne's heroic qualities. You know, she does have some social problems."

"I don't know," John comes back. "I don't see how we can *not* read her as a hero. She's a hero to me, and I think Bass intended her to be a hero. I mean, look how close she is to Bass's own position. Remember his essay 'On Willow Creek' about the death of his mother and the picnics in the Hill Country and all? She *is* Rick Bass to some extent; don't you think? Look how he lives so secluded in the Yaak Valley in Montana now, somewhat like Anne on her hill-country ranch."

"Well, maybe," says Jimmie, hitting his stride, "but he does distance himself by making her a girl, for starters, and then she's not just alienated but positively antisocial. She can't form a relationship that satisfies her because all her men let her down in the way they look at the land, or lack sympathy with it, or go off someplace else to study without regard to her attachment to her place. . . ."

"Yeah, that's true; Bass seems to be pretty thoroughly bonded with other people in the Yaak community, and he shows in his books how he enjoys his camaraderie with naturalists and his other alienated pals. And you know, there's no way Anne would involve herself in Bass's social/political activism."

"and Anne's loss of her mother is important, too. In fact, now that I think of it, the land becomes a kind of substitute mother. . . ."

John smirks; "That's so obvious; I didn't give it a second thought. . . ."

"Maybe you ought to rethink, then," Jimmie's rolling now. "Because Anne, however much *we* love her, has formed a neurotic attachment to the land. Even if *Bass* doesn't realize it himself—I mean, come on, reader response is our game—she's really pretty fucked up!"

"Hold on; hold on; I can't go that far," says John.

Jimmie presses him with his usual tenacity, but John's too stubborn himself to follow this turn of argument. He switches the conversation to questions of grading the journals. Jimmie relents grudgingly.

That night, John talks with his wife, Marnie, an elementary school language arts teacher who read Bass's novella with her husband when he was preparing for the course: "Jimmie argues that Anne is neurotic in her attachment to the land. I'm not really convinced. Maybe I *like* her too much to see it." But he finds no support on the home front. Marnie says, "I told you that when *I* read the book, and you didn't want to listen then either." Still resisting, John e-mails Jimmie, defending the character with wonderful gallantry. But by now Jimmie's got his mind made up and won't give in: "Face it, man, she's fucked up."

Next time the class meets, John, frustrated with his reading companions, puts a more open question to his students: "Tell me what you felt when you read Anne's story."

Front-row Dallas is ready: "It made me sad. I mean, this girl can't form any friendships and she chases off all her men. She's so smart and everything, but she doesn't have anybody after her grandfather and Chubb die and her brother and father move away at the end. She's all alone on her land."

"OK," John probes, "What does Bass seems to be saying about her?"

Front-row Dallas: "I think it's all about her mother, about how she doesn't get over the death of her mother." The class stirs in agreement.

"Yeah," a voice comes from the back of the room. "It's like she loves the land so much because she can't love her mother anymore. She even says she 'looks for her mother's spirit in the land.'"

John begins to feel energized: "Jimmie and I have been talking about this," he says, feeling himself pulled into the flood of ideas: "We're really interested in what you think about it." The insights continue to flow now that he's tapped a position of sympathy. He asks about a peculiar scene in the book, in which Anne finds a dead golden eagle, shot by a rancher, and with great effort carries the giant bird to the top of a high cliff, and mounts it, wings outspread, upon the skeleton of a lightning-struck old tree, forming a kind of defiant altar, which she visits regularly until nothing is left but a ragged skeleton and finally nothing at all but dust. One student says, "The eagle is like her mother. She can't accept that it's dead. She sets it up as if it's alive and almost worships it." The class goes so well that three students come up after class and want to change their paper topics so that they can write about Anne.

The insights flow toward the papers, which are due the following week. The students write well, for example, about how shifting genre, from argumentative essay to suggestive narrative, can make environmental arguments more palatable to the unconverted audience. And they also write about the character type of the environmentalist, probing psychological sources and personal connections. One paper, entitled "The Healing Connection," begins with this paragraph:

> Throughout my life, I have lost many things that I love very much. The murder of my brother when I was ten, was definitely the greatest loss I have experienced. It created a huge whirlwind of grief, anger, sorrow, and questions that I had no answers to and made my life empty. I constantly find myself searching for reasons or answers but usually fall short before I find them. This search is never-ending just like that of Anne, the narrator in *The Sky, the Stars, the Wilderness,* by Rick Bass. Anne's connection with nature helps her to find peace and reassurance and to answer many questions. She uses life to . . . fill the void placed in her life by the death of her mother.

Despite Anne's eventual loneliness, the student-writer makes a strong case for the character in her own terms and suggests that, contrary to the way in which a conservative antienvironmentalist might read this story (see Killingsworth and Palmer, "The Discourse of Environmentalist 'Hysteria'"), the strength of the environmentalist character cannot be reduced to a simple perversity or obsession. On the topic of the dead eagle, the student writes;

> In many ways this eagle was her mother. After her mother died, they buried her in a place she chose, one that she would like the best. Anne clutched onto her mother's presence as the eagle's talons did to the branch. Her grip was strong and wouldn't let go because her mother was her life. This represents a lot about Anne and her level of faith in existence. She had a strong will and determination to hang onto life in all she could grasp, while at the same time she tried to help others see it too. She attempted many times to show her younger brother Omar the beauty and life around them, hoping that he too would find meaning and the presence of her mother as she had.

The student concludes that her life is similar to Anne's but that she lacks the latter's "obsessive strength." Her comments lead us to acknowledge the possibility of a complex neurosis at the heart of the environmentalist character, the flip side of heroism. This acknowledgment has many positive values, from helping us as activists to anticipate the arguments of antienvironmentalists with their contempt for tree-huggers, to helping us see deeply into the possible resistances of students. One interesting possibility is that when the neurosis is allowed to surface and offers itself to the reader for investigation, as in the story by Bass, it creates an appeal for sympathy that is lacking in aggressive arguments like those of Dodge or in scientifically oriented descriptions like those of Muir, which, though they may seem to be "personal" enough in their use of autobiographical or conversational conventions, aren't confessional enough to allow motives that might be considered damning to their cause to rise to the surface of discourse. What if Rachel Carson had revealed that one of her motives for writing *Silent Spring* was that she had been diagnosed with a type of cancer likely to have been environmentally induced? Would such a confession have brought even more sympathy to her cause, even though it would certainly have bolstered the opposition to her that claimed she was overly biased and unscientific anyway? (See Killingsworth and Palmer, "*Silent Spring* and Science Fiction"; and the other essays in Waddell.)

With these students, then, we gradually come to see that the exalted triad in whose presence *we* have worshiped—ecology, alienation, and literacy—may have a peculiarly neurotic flavor to its ethos. Is it not true that environmentalists of this particular breed are all orphans in one sense or another? As we work in our conversations to understand this viewpoint,

John reminds Jimmie that our initial sympathy for the character of Anne and our love of the novella grew up under very specific circumstances of reception. John had read the book for the first time just after his mother had died the summer before. Jimmie read it on the airplane on the way to his own mother's funeral.

In class today, we're discussing the prototype of the ecologically informed, alienated, and literate ethos, as represented in Thoreau's chapter "Solitude" from *Walden*. Thoreau is making one of his favorite rhetorical moves, contrasting his own deep connection with nature with the relatively superficial relation of those who come to visit him from town: "I come and go," he writes, "with a strange liberty in Nature, a part of herself": "all the elements are unusually congenial to me. The bullfrogs trump to usher in the night, and the note of the whippoorwill is borne on the rippling wind from over the water. Sympathy with the fluttering alder and poplar leaves almost takes away my breath; yet, like the lake, my serenity is rippled but not ruffled" (87). His complete identification with nature stands in contrast with the visitors, who far from identifying with the woods, take tokens of it in their hands, shape them to their own character, and leave them behind when they return to their preferred places, where their true identification belongs: "They who come rarely to the woods take some little piece of the forest into their hands to play with by the way, which they leave, either intentionally or accidentally. One has peeled a willow wand, woven it into a ring, and dropped it on my table" (87). These meditations on his difference from others lead ultimately to his famous thesis that "Society is commonly too cheap" (92): "I find it wholesome to be alone the greater part of the time. To be in company, even with the best, is soon wearisome and dissipating. I love to be alone. I never found the companion that was so companionable as solitude" (91).

The students' reception of Thoreau is mixed; most of them have read him before. One says, "I hate Thoreau, always have, ever since high school." John urges him to elaborate on his dislike. He says he can't put his finger on the problem exactly, but the Front Row is ready when he's not. They leap into the breach with their by-now predictable chorus:

"Really wordy!"

"I agree: Entirely too wordy!"

"It's hard to concentrate on what he's trying to say when he goes on and on like this. My brain can't hold all the information. My head is wanting to explode."

One student associates the demands Thoreau makes upon the audience's concentration with the challenges he offers to the reader's consciousness, connecting form to content. Agreeing that he's hard to read, she adds, "He makes a double standard, like all these people don't understand nature like I do. I'm special and they're shallow. Nature is for me, not them. But how does he know what they think?"

After our experience with the character of Anne, we are more open to the Front Row, more mistrusting of our own dismissive attitude, evident in our pet name for them, "Front Row Dallas Republican." Thoreau's rhetoric, we must admit, not only presents us with a socially alienated persona, but may also produce an alienated reception in the demands it makes on its reader and in its use of irony. The rhetoric of irony turns on the development of what has been understood as a *triple persona* (Aune, Black, and Wander). The First Persona is that of the alienated author, the first-person "I" of the discourse. The author's ideal audience can be viewed as a Second Persona, a character that plays the role of the intimately addressed second-person "you" for the author's knowledgeable "I." For Thoreau and for followers like Dodge, the Second Persona is the aspiring novice or fellow-initiate into nature's chosen few. The development of an ideal audience or Second Persona already hints at an excluded audience, a Third Persona, which stands as "they" to the author's "I" and to the ideal audience's "you." Identification forms between the First and Second Persona as together they ironically contemplate the ignorance of the Third Persona: "You and I can see how stupid and misguided they are. It's up to us to save the world."

Many of our students feel themselves placed into the position of Third Persona by the habitual irony of the deeply ecological, literate, alienated First Persona of Romantic nature writing while we, as purveyors of ecocomposition, happily assume the role of Second Persona. What we have realized is that we must, at various points in the reading and writing process of the course, assume the role of a Fourth Persona. Barely even perceived by the author or First Persona, this Fourth is that of the critic, the one who at least momentarily stands apart from full participation in the charged ideological action embodied in the text and its reception. The very act of identifying the First, the Second, and the Third Persona places the reader in the position of the Fourth. At any point, one may return to the fray and assert one's position as Second or Third, but having identified the ironic processes at work, the reader is not likely to be quite so naive about either of those two positions.

From the start, several of our students are willing to participate as Second Persona to Thoreau's First. They defend him against the attacks of those who would place him in the camp of the woodsy and wordy: "No," says one, "Thoreau is not just wordy; he's poetic. You have to read him slowly and take the meaning from each word. He's slow to read, but rewarding." John and Jimmie sneak smiles at one another, which quickly fade as the young defender continues. "Reading Thoreau is like reading *Chicken Soup for the Soul*. It makes you a deeper, more thoughtful person. I just love it."

After class, John says to Jimmie, "Good God! Thoreau would be horrified to be compared with a cheesy book like *Chicken Soup*, little snippets of writing that people read at bedtime so they can sleep better."

"Deeply literate it's not," Jimmie agrees, "but at least the student got the genre right: *Walden* and *Chicken Soup* are both wisdom literature. One's for the deeply literate; the other's for the secondarily oral, the mass audience."

But John's right in the big sense. Thoreau demands close attention over a long span of time, and *Chicken Soup* demands next to nothing of the reader's time and energy. The single chapter from *Walden* is far too taxing for most of our students. Their journals bear this out. He is our hero, not theirs. The combination of his elitism with his ironic style drives them away, makes him seem distant, old, cold, unsociable, not applicable to their lives.

Still, we can't give in. We might ultimately throw Jim Dodge to the secondarily oral urban wolves of mass-cultured Dallas, but we want even our most resistant students to come to appreciate Thoreau. Our own resistance is engaged. So we turn hopefully again to the students who seem to value his work.

Interestingly, those who defend Thoreau tell us that they associate him with Ghandi and with Martin Luther King Jr. They tell us that they read Thoreau in high school, only a little of *Walden*, but all of *Civil Disobedience*. They come back to *Walden* with a receptive attitude. It is the social and political Thoreau, the radical, who engages them first and helps them make sense of the poetic hermit whose own neighbors thought of his concern with nature as "absurd" (Buell 104-5).

A similar viewpoint comes out in a bold new book by Hephzibah Roskelly and Kate Ronald that attempts to reconnect the teaching of composition in America to roots in romanticism and pragmatism. American romanticism, the forerunner of pragmatism, is different from European romanticism in precisely its sociability and political engagement, according to Roskelly and Ronald: "The ideal of Nature and the importance of the individual took on different—more conscious and rhetorical—dimensions in a land where individuals were required to shape national, as well as individual, identities and where the natural world was as often experienced as a combatant as a refuge" (38). In America, there have been no established relations to the land and to the society into which a person is born. You learn to define yourself against the background of a dynamic society and of a dynamic natural environment. The struggle to define the self makes ripples out into society as others adjust to make places for the newly defined one. In developing "a *method* for communing, as though the solitary personal struggle is at one with other personal struggles," writers like Emerson, Whitman, Fuller, Dickinson, and even Thoreau "dissolve the dichotomy the Europeans seem to embrace by considering the self's relationship to society" (59). In *Walden,* "Thoreau's experience . . . is, in fact, not primarily isolated or self-involved but communal and dialectical" (60). Indeed there are moments in *Walden* when Thoreau seems deliberately to collapse the rhetorical distinction between the Second and the Third Persona. He does so in his introduction to the first chapter:

> In most books, the *I,* or first person, is omitted; in this it will be retained; that, in respect to egotism is the main difference. We commonly do not remember that it is, after all, the first person that is speaking. I should not talk so much about myself if there were any body else whom I knew as well. Unfortunately, I am confined to this theme by the narrowness of my experience. Moreover, I, on my side, require of every writer, first or last, a simple and sincere account of his own life, and not merely what he has heard of other men's lives; some such account as he would send to his kindred from a distant land; for if he has lived sincerely, it must have been in a distant land to me. Perhaps these pages are more particularly addressed to poor students. As for the rest of my readers, they will accept such portions as apply to them. I trust that none will stretch the seams in putting on the coat, for it may do good service to him whom it fits (1-2).

The passage fairly brims with irony. But its potential exclusions are full of invitations to join the author in his playful contemplation of what it means to say the word *I* in writing and to know the self. Those who omit the first person, he suggests, do so in the name of foregoing egotism but end up more egotistical yet by seeming to speak for something larger than their own experiences. Thoreau makes no claim to speak for others and says he asks of other writers that they address him sincerely, as kindred in a distant land—the voice of the alien who is nevertheless a kinsman.

Worn-out then with the role of the writer, he turns to the reader and names forthrightly his ideal audience, the "poor student" who wears the hand-me-down coats of others. But he is hardly unkind to "the rest of [his] readers" whom he invites to "accept such portions as apply to them." He hopes no one will stretch the seams of his coat, his book—misinterpret him? try to fit him to a context too large?—for the poor and slender reader, the one in need of self-definition, comfort, warmth, and yet the one hearty enough to accept hard lessons, the student, will get good service from this tight-fitting coat.

The students listen patiently to our defense of Thoreau. The journals and the class discussion show some movement of the students from Third Persona to Second. They learn to look for the invitations he offers. They learn to think about him as a critic in a land still saddled with slavery, a land whose growth threatened the lives of its native inhabitants, both human and animal, flora as well as fauna, a land embarking on a technological experiment unparalleled in human history, embodied for Thoreau in the railroad. But most still find him too daunting of a messenger, the coat too tight a fit: "I know he's important, but he's just too hard to understand," one student concludes.

Despite our own defense and that of Roskelly and Ronald, Thoreau's rhetoric may have no more than a limited appeal in our times. He may well contain the seeds of a more sociable literacy and a more open political participation, but the ironic mode of the exclusionary alien predominates in his work. He is primarily the father of "deep ecology" and only the distant uncle of "social ecology." As Killingsworth and Palmer have argued in *Ecospeak: Rhetoric and Environmental Politics in America*, "social ecology" is more likely than "deep ecology" to expand political participation in the environmental protection movement. The rhetoric of deep ecology tends to narrow the scope of the Second Persona ("you") and to expand the scope of the Third ("they"). But social ecology does the opposite. It connects environmentalism to issues of public health and human economy; it undergirds the most critical understanding of sustainable development and environmental justice. The movement against environmental racism, for example—from Murray Bookchin's early efforts in critical theory to recent experiments in practical politics in the Rio Grande Valley of Texas and Louisiana's Cancer Alley (see Ashe, Bullard, and Peterson)—requires broader participation and a rhetoric that recognizes the need of people to "make a living" and "pay the bills," a need always near to the top of consciousness among our students—both Front Row Dallas and Back Row Farm and Ranch—as well as the working people victimized by race and class prejudice. The environmental justice movement has only recently caught the notice of scholars in ecocriticism and environmental rhetoric (see Ashe; Buell's comments on Leslie Marmon Silko; Killingsworth and Palmer, "Ecopolitics";and Peterson). And only a few of the movement's writers find their way into textbooks still dominated by the nature writer's preference for deep ecology. In the text we are using for this course, writers like Terry Tempest Williams and Tino Villanueva appear only briefly, leavening the dominant presence of nature writing as it has become canonized, largely in the woodsy and wordy tradition of Thoreau.

The tendency of woodsy and wordy writers to favor slow-paced contemplative writings, to project alienated and idiosyncratic individualism, and to retreat from rather than engage society at large limits the rhetorical reach and the political efficacy of environmentalist discourse. The sad truth about heavily ironic writing that constricts the Second Persona and enlarges the Third is that, as James Arnt Aune suggests, when it is "extended into a worldview by habitual practice"—as it is in the conceptual triad of ecology, alienation, and literacy—it "is essentially *conservative* ideologically"; it suggests elitism and projects a "Mandarin-like disdain" for the mass of humanity (20).

A recent issue of *Sierra* magazine reports on the promising trend of a coalition of strange bedfellows—labor unions and environmentalists—and argues that if this potential alliance is "built up carefully over time . . . they may find that they have more in common than they think" (Moberg 114). Likewise, if the modernist vision of the alienated voice crying from the wilderness does not play well with our students, rather than unilaterally forcing that vision, we should recognize the opportunity of participating in the development of a more socially conscious environmental rhetoric, which advances both environmental protection and social justice. Rather than stubbornly resisting our students' resistance, rather than merely attempting to indoctrinate, we might not only teach our students something about composition and literacy, but in the process, also contribute to an environmental rhetoric constructed in a climate of sociable literacy.

Sociable literacy is an idea that comes directly from our encounters with our students. It fits with the "process approach" that has dominated college composition classrooms since the 1980s. In the arena of ecocomposition, sociable literacy provides a companion concept for social ecology.

We arrived at the concept one evening in very early Spring sitting in the growing darkness on the patio of Jimmie's suburban Texas home. It was the very day the barn swallows were returning to take up residence in the mud nest they abandon each August. They fluttered overhead as John told Jimmie about his recent work with the Sierra Club. Then as we turned to analyzing the journals and papers from our students, we got to talking about how the students were such social animals and how the writings of Thoreau, Dodge, and Jack Kerouac ("Alone on a Mountaintop") filled them either with antipathy or wonder ("I just couldn't live like that, all alone and all").

Jimmie cranked up a train of thought about how the very idea of literacy requires aloneness. If students are so estranged from the idea of solitude, can they ever attain the concentration and attention span needed to become devoted readers and writers? He was on the way to mourning the loss of literate culture, when John hit upon an important insight: "We're really not that different from them, man. Look at how we write. I read something and say, 'This is cool, check it out,' and you read it, and then one of us works it into our text and shows it to the other and asks how it fits, and on and on."

Building on the insight, we recalled the sociability of our recent work. John's wife read with him as he prepared his syllabus. Jimmie read with him to prepare for teaching the course. Our students read and argued with us in class discussions, in journals, and in at least two drafts of every paper. Jimmie's wife Jackie Palmer read the abstract and early versions of *our* paper and offered comments and suggestions. Other faculty and graduate students were enlisted as readers and commentators. Music rehearsal and family dinners got interrupted when an insight emerged. Telephone calls and e-mail messages broke the silence and solitude of the writing and reading experience on a daily basis. Then we passed the essay to the energetic editors of this volume, who prepublished it on a web site and invited other contributors to read and respond to it.

We are members of a writing community. From this perspective, the old romantic concept of the alienated, decontextualized writer appears almost pathological. And yet, we cling to it and expose our students to it. Why? The short answer is that it gives us strength; it is heroic and has a powerful place in our mythology as writers and environmentalists. When we retreat to our studies to face the blank page, to write the wordy texts that our companions in literacy will ultimately help us make more sociable, we remember Thoreau and Bass, just as we think of them when we walk alone in the woods. Our heroes endured the necessary solitude and brought us back the words that lead us to identify with them and to trust in our own literacy. The movement inward and outward, from solitude to society and back again, is the very motion of literacy. Like literacy, environmentalism could not be sustained without both alienated individuals and mass identification, indeed without a degree of alienation and identification within each individual. Some of our students in ecocomposition lack sufficient alienation or critical distance, just as we and our heroes may well lack sufficient socialization (or awareness of our need for socialization). To move from deep to social ecology (and back again), from alienation to engagement (and back again), from literacy to orality (and back again): These are the necessary rhythms of the environmentalist in contemporary life.

WORKS CITED

Anderson, Lorraine, Scott Slovic, and John P. O'Grady. *Literature and the Environment: A Reader on Nature and Culture.* New York: Longman, 1999.

Ashe, Diana. "Generic and Institutional Constraints in Environmental Advocacy Discourse." Ph. D. diss., Texas A&M University, 1999.

Aune, James Arnt. *Rhetoric and Marxism.* Boulder, CO: Westview, 1994.

Bass, Rick. *The New Wolves.* New York: Lyons Press, 1998.

———. "On Willow Creek." In Anderson, Slovic, and O'Grady, 249–58.

———. *The Sky, the Stars, the Wilderness: Novellas.* Boston: Houghton Mifflin, 1997.

Black, Edwin. "The Second Persona." *Quarterly Journal of Speech* 56 (1970): 113–19.

Bookchin, Murray. *The Ecology of Freedom.* Palo Alto, CA: Cheshire, 1982.

Buell, Lawrence. *The Environmental Imagination: Thoreau, Nature Writing, and the Formation of American Culture.* Cambridge; Harvard University Press, 1995.

Bullard, Robert D., ed. *Confronting Environmental Racism: Voices from the Grassroots.* Boston: South End, 1993.

Cantrill, James G., and Christine Oravec, eds. *The Symbolic Earth: Discourse and Our Creation of the Environment.* Lexington: University Press of Kentucky, 1996.

Cooper, Marilyn. "An Ecology of Writing." *College English* 48 (1986): 364–75.

Dodge, Jim. "Living by Life: Some Bioregional Theory and Practice." In Anderson, Slovic, and O'Grady, 230–38.

Herndl, Carl, and Stuart Brown, eds. *Green Culture: Environmental Rhetoric in Contemporary America.* Madison: University of Wisconsin Press, 1996.

Kerouac, Jack. "Alone on a Mountaintop." In Anderson, Slovic, and O'Grady, 191–99.

Killingsworth, M. Jimmie, and Jacqueline S. Palmer. "The Discourse of Environmentalist 'Hysteria.' " *Quarterly Journal of Speech* 81 (1995): 1–19.

———. "Ecopolitics and the Literature of the Borderlands: The Frontiers of Environmental Justice in Latina and Native American Writing." *Writing the Environment: Ecocriticism and Literature.* Eds. Richard Kerridge and Neil Samuells, London: Zed, 1998. 196–207.

———. *Ecospeak: Rhetoric and Environmental Politics in America.* Carbondale: Southern Illinois University Press, 1992.

———. "*Silent Spring* and Science Fiction: An Essay in the History and Rhetoric of Narrative." In Waddell, forthcoming.

McLuhan, Marshall. *The Gutenberg Galaxy.* Toronto: University of Toronto Press, 1962.

————. *Understanding Media: The Extensions of Man.* New York: McGraw-Hill, 1964.

Moberg, David. "Brothers and Sisters." *Sierra* 84.1 (January/February 1999): 46-51, 114.

Muir, John. "A Wind-Storm in the Forests." In Anderson, Slovic, and O'Grady, 178–84.

Ong, Walter J. *Orality and Literacy: The Technologizing of the Word.* London: Metheun, 1982.

Peterson, Tarla Rai. *Sharing the Earth: The Rhetoric of Sustainable Development.* University of South Carolina Press, 1997.

Roskelly, Hephzibah, and Kate Ronald. *Reason to Believe: Romanticism, Pragmatism, and the Teaching of Writing.* Albany: State University of New York Press, 1998.

Thoreau, Henry David. *Walden and Resistance to Civil Government.* Norton Critical Edition. 2nd ed. Ed. William Rossi. New York: Norton, 1992.

Waddell, Craig, ed. *"And No Birds Sing": The Rhetoric of Rachel Carson.* Carbondale: Southern Illinois University Press, forthcoming.

Wander, Phillip. "The Third Persona: An Ideological Turn in Rhetorical Theory." *Central States Speech Journal* 35 (1984); 197–216.

Whitman, Walt. *Complete Poetry and Collected Prose.* Washington, DC: Library of America, 1982.

The Politics of Place:

Student Travelers and Pedagogical Maps

Julie Drew
University of Akron
Akron, Ohio

INTRODUCTION: ECOCOMPOSITION

Although pleased, I was initially troubled by the editors' invitation to contribute to this book. I knew early on that I would not write about the various relationships among nature and discourse. I had no desire to stake out
a position regarding whether or not compositionists ought to work to con-
serve and protect natural environments by teaching students to produce
and analyze texts about nature and environmentalism. While these are increasingly interesting and complex topics within composition studies, they
are not areas in which I feel drawn to write. After talking with Dobrin and
Weisser, however, it became clear to me that my discomfort was a result of
my own limited understanding of the ways in which ecocomposition
might offer a broad and generative theoretical framework. Consequently,
after much reading and many conversations, what has become most interesting to me about this category of theories and practices called "ecocomposition" is what I would call *"the politics of place"* for teaching, learning,
and—perhaps most importantly—for research in composition studies.

A politics of place is certainly locatable at the theoretical core of any
conception of environmental theory or ecocriticism. But compositionists
are interested in more than reading and writing texts that deal in some way
with nature as subject matter. We don't have to go far—indeed, we don't
have to go anywhere at all—to think about the ways in which *place* plays a
role in producing texts, and how such relationships affect the discursive
work that writers attempt from within the university. In fact, the very idea
of nature, or natural environment, in the composition classroom might arguably be subsumed within a larger notion of place that certainly includes,
but is not limited to nature. So, while I remain somewhat disinterested in

thinking and writing about natural places, and about how such concepts and realities might pertain to writing instruction, I am profoundly interested in *the place of writing instruction itself*.

The place of writing instruction, almost exclusively understood by teachers as the writing classroom, has been, and continues to be, examined by scholars in the field as a politicized space, and in that sense a politics of place is by no means a new idea. From David Bartholomae's "Inventing the University" to Nedra Reynold's "Composition's Imagined Geographies," compositionists have become increasingly interested in understanding the ways in which particular spaces are politicized, and the effects of those politicized spaces on writing and writers. For Bartholomae, Reynolds, and for other theorists, the politics of the classroom as embodied location plays a vital role in our understanding of how writers—especially basic writers—write in institutional settings. I hope to begin exploring the possibilities for both teaching and research that may be found in a conviction that first, the classroom, as institutional/pedagogical space is also necessarily informed in multiple and conflicting ways by other places in which discursive pedagogies also abound. And second, that that conviction *must* be accompanied by a commitment to include students in composition research and to view our epistemological projects as coproductions. I will suggest here that the figure of *traveler* and the metaphors of both *geography* and *cartography* may prove useful toward that end, both as a persuasive rationale and as a springboard for methodological reform.

LOCATING WRITING: WHY SPATIAL THEORY?

Before we can understand the ways in which social space may impact the research, teaching, and practice of writing, we must first have some sense of a theory of place, or spatiality itself that addresses social relations. Edward W. Soja argues that critical social theory is "still enveloped in a temporal master-narrative, in a historical but not yet comparably geographical imagination" (137). Unlike the temporal, the spatial has generally not been used by social theorists as a critical lens through which to observe and understand social relations and the political struggles that mark them. Michel Foucault and Henri Lefebvre identify the nineteenth century's myopic obsession with history, an obsession that necessarily suggests a temporal, and thus linear sense of social movement. The twentieth century was also marked by this predominant critical perspective—a perspective that serves to erase the politicization of space itself in its suggestion that social structures are built upon a fixed and extra-ideological geography.

In order to address this theoretical and material oversight, Patricia Yaeger notes that the postmodern insistence that power is discursively produced and maintained is only partially correct, since it does not also consider that sovereign power necessarily implies space (8). Politicized space is both the location of hegemony and, importantly, the location of the veiling of power. And, since "sovereignty requires space to survive, its politicized places—those everyday sites where power is promulgated—become the very domain where the politics of space is forgotten" (ibid). Soja, also interested in an intellectual move toward understanding the continual structuring and restructuring of "human geographies," identifies a critical need for the "social being actively emplaced in time *and* space in an explicitly historical *and* geographical contextualization" (136).

Such notions clearly contend with traditional intellectual reliance upon the temporal in critical social theory—the reliance, that is, upon history and a notion of the progressive. A historical perspective traditionally views time as acting upon space, time as actor/subject and space as object, fixed and knowable in a linear, timely fashion. For while the "historical imagination is never completely spaceless . . . it is always time and history that provide the primary 'variable containers'" in which we intellectually and critically address the social. An "already-made geography sets the stage," Soja argues, "while the willful making of history dictates the action and defines the story line" (139). The unquestioned primacy of history for social critique, however, is changing: "A distinctively postmodern and critical human geography is taking shape, brashly reasserting the interpretive significance of space in the historically privileged confines of contemporary critical thought" (137). It is within this movement in critical theory that a politics of place for composition may be located.

The traditional and consequential submergence of the spatial within the temporal for critical social theory, then, effectively helps to veil institutional power within politicized spaces such as classrooms. Such an understanding is important for composition studies because critical social theory—the "search for practical understanding of the world as a means of emancipation versus maintenance of the status quo"—is an indispensable component of radical pedagogical theory and practice (139). Compositionists, of course, have long been concerned with the power relations that reside at the site of literacy work: the university, and particularly the writing classroom.[1] The geographic space of the composition classroom is, for many in the field, a space in which social relations may be variously reproduced or called into question. Thus, for composition, identifying and working within a politics of place for writing instruction is an ongoing project. What may be problematic, however, in our current thinking about the place of discursive learning, is that students often exist for compositionists *exclusively* within the classroom, when the material reality of their lives, and the spaces they inhabit, would suggest that this is only a partial picture at best. And if the places of discursive pedagogy are not only multiple, but in conflict as well, then the classroom itself may be more complex, and simultaneously less effective as a location of learning than we might have assumed.

Part of the problem lies in the figure of "student" itself, a figure that resonates within the culture as the novice, young and as yet un(in)formed. Any attempt to construct a pedagogy based on such an unexamined understanding of *student* is necessarily saddled with such cultural baggage and is therefore likely to exclude most knowledges and experiences outside classroom walls. But students pass through, and only pause briefly within, classrooms; they dwell within and visit various other locations, locations whose politics and discourse conventions both construct and identify them. By reimagining students as *travelers* we may construct a politics of place that is more likely to include students in the academic work of composition, and less likely to continue to identify and manage students as discursive novices. Modifying our notions of what students are and do to include traveling may create opportunities for students to acknowledge and use the power relations that exist in the often conflicting discourse communities they traverse, and for compositionists to improve pedagogical practices in ways that have positive material consequences for writers. And, by including students in our research—not as objects of study, but rather as coinquirers—we stand a better chance of locating and understanding the multiple discursive pedagogies at work in both classroom and other spaces.

OUT OF PLACE: STUDENT TRAVELERS

Patricia Yaeger's contention that power "requires space to survive," and that everyday spaces are the "domain where the politics of space is forgotten" has a familiar ring to it in composition studies (8). Much contemporary work in composition theory examines the role of writing instruction as a purveyor of cultural capital within the larger framework of institutional education. If the classroom is, indeed, where the politics of that space is forgotten, it stands to reason that the politics of *other* spaces— spaces that impact the mission of institutional education—are *also* forgotten in the classroom. In other words, any understanding of the power relations that are maintained and reproduced within institutional educational settings must necessarily be veiled in institutional spaces, including the politics of *other* spaces that might call institutional power into question.

I want to locate the classroom within the pedagogical, rather than locate the pedagogical within the classroom. In order to understand the pedagogical implications of politicized space for teaching writing, we often constitute our students and their textual productions as objects for analysis, rather than engaging them to help us identify the pedagogical implications of the spaces they variously inhabit. It is my contention here that we must do more than focus on the classroom as a politicized space that participates in constructing both students and their texts.[2] We must also expand the role of place in the pedagogical, and the politics that work within and around identifiable spaces, to include the material realities of movement—of travel—and the multiple spaces within which students reside and learn. The pedagogical is not located exclusively within the classroom; rather, the classroom is one location in which pedagogical moments occur. And those other places, those other pedagogies, are embodied in the students we see for a few hours each week. We may discover some interesting possibilities for an increasingly multicultural population of writers within university settings by thinking of those writers as travelers. Looking at postcolonial literature and literary criticism, as well as cultural anthropology, may prove a useful first step.

Postcolonial literature offers some insight into the kinds of fragmented and hybrid subjectivities that such a notion of traveling and spatial construction of identity suggest. Derek Wright, in speaking of characterization in much postcolonial literature, notes that "those who live fragmentarily, through a number of cultures . . . always have missing parts of themselves elsewhere, on the other side of some border" (382). This "irretrievable hybridization" that Wright speaks of may be useful for thinking about the ways in which the places students inhabit help to define both the social and political constraints under which they work in school, and the texts they produce within the classroom.[3] Basic writers, as a population of students identified by institutional assessment, are easily read into such a notion of multiple cultures and hybrid subject positions. Working *with* basic writers to locate themselves both in and in-between pedagogical locations where discursive abilities are assessed in very different ways, and power is distributed accordingly, may serve to motivate students grappling with unfamiliar discourse conventions. It may also help to improve the teacher-researcher's ability to develop and institute more effective classroom practices.

Understanding students as traveling between and dwelling in multiple locations whose discursive pedagogies help to construct them as writers is one important component of what ecocomposition might engender. Equally important—especially for research—is gaining a more complex understanding of the classroom as an artificially bordered location where research is conducted and conclusions are drawn. James Clifford's work in cultural anthropology addresses these very issues.

Clifford speaks of the "village" as research site; for our purposes here, I want to think of the composition classroom as Clifford's village. The writing classroom is inhabited by students and teachers , and, as such, is a "bounded site" that serves as a "mappable center" for knowledge-production—for teaching and for learning. The classroom is too often seen as a "manageable unit," quarantining as it does students and teachers in order to "centralize a [pedagogical] practice" and observe its results (98). And, not unlike traditional anthropological fieldwork that locates culture within the boundaries of the village, when we locate the pedagogical moments of discourse production simply, easily, and exclusively within the classroom, "the sites and relations of *translations* are minimized." Localizing students, and the pedagogical, exclusively within the classroom tends to "marginalize or erase several blurred boundary areas, historical realities that slip out of the [pedagogical] frame." What is lost is "the wider world of intercultural linguistic import-export in which the [classroom] experience is already enmeshed" (100).[4]

Traditionally, students are not asked to examine either the political realities of the classroom that in fact shape that space, or the texts they are asked to produce in particular ways. Nor are students asked, by extension, to examine the political *other* spaces they inhabit, the discourses of those spaces in which they participate, and the ways in which all of those places interact to create power relations within which they must operate. The issue of translation is one that might be more likely addressed if students are seen as traveling to and from various other discursive locales, and as always negotiating those spatial and discursive geographies.

Naming the writers in our classrooms "students" is a way of confining them, reducing them to knowable objects, by intimating that one aspect of their discursive and intellectual lives is accurately representative of the whole. But students, like villagers, "unsullied by contact with and knowledge about a larger world have probably never existed" (100). Composition pedagogical theory tends to localize in the classroom "what is actually a regional/national/global nexus," and thus relegates "to the margins a [student's] external relations and displacements" (100). Classroom sites of intellectual interaction are only a partial story of teaching and learning and engaging with discourse conventions; classrooms are only one site among many where these activities occur. Understanding the pedagogical as politicized and locatable in all of the many locations students inhabit and travel between may expand the possibilities of classroom practices that revolve around difference. We might focus on hybrid experiences as pedagogical, not just those that take place within the confines of the classroom, the traditionally understood site of learning. We might also focus on what Clifford calls the "concrete mediations" of the cultural figure *student* and the intercultural figure *traveler* in "specific cases of historical [and spatial] tension and relationship (101).

The roles of student and of traveler, then, could be constitutive of what counts as both teaching and learning, in the multiple spaces in which those figures operate. The classroom is thus both politicized and contextualized as one "constructed and disputed" bounded territory among many others, and thus "sites of displacement, interference, and interaction, previously occluded, come into view" (101). In this way we may actually come to include students, because we must, in understanding what and how various discourses construct their social selves, and how we might together teach and learn in academic settings. We might also begin to move beyond composition's reliance on such notions as contact zones, which exist (for teachers) in the classroom, and move instead toward notions of coproductions, hybrid experiences as pedagogical, and the practices of various discourses as travel, best understood by mapping.

PEDAGOGICAL POSSIBILITIES: MAPPING DISCOURSE

Thinking of students as travelers may be useful in two very specific ways. First, it brings into focus the mere fact that they *do* inhabit external, politicized spaces, as well as the particular pedagogies embodied in those sites. Attempting as teachers to identify the social relations and implicit and explicit power relationships within the various locations students inhabit is an impossible task and, I suspect, one reason why we avoid fully incorporating a notion of students' multiple external connections into our pedagogical thinking. This is not to say, of course, that compositionists do not recognize that students have discursive lives external to the classroom. Unfortunately, when we do attempt to account for the politics of place we tend to stall at the door of the classroom. We fix students in classrooms, imagining through such pedagogical norms as race, class, and gender writing topics that we've placed academic writing within a cultural context that will both attract and challenge students to think and write critically. Students-as-travelers, however, are *already* engaged in various forms of critical thinking and would best be served by an increased understanding of theories and practices of discourse that will help them move more successfully between and among the various spaces they inhabit. And second, thinking of students as travelers may in some small way disarm the often destructive tags of varying degrees of literacy with which we identify student writers who are native English speakers.

One way of incorporating the notion of academic writers-as-travelers into the composition classroom is to engage students in a form of discursive map-making. Such an activity might serve not only to highlight the fact that academic discourse conventions are just that—conventions— but also to help students grasp both the politics of place and the styles and genres of academically powerful writing. I believe that by contrasting the conventions of specific forms of academic discourse to those of discourses in which students may feel both more familiar and more privileged will de-emphasize their status as novices and emphasize the political realities and meanings of translation and movement. In this way, they are less likely to feel or be identified as deficient or incompetent. Instead, they will more likely—and more accurately—be viewed as travelers who, to varying degrees, have arrived in a place where power relations are obscured, the discourse is unfamiliar, and the conventions as yet unmastered.

Each student would, of course, be responsible for identifying the various locations she or he inhabits, the power relations indicated by language use that reside in those locations, and the discursive conventions familiar to insiders. In identifying these categories for students as always already locatable, and varying from location to location, we pave the way for introducing the particular conventions and forms of academic discourses students must learn. Academic discourses then become for students exactly what they are: the dominant discourse of *this* place (and perhaps other places within which they might wish to effectively dwell). The whole notion of "literacy" thus becomes for students a construct rather than a condemnation, as they identify specific geographic locations they inhabit and map the various and competing power relations signified by differences in vocabularies, modes of communication, discursive forms, and so on.

When students produce texts in an academic setting they are asked to practice the forms and conventions of particular genres, and to gain a level of proficiency in manipulating those genres deemed appropriate by school culture. By producing discursive maps, students might expand what we think of as their writing process to include not only invention, drafting, and revising practices, but the practice of analyzing the cultural forces within which they are situated and that directly affect the production of their texts. Student writing itself may then be viewed as a material connection among various forces at work in the moment of student authorship. When students write, they do so out of particular conjunctures of social and material forces, indicated by their very presence in the college classroom. Furthermore, the normalizing presence and judgment of instructors who evaluate student writing help students learn to write in ways that support particular social relations. Student writing and writing instruction both express and connect, as their texts link, in the moments of both production and reception, the economic, political, social, and other forces that work to produce and reproduce cultural meaning.

A pedagogy that articulates both the conventions of particular, institutional discourses and the politics of institutional and other spaces, then, would locate student-written texts at the matrix of a host of intersecting social forces that authorize students as writers and that simultaneously support, reproduce, or subvert particular social relations. Such a pedagogy might avoid the privileging of historical over spatial critical theory that serves to further veil the power relations residing in geographic and discursive locations. A pedagogy that attempts to simultaneously articulate these notions would ask students, as part of their writing process, to identify those forces that are working for and against their authorship.

In attempting to understand the politics of classroom space, for example, students might explore forces such as their own linguistic backgrounds in relation to institutional discourse; gender differences in communication patterns; who and what may be silenced by various, competing genres that they must, nevertheless, emulate and manipulate; and the subjectivity of both peers and teachers in reading and evaluating writing. Recognition of both their authorship *and* the power of the conditions of that authorship would demand identification and analysis of those aspects of both the institutional process of literacy instruction and their own locations in various cultural spaces that either aid or hinder their attempts to author academically successful texts. And, finally, those texts, authored by students, which have been deemed powerful and effective, or weak and unsuccessful, respectively, by the instructors and the institutional machinery that produces such evaluations and their consequences, would also be taken into account. Such analyses, coupled with intensive practice in writing—in making statements, in stylistics, and in manipulating genres—could avoid the tendency in composition to construct students without their participation. That is to say, we might avoid taking on the task of naming students in relation to dominant discourse and literacy—a task that leads us to fix them within the classroom as the most obvious and knowable place in which they reside as an identifiable group.

Erasing those exterior-to-the-classroom places that students variously inhabit and travel among ignores the "prior and ongoing contacts and commerce with exterior places and forces which are not part" of the object of study—institutional, sanctioned writing, performed under surveillance (Clifford 99). If the pedagogical moment for student travelers is at once locatable in various spaces and in multiple and competing ways, however, we might expand our ability both to understand the power of translation in monolingual competence, and thus teach writing in more effective and meaningful ways. Nedra Reynolds asks us to "attend to the negotiations of power that take place across and within a number of spaces: regional or topographical, domestic or institutional, architectural or electronic, real or imagined" (13). It is not only those localized negotiations of power that occur within and across the institutional space of the composition classroom to which pedagogical theorists and practitioners ought to attend; as Reynolds rightly notes, other spaces impact our work. But these multiple, endless number and kinds of spaces are only bordered and named in our constructions of them. If we are truly interested in the pedagogical, in teaching and learning, then students must be invited to name and explore the ways in which they embody the many spaces they inhabit, and the discourses in which they both do and hope to participate. A politics of place that not only invites but *needs* student participation in identifying and understanding the simultaneity of both ordinary and politicized spaces that impact learning is made possible by the theoretical spaces currently being mapped by ecocomposition.[5]

CONCLUSION: TEACHING ON THE ROAD

Perhaps the difficulty in letting go of a notion of fixity and singularity in regard to where and how learning happens, and of students as such existing primarily within the classroom, lies in our own reluctance to see ourselves as performing our work, in a sense, on the road, in seeing ourselves as occupants of a place where students briefly pause—a roadside stand, perhaps—in their lifelong relationships with multiple discourses. Those who write for and within the university do so, to varying degrees of success, by securing some fluency in the various modes of discourse required by the academic community. But they also, necessarily, have and continue to secure varying degrees of fluency in other discourse communities, a process that no doubt brings very different pressures to bear on those who operate within them. It is not in the conflict, however, that the pedagogical moment survives and flourishes, but rather in the coproductions, the mediations, and the hybrid literacies that result from life within and between politicized spaces. It is interesting, and perhaps productive, then, to imagine the university, to imagine the classroom, as a politicized location on the road between various other places whose political and discursive relations students wish to successfully negotiate.

I have suggested here that in furthering our work in composition we consider the possibilities of a politics of place, of moving beyond thinking of pedagogical space as fixed, and thus of students as fixed. I have suggested some ways in which relatively new metaphors might offer pedagogical possibilities. Shifting human geographies, if mapped by those whose travels constitute discursive challenges for them, may lend themselves to the formulation of a transgressive and productive pedagogy that builds on student travelers' knowledge and experience of the politics of place for writing.

NOTES

1. For discussions of the ways in which teaching reading and writing maintains and reproduces particular social relations, see, for example, David Bartholomae, Lynn Z. Bloom, Paulo Freire, and Elspeth Stuckey.

2. Bartholomae, in "Inventing the University," argues that students writing within the politicized space of the university must grapple with the veiled politics of that space in learning the discourses of the academy. His contention that students must first learn the commonplaces of a given discourse, and traverse various stages as they attempt to write their way into a privileged position has been key to composition's understanding of the politics of place for writing in institutional settings.

3. This is not to say that college students commonly experience the degree of displacement and cultural fragmentation one might attribute to the diasporic experience. The experience of fragmentation, of cultural and linguistic diversity, however, are readily apparent in students' lives—especially, perhaps, in the case of basic writers. Furthermore, the power relations embodied within the various locations in which students dwell has, arguably, a significant effect on their discursive practices, in much the same way that Derek Wright describes the postcolonial literary character.

4. Portions of this section were developed in Julie Drew, "Cultural Tourism and the Commodified Other: Reclaiming Difference in the Multicultural Classroom."

5. Portions of this section were developed in Drew, "(Teaching) Writing: Composition, Cultural Studies, Production."

WORKS CITED

Bartholomae, David. "Inventing the University." *When a Writer Can't Write: Studies in Writer's Block and Other Composing-Process Problems.* Ed. Mike Rose. New York: Guilford, 1985. 134–65.

Bloom, Lynn Z. "Freshman Composition as a Middle Class Enterprise." *College English* 56 (1996): 654–75.

Clifford, James. "Traveling Cultures." *Cultural Studies.* Eds. Lawrence Grossberg, Cary Nelson, and Paula Treichler. New York: Routledge, 1992. 96–116.

Drew, Julie: "Cultural Tourism and the Commodified Other: Reclaiming Difference in the Multicultural Classroom." *The Review of Education/Pedagogy/Cultural Studies* 19 (1997): 297–309.

———. "(Teaching) Writing: Composition, Cultural Studies, Production." *JAC: A Journal of Composition Theory* 19.3 (1999): 411–29.

Freire, Paulo. *Pedagogy of the Oppressed.* New York: Seabury, 1973.

Reynolds, Nedra. "Composition's Imagined Geographies: The Politics of Space in the Frontier, City, and Cyberspace." *CCC* 50.1 (1998): 12–35.

Soja, Edward W. "History: Geography: Modernity." *The Cultural Studies Reader.* Ed. Simon During. New York: Routledge, 1993. 135–50.

Stuckey, Elspeth. *The Violence of Literacy.* Portsmouth, N.H.: Boynton/Cook, 1991.

Wright, Derek. "Parenting the Nation: Some Observations on Nuruddin Farah's *Maps.*" *Order and Partialities: Theory, Pedagogy, and the "Postcolonial."* Albany: State University of New York Press, 1995. 377–90.

Yaeger, Patricia. "The Strange Effects of Ordinary Space." *The Geography of Identity.* Ed. Patricia Yaeger. University of Michigan Press, 1996.

The Ecology of Genre

Anis Bawarshi
University of Washington
Seattle, Washington

In the last thirty or so years, teachers and scholars of writing have made great strides in exploring the cognitive dimensions of textual production, to the extent that the "writing as process" (see Crowley) movement is now recognized as central to the intellectual and pedagogical enterprise of composition studies. Only more recently, however, have teachers and scholars of writing fully begun to consider the social dimensions that contribute to how and why cognition and texts are produced. This "social turn" (Trimbur) recognizes that there is more at work on the text than just the writer's autonomous cognition; there are also various social forces that constitute the scene of production within which the writer's cognition as well as his or her texts are situated and shaped. Within composition studies, this scene of writing is most commonly identified as a discourse community—the social and rhetorical environment within which goals, assumptions, and values are shared by participants who employ common discourse strategies for communicating and practicing these goals, assumptions, and values. Those teachers and scholars who espouse such a social constructionist position shift the balance of power from the writer's cognition to the writer's context, hence creating a dichotomy between those who argue for the primacy and cognitive authority of the writer and those who argue for the primacy and discursive authority of the writer's social environment.[1]

Of course, this dichotomy is pedagogically and theoretically limited. Neither the writer nor his or her social environment exists independently of one another. Neither is artificial nor static enough so as to remain self-sufficient. Rather, communicants and their social environments are constantly in the process of reproducing one another, in much the same way that biologic ecosystems sustain, and are sustained by, their organisms. Composition studies for the most part lack the ecological vocabulary to conceptualize and describe such a dynamic relation between communicants and their environments. While we recognize that the self and the social inform one another in some way, we still perceive them as fundamentally separate: the self is one thing; the social is another. The self is inside; the social is outside. The self is subjective; the social is constructed. What we lack is a theoretical perspective for perceiving the self and the social as recursively at work on one another, as engaged in an ecologically symbiotic relationship. Ecocomposition can supply such a perspective by helping us recognize that a writer and his or her rhetorical environment are always in the process of reproducing one another, so that "environment" is not some vague backdrop against which writers enact their rhetorical actions; instead, the environment becomes in critical ways part of the very rhetorical action that writers enact. We create our environments—our rhetorical situations—as we write within them; that is, we create our contexts as we create our texts. And genre is at the heart of this ecological/rhetorical process.

In the "Ecology of Writing," Marilyn Cooper describes what she calls "an ecological model of writing" (7) in which a writer is continually engaged with a variety of socially constituted systems. These social systems are not merely contextual backdrops; they are "dynamic interlocking systems that structure the social activity of writing" (7). Thus, writing is not a social act simply because it takes place in some social context; it is social because it is at work in shaping the very context within which it functions. A writer's response to, and interaction within, a social context affects that social context. It is not that a writer merely functions within a context, but that a writer participates in the construction of that context. Writing is both constituted by, and constitutive of, ever-changing social contexts (12). This is why writing is ecological.

In much the same way, genres are ecological. As what I am calling "rhetorical ecosystems," genres help communicants recognize, act within, and reproduce recurring environments (see Bazerman, Devitt, and Miller). Following Carolyn Miller ("Genre as Social Action"), for instance, Charles Bazerman defines genres as social actions. He writes:

> Genres are not just forms. Genres are forms of life, ways of being. They are frames for social action. They are environments for learning. They are locations within which meaning is constructed. Genres shape the thoughts we form and the communications by which we interact. Genres are the familiar places we go to create intelligible communicative action with each other and the guideposts we use to explore the unfamiliar. (19)

To claim that genres are environments within which familiar social actions are rhetorically enacted and reproduced is to reject traditional notions of genres as artificial forms or arbitrary classification systems for organizing and defining kinds of texts. Indeed, over the last fifteen years, genre scholars in speech communication, applied linguistics, and composition and rhetoric have reconceptualized genre so that it includes not only ways of organizing and defining kinds of texts, but also ways of organizing and defining kinds of social actions, social actions that genres rhetorically make possible. As such, genres are now understood as containing both a functional and an epistemological dimension; they are both the familiar rhetorical tools communicants use to respond to recurring situations as well as the ways in which communicants come to know and define recurring situations. Genres, in short, are the sites in which communicants rhetorically reproduce the very environments to which they in turn respond—the habits and the habitats for acting in language. This is why I argue that genres are rhetorical ecosystems that allow communicants to enact and reproduce various environments, social practices, relations, and identities. In the rest of this chapter, I make the case for such an ecological view of genres.

GENRES AS RHETORICAL ECOSYSTEMS: HOW

Human beings are rhetorical beings. We are not only different from other animals because of our capacity to use language as symbolic action or because we can use language to express ourselves in rhetorical ways; more significantly, we use language to construct rhetorical environments in which we exist, interact with one another, and enact social actions. We are constantly in the process of reproducing our contexts as we communicate within them, speaking and writing about our realities and ourselves to the extent that discourse and reality cannot be separated. Within these rhetorical constructs, we assume different rhetorical identities and perform different social activities as we negotiate our way from one environment to the next, often balancing multiple identities and activities at the same time. While on a recent visit to Florida, I was struck by the extent of this fact. Seemingly everywhere, the geography of Florida is rhetorically demarcated by such slogans as The *Real* Florida or billboards that promise real estate that allows one to Experience the *Wild* in Your Backyard. These slogans and billboards ironically stand interspersed between billboards advertising the staged realities of Disney's EPCOT Center and Universal Studios. Marking Florida's highways, these signs appear to be engaged in a grand rhetorical argument with one another: the "real" Florida versus the "tourist" Florida. But this binary does not really hold.

The "real" Florida is as much a simulacrum as is the "tourist" Florida.[2] Both are rhetorical demarcations, ways of defining and conceptualizing our notions of place. Certainly, Epcot is more overtly rhetorical in its construction, but really the difference between what we call "wild" and "staged" environments is as much rhetorical as it is geographic. We recognize a place as wild mainly because we discursively designate it as such, and we act in such a place according to accepted social norms. These norms are rhetorically rehearsed for us in such places as National Parks' visitors centers that not only narrate the nature of the wilderness we are about to enter—and how, subsequently, we should behave in this environment—but also place us conceptually within this narrative/environment. In short, even in places ostensibly outside of rhetoric, places we call "wilderness" or "nature," we cannot escape the power of rhetoric in shaping how we socially define, recognize, and experience our environments and ourselves in relation to them. Discourse and reality are deeply, ecologically, interconnected, so much so that we create the rhetorical conditions within which we perform and come to understand our environments, our social activities, and our identities. This is why we are rhetorical beings.

The ancient Greek Sophists recognized the contingent and rhetorical nature of human reality. Like the New Rhetoricians who followed them in our own century, the Sophists recognized that rhetoric is epistemological, involved not just in how we order particular arguments, but more significantly in how we order and experience reality, which itself becomes a cultural argument or mythos writ large. The Sophists described this rhetorical construction of reality as *nomos,* what Susan Jarratt defines as "rhetorical construct" or "habitation" (42). Within this rhetorical habitation, human customs of social and political behavior are historically and provisionally constructed and reproduced through cultural narratives, which, according to Kenneth Burke, shape the rhetorical contexts in which we identify and relate to one another. These cultural narratives maintain the rhetorical conditions that enable and shape our social relations and actions. Our interactions with others and with our environments, therefore, are always already mediated not only by physical contexts but also by rhetorical contexts which, as I mentioned earlier, are ideologically and discursively embodied and reproduced by genres. Genres—what Catherine Schryer defines as "stabilized-for-now or stabilized-enough sites of social and ideological action" (108)—thus become the typified rhetorical sites or *habitations* in which our social actions are made possible and meaningful as well as in which we are rhetorically socialized to perform these actions.

Within material constraints, then, our social relations and actions are rhetorically mediated by genres, which maintain and reproduce the socio-rhetorical conditions within which we perform our social relations and actions. In this way, genres are more than simply conduits or backdrops for our actions; they are not only familiar communicative tools we use to convey or categorize information. Rather, genres are more like rhetorical ecosystems in which communicants reproduce the very conditions that in turn call for certain typified responses, that is, genres help reproduce so-ciorhetorical environments by providing communicants with the rhetori-cal conventions for enacting them. This is why they are ecological. Through genres, our typified rhetorical actions reproduce the very recur-ring environments that subsequently make these rhetorical actions neces-sary and meaningful. For this reason, generic conventions are not inno-cent or arbitrary, but are at work in rhetorically shaping and reproducing our social environments, our practices, and our identities as social ac-tors—how, that is, we become socialized by genres to assume and perform certain situated roles and actions.

We notice the extent to which genres function as rhetorical ecosys-tems (rhetorical habits as well as social habitats) in the example of the physician's office. A physician's office is not a rhetorically unmediated en-vironment, a purely physical site in which doctor and patient interact. We might be tempted to think that it is because the doctor-patient relation-ship is such a sensual, tactile one, but this would be to underestimate the power of genre in shaping and enabling this very physical relationship. Prior to any interaction between doctor and patient, the patient has to complete what is generally known as the "Patient Medical History Form" (PMHF). Patients recognize this genre, which they encounter on their ini-tial visit to a physician, as one that solicits critical information regarding a patient's physical statistics (sex, age, height, weight, etc.) as well as medical history, including prior and recurring physical conditions, past treat-ments, and, of course, a description of current physical symptoms. This is followed by insurance carrier information and then a consent-to-treat statement and a legal release statement, which the patient signs. The genre is at once a patient record and a legal document, helping the doctor treat the patient and presumably protecting the doctor from potential lawsuits. But these are not the genre's only functions. The (PMHF) also helps re-produce the social and rhetorical environment within which the patient and doctor interact. The genre, for instance, reflects how our culture and science separate the mind from the body in treating disease, constructing the patient as an embodied object. It is mainly rhetorically concerned with a patient's physical symptoms, suggesting that we can treat the body separately from the mind—that is, we can isolate physical symptoms and treat them with little to no reference to the patient's state of mind and the effect that state of mind might have on these symptoms.[3] In so doing, the PMHF reflects Western notions of medicine, notions that are rhetorically preserved and reproduced by the genre and that in turn are physically embodied in the way in which the doctor recognizes and treats the patient as a synecdoche of his or her physical symptoms (for example, "I treated a knee injury today" or "The ear infection is in room 3"). The PMHF, then, is at work on the patient, socializing or scripting the individual into the role of "patient" (an embodied self) prior to her meeting with the doctor at the same time as it is at work on the doctor, preparing her to meet the individual as an embodied "patient." So powerful is the socializing power of genre in identity formation that we more often than not accept and act out our genre roles. As Teresa Tran explains, "Also on the [PMHF], there is a part that says 'other comments' which a patient *will understand* as asking whether or not he or she has any other physical problems, not mental ones" (2; my emphasis). Even when a patient ostensibly has a choice, the genre and the cultural ideology that it reflects and reproduces are already at work in constituting the patient's subject position in preparation for meeting the doctor. The genre, thus, helps us assume certain social roles, roles established by our culture and rhetorically reproduced and enacted by the genre, which in turn help us perform certain activities in certain ways.

The PMHF, then, rhetorically helps to shape and enable the social interaction between doctor and patient. As a genre, it is both a habit and a habitat—the conceptual habitat within which individuals perceive and experience a particular environment as well as the rhetorical habit by and through which they act within that environment. But the PMHF does not function in an ecological vacuum. It is one of a number of genres that enables its users to maintain and reproduce the sociorhetorical conditions shaping and enabling the larger environment or "ecosystem" we call the "physician's office." These genres individually constitute their own microenvironments—their own social situations, practices, and relations (relations between doctors and patients, nurses and doctors, doctors and other doctors, doctors and pharmacists, etc.)—and together, these related genres—what Amy J. Devitt calls "genre sets" ("Intertextuality") and what Charles Bazerman calls "systems of genre" ("Systems")—interact to constitute the macroenvironment we recognize as the physician's office. As a result, the physician's office becomes, so to speak, a "biosphere of discourse," one constituted by various interconnected, sometimes competing, genre habitats.[4] Within this genre-constituted and genre-mediated environment, communicants assume and enact various genre identities, social practices, and relations—ways of scripting and speaking themselves into existence in particular environments—much like we write ourselves into and enact the role of patient in the PMHF and, in so doing, shape and enable the rhetorical ecosystem of the physician's office.

GENRES AS RHETORICAL ECOSYSTEMS: WHY

In "Building, Dwelling, Thinking," Martin Heidegger writes that "a boundary is not that at which something stops but . . . the boundary is that from which something begins its presencing"—its coming into being. So far, I have been arguing that as human beings, our presencing takes place within rhetorical and social boundaries or environments we call "genres." As we move from one sociorhetorical environment to the next, we shift genre boundaries, which maintain and reproduce certain ways of perceiving a particular social activity, ways of relating to others, and ways of lexicogrammatically and rhetorically interacting with one another within the environment. The ways in which we use language to perform certain social activities and to enact certain social relations and identities changes as we adjust from one genre-constituted environment to the next.

The environment and its participants' activities and identities are, therefore, always in the process of reproducing each other within genre: the PMHF rhetorically maintains the social conditions within which we enact our roles and activities, and our roles and activities in turn reproduce the very conditions that make such roles and activities possible and meaningful.[5] This ecological process is what Anthony Giddens, in *The Constitution of Society: Outline of the Theory of Structuration,* refers to as the "duality of structure." Giddens's theory of structuration is largely an attempt to reconcile what he perceives as inaccurately dichotomized views of human agency and social systems, what he calls "hermeneutic sociologies" ("the imperialism of the subject") versus "structuralist sociologies" ("the imperialism of the social object") (2). Both sociologies are inaccurate, Giddens argues, because they overlook the extent to which human actions both enact and reproduce social structures. In their social practices, human agents reproduce the very social structures that subsequently make their actions necessary, possible, recognizable, and meaningful, so that their practices maintain and enact the very structures that consequently call for these practices. In all this, genre plays a critical role.

For Giddens, structures, as I have been arguing about genres, do not merely function as backdrops for social activities; instead, they are "fundamental to the production and reproduction of social life" (36). Structures function on two simultaneous levels: the conceptual and the actual. On the one hand, structures are concepts; they function on the level of ideology, a kind of social collective or what Thomas Kuhn calls "paradigm" that frames the ideological and epistemological boundaries of what we assume to be knowable, doable, and possible in any given situation. On the other hand, structures do not just have a conceptual existence; they are also actualized as social practices. According to Giddens, social practices are what give structures ontological life, manifested as certain technologies, conventions, rituals, institutions, tools, and so on. Social practices, thus, allow human agents to enact and hence reproduce ideological structures—the two recursively interact to form a "duality of structure" on both an epistemological and ontological level. Structures, in short, are both the ideology and the enactment of the ideology at once. As Giddens explains: "the rules and resources drawn upon in the production and reproduction of social action are at the same time the means of system reproduction" (19). Structures constitute the potential for action, and social practices, recursively working within structures, constitute the actualization of that potential, so that structures both provide a defined, socially recognized, and virtual action-potential as well as the means of instantiating that potential as actualized social practice in space and time.

Because structure represents the ideological potential for action, it is related to motive. According to Giddens, "Motivation refers to potential for action rather than to the mode in which action is chronically carried out by the agent. . . . For the most part motives supply the *overall plans or programmes* . . . within which a range of conduct is enacted" (6; my emphasis). Motive exists on the conceptual level of structure; it frames the possible ways of acting and meaning in any given time and space. Operating on the conceptual level of structure, motive comes to frame the ideological boundaries that socially define and sanction a certain appropriate range of conduct within a particular situation. This notion of motive is linked to what Carolyn R. Miller, in "Genre as Social Action," has defined as exigence.[6] Like motive, exigence frames part of how we recognize a situation as requiring a socially sanctioned immediate attention or remedy, and so shapes and enables any subsequent actions we might perform in response to that situation. In fact, like motive, exigence is so entrenched a part of our social knowledge, so ideological in nature, that we as social actors are often unaware of its constitutive presence. Motive becomes such a part of what seems to be "natural" or common sensible that we no longer consider the ideologies that sanction and enable our actions. We just act.

We function, then, in motive-potentials that constitute in part what Giddens calls "structures." But, as we discussed earlier, structures are not just potentials; they are also actualizations of potential. In order for us to transform the potential for action into its actualization—in order to act— we must transform the motive into agency, and this is where intention plays a role. Intention is where motive-potentials become internalized by actors and then actualized as agency. Whereas motive is socially defined, intention is an interpretation and instantiation of social motive. Intention is a form of social cognition, an embodiment of social motive and the means by which individuals become social agents, interpreting and carry- ing out the social motives available to them. According to Giddens, inten- tion can only exist *in relation to* motive, since "for an event to count as an example of agency, it is necessary at least that what the person does be in- tentional *under some description,* even if the agent is mistaken about that description" (8; my emphasis). Intention must have some socially defined motive in order to be recognized as a meaningful social action, something that gives it generalizable meaning and value within a particular environ- ment. It must be intentional under some *described* social motive.

The "motive-intention" dialectic just described is situated within and in turn reproduces structure, which provides both the ideological condi- tions and the institutional conventions agents need for recognizing and enacting their social practices. This recursive process at work in what Gid- dens calls "structures" is the same one I have been describing as work in genres. Genres are structures in that they maintain the ideological poten- tial for action (in the form of genre motive or exigency) and the typified rhetorical means of actualizing that potential. They are ideological con- cepts and rhetorical actualizations at the same time, both the way in which we recognize a sociorhetorical environment as requiring a certain response and the way in which we actually rhetorically respond to, and act within, it. This actualized activity—the patient completing the PMHF, for in- stance—reproduces the ideological conditions—how physicians concep- tualize their practices and respond to their patients—that in turn results in the kind of patient-physician interaction that prompted the PMHF in the first place. Genre is at the heart of this ecological process, maintaining a symbiotic relationship between social habitats and rhetorical habits.

Genres, therefore, recursively operate on two levels at once: the ideo- logical and the textual. At the ideological level, genres maintain the ways in which we perceive particular environments as requiring certain imme- diate and "appropriate" attention and response—in short, exigencies or motives for potential action. At the textual level, genres maintain the rhetorical and lexicogrammatical conventions that allow their users to participate in these environments in meaningful and recognizable ways. In short, genres are the ways in which we perpetuate particular environments by treating them as particular exigencies. Returning to Heidegger, then, we notice that genre is both the boundary and the presencing, both the ideological construction of an environment and its rhetorical enactment—in short, the habitat that makes habit possible and the habit that makes habitat possible.

CONCLUSION

Writing is not only about learning to adapt, socially and rhetorically, to various contexts via genres; it is also about reproducing these various contexts via genres. When we write, we are enacting these contexts at the same time as we are enacting ourselves, our social practices, and our relations to others within them. The physician's office bears this out. As a rhetorical ecosystem, it is sustained by its genres. Communicants assume ways of being in this environment not only because of its material setting—although that certainly does play a major part—but also because of its sociorhetorical conditions as they are mediated by the available office genres. At the same time, these communicants are also engaged in tacitly reproducing this environment, reproducing it socially as they enact it rhetorically. Clearly, within the ecology of genre, the self/social dichotomy does not hold.

We need to pay more attention to the sociorhetorical ecosystems within which communication and communicators take place and are made possible—the conditions that prompt us to write and that our writing makes possible. And genres are one significant way to do it, since genres rhetorically embody and help communicants reproduce these ecosystems. As such, the environment of the physician's office or any other setting for that matter (think, e.g., of the First-Year Composition classroom with its various genres: syllabi, student themes, teacher end comments, writing prompts, conferences, journals, peer review handouts, etc.) is not only an ontological fact but also a generic fact. It exists largely because we reproduce it in our genres. When communicants use genres, they are interpreting and enacting the social motives (embedded rhetorically within it) that sustain an environment and make it meaningful, and so are becoming socialized into producing not only certain kinds of texts, but also certain kinds of contexts, practices, and identities—ways of being and acting in the world, socially and rhetorically.

NOTES

1. For more on the self-social dichotomy, see the exchange between Peter Elbow and David Bartholomae in *College Composition and Communication* 46 (1995): 62–83.

2. I am indebted to Sidney I. Dobrin for these observations on the rhetorical construction of Florida. For more on this topic, see Dobrin's essay, "Writing Takes Place," in this collection.

3. My conclusions regarding the PMHF and its role in shaping the doctor-patient relationship are largely based on, and extend, the research of Teresa Tran, a premed student who was enrolled in a genre analysis course I taught in 1997 at the University of Kansas.

4. I am indebted to Christian R. Weisser for the use of the term *biospshere of discourse.*

5. I use the term *reproduce* deliberately throughout this essay to emphasize the ecological interaction between human actions and social systems. In using the term, however, I certainly do not mean to suggest that human actions and social systems duplicate one another. Reproduction is not the same as duplication or replication because reproduction always involves some variation. This is the case biologically, linguistically, and rhetorically. Ecosystems are not static mainly because they evolve as their organisms evolve. The same is true for genres. In helping communicants reproduce rhetorical environments, genres also help communicants change rhetorical environments because on some level genres always involve some interpretation, which involves some variation.

6. Carolyn R. Miller defines exigence as "a form of social knowledge," involved not only in how we recognize but also in how we respond to a particular situation or event, so that exigence becomes "an objectified social need" (1984, 157).

WORKS CITED

Bartholomae, David. "Writing with Teachers: A Conversation with Peter Elbow." *College Composition and Communication* 46 (1995): 62–83.

Bazerman, Charles. "The Life of Genre, the Life in the Classroom." *Genre and Writing: Issues, Arguments, Alternatives.* Eds. Wendy Bishop and Hans Ostrom. Portsmouth, N.H.: Boynton/Cook, 1997. 19–26.

———. "Systems of Genres and the Enactment of Social Intentions." *Genre and the New Rhetoric.* Eds. Aviva Freedman and Peter Medway. Bristol: Taylor and Francis, 1994. 79–101.

Cooper, Marilyn, and Michael Holzman. *Writing as Social Action.* Portsmouth, N.H.: Boynton/Cook, 1989.

Crowley, Sharon. "Around 1971: The Emergence of Process Pedagogy." *Composition in the University: Historical and Polemical Essays.* Pittsburgh: University of Pittsburgh Press, 1998.

Devitt, Amy J. "Generalizing about Genre: New Conceptions of an Old Concept." *College Composition and Communication* 44 (1993): 573–86.

———. "Intertextuality in Tax Accounting: Generic, Referential, and Functional." *Textual Dynamics of the Professions: Historical and Contemporary Studies of Writing in Professional Communities*. Eds. Charles Bazerman and James Paradis. Madison: University of Wisconsin Press, 1991. 335–57.

Elbow, Peter. "Being a Writer vs. Being an Academic: A Conflict in Goals." *College Composition and Communication* 46 (1995): 72–83.

Giddens, Anthony. *The Constitution of Society: Outline of the Theory of Structuration*. Berkeley: University of California Press, 1984.

Jarratt, Susan. *Rereading the Sophists: Classical Rhetoric Refigured*. Carbondale: Southern Illinois University Press, 1991.

Kuhn, Thomas. *The Structure of Scientific Revolutions*. Chicago: University of Chicago Press, 1970.

Miller, Carolyn R. "Genre as Social Action." *Quarterly Journal of Speech* 70 (1984): 151–67.

———. "Rhetorical Community: The Cultural Basis of Genre." *Genre and the New Rhetoric*. Eds. Aviva Freedman and Peter Medway. Bristol: Taylor and Francis, 1994. 61–77.

Schryer, Cathy. "The Lab vs. the Clinic: Sites of Competing Genres." *Genre and the New Rhetoric*. Eds. Aviva Freedman and Peter Medway. Bristol: Taylor and Francis, 1994. 105–24.

Tran, Teresa. "A Patient as an Object." Manuscript, 1997.

Trimbur, John. "Taking the Social Turn: Teaching Writing Post-Process." *College Composition and Communication* 45 (1994): 108–18.

Ecocomposition
and the Greening of Identity

Christian R. Weisser
University of Hawaii (Hilo)
Hilo, Hawaii

To speak, people must first listen to what the world has to say.
—Judith Halden-Sullivan, "The Phenomenology of Process"

If we want to be at home on this earth, even at the price of being at home in this century, we must try to take part in the interminable dialogue with its essence.
—Hannah Arendt, "Understanding and Politics"

Writing instruction has been dramatically transformed in the past forty years. Before the 1960s, writing was seen only as a skill to be modeled and learned, and most English professors saw writing as either a preparation for practical living or as a foundation for the production or critique of literature. Since then, one of the most pervasive theoretical subjects—particularly in composition studies—has been how students explore, define, and extend their identities through discourse. In other words, I think it's fair to say that most of the research, scholarship, and teaching in composition that we've done in the past four decades has intended to enable students to better understand who they are and how language shapes their conceptions of themselves and the conceptions others have of them. The ways in which we envision identity have evolved in accord with the dominant theoretical stances of the time. Specifically, our conceptions of how identity is formed have corresponded to our personal, social, and more recently, political theories of discourse. While this evolution has helped us to conceptualize identity in more constructive ways, we have failed to account for the ecological dimensions of selfhood. Our discussions of identity has been, thus far, constricted by the underlying premise that our identities are fashioned only through our connections with other humans. In fact, this premise is so integral to our belief system that we hardly perceive it. Our current conceptions of identity are *pre-ecological*; we have not yet recognized that the whole spectrum of the nonhuman physical environment is embedded in each of our identities. Other contributors to this volume have realized that a more extensive understanding of how our identities are shaped by the world around us is perhaps one of the most significant goals we might accomplish through ecocomposition. Sid suggests that "when we question the construction of identity, we must include a stronger sense of physical place when we contend that identity comes from other places, that we know ourselves through the surrounding world"(12). Colleen Connolly suggests that composition teachers might "expand their notions of diversity—of society as an immensely complex global system, in which power, matter, and ideas interact—to include the natural world"(186). Bradley John Monsma writes that "ecocomposition might encourage a better understanding of the role of ecosystems and environments in the dialogic relationships that form between ourselves and our words"(286).

While these authors and others like them have begun to realize that our identities—and how they are manifested through discourse—are inextricably linked to the larger biosphere that we live in, such perspectives have had little impact on composition theory in general. The manner in which we've theorized, perceived, and discussed identity has developed in more sophisticated and holistic directions over the past forty years, but composition has thus far failed to account for the ecological dimensions of identity. This essay traces the recent history of composition theory to show how our focus has expanded to account for a greater number of influences in the shaping of the individual writer's identity. While this expansion has been progressive, reformative, and (dare I say it?) evolutionary, I argue that it is still incomplete. In order for composition theory to fully account for the many ways in which human subjectivity is constructed, we must begin to recognize that our own personal, social, and political lives are wholly dependent upon the biological matrix of life on this planet. Recognizing our own "green identities," I argue, moves us closer toward realizing exactly who we are in relation to the rest of the world.

THE EVOLUTION OF IDENTITY IN COMPOSITION STUDIES

Named by James A. Berlin as "the Renaissance of Rhetoric," the period from 1960 to 1975 witnessed the gathering momentum of a new perspective that was to change the discipline of composition fundamentally in years to come *(Rhetoric and Reality)*. In the early 1970s, this new perspective blossomed into what many compositionists perceived as a revolution in teaching writing. The most widely accepted account of this revolution is the paradigm shift theory, and one version of it has been particularly influential: Maxine Hairston's 1982 "Winds of Change: Thomas Kuhn and the Revolution of Teaching Writing." In her article, Hairston suggested that the traditional paradigm, with its emphasis on the composed product rather than the composing process, its focus on the teacher as a depositor of knowledge, and its assumption of an unchanging reality which is independent of the writer and which all writers are expected to describe in the same way regardless of the rhetorical situation, was becoming increasingly problematic, that is, the traditional paradigm was seen as a perspective that saw no differentiation in the ways separate individuals encountered, conceptualized, and interpreted the world around them. As a result of the many questions the traditional paradigm raised, many writing teachers began turning to newer student- and process-centered approaches to writing instruction.

Perhaps the most significant of these new approaches were cognitivism and expressivism. What is most striking about the new approaches to writing instruction at this time is that despite their many differences in both epistemology and practice, they were marked by a common and profound dedication to the student—a commitment that was much more explicit than it had been during earlier decades of writing instruction. The cognitivist's interest in writing as a process shifted the focus of writing instruction to the internal experiences and perspectives of the student. These approaches began to envision identity as emerging internally, and urged compositionists to recognize that each individual interpreted the world around them in ways quite distinct from others. Similarly, expressivists saw writing as an act that authenticates and affirms the self. The two approaches are closely related, since both have to do with the stance an individual takes toward reality. Despite the differences between the two perspectives, both hoped to change the classroom to help students extend their identities and make better sense of their place in the world by looking inward.

In contrast, scholarly investigations of discourse and composition in the 1980s began to view writing as a complex process that conveys and creates knowledge. Composition theorists and researchers began to focus on the social nature of writing and suggested that the correlation between social experience and writing ability is palpable. These theories—often called "social constructionist theories"—shifted our focus from the individual to an understanding of facts, texts, and selves as social constructs. Social constructionist approaches to composition expanded the way we thought of identity, asserting that it emerged not just from the internal processes of the individual, but also from a wider variety of influences: the social conventions we share with other human beings. These perspectives suggested that what we know about our world and ourselves is manufactured primarily through our interactions with others. As one of the most influential compositionists in the 1980s, Kenneth Bruffee argued that "entities we normally call reality, knowledge, thought, facts, texts, selves, and so on are constructs generated by communities of like-minded peers" ("Collaborative Learning" 774); that is, social constructionists urged us to see identity not as something internal, singular, and centered, but as a language construct generated by discourse communities and used by them to maintain community coherence. Bruffee describes perception, expression, and identity as functions of the social contexts in which they occur. The social constructionist approach suggests that since knowledge and identity do have social and communal dimensions, compositionists must begin to see "teaching and learning not just as activities which occur in a social context, but as activities which are themselves social in nature" ("The Way Out" 458). Social constructionist theories suggested that through discourse with others, our identities—ourselves—are constructed and defined. Social constructionism shifted the locus of subjectivity from the solitary, detached writer to the interconnected network of other humans.

These social constructionist theories have brought about important changes in composition and initiated a long conversation on the social context of writing—a conversation that continues today. In the 1990s, the social constructionist approach has been a useful starting point for examining the ways in which discourse is political and ideological—as evidenced by feminist, postmoderninst, postcolonial, and cultural studies approaches to composition. These investigations have begun to examine an even wider scope of influences on the construction of identity. They have urged us to look at the greater political and ideological forces that structure our ways of thinking, and, consequently, our conceptions of who we are in relation to the rest of the world. They have introduced discussions of diversity and difference, which recognize the degree to which our identities are constructed through encounters and negotiations with others. Radical theories suggest that there is perhaps more at work in the construction of identity than just the interaction and negotiation of individuals in social settings.

I don't offer this account as an attempt to define composition studies as a discipline; others (Berlin, Miller, North, and Harris) have already done this quite well. What I would like to suggest, however, is that all of these approaches over the last forty years have had essentially the same purpose—to enable students to develop a greater understanding of their own identities through discourse. Cognitivist and expressivist perspectives—with their emphasis on students' composing processes and inner voices—envisioned writing as emerging from an internal dialectic that enables writers to arrive at self-understanding and personal growth. Social constructionist approaches built upon these individualistic notions of identity and suggested that the correlation between social experience and knowledge is palpable. More recent theories, influenced by postmodernism, feminism, and cultural studies, have led compositionists to define a writer's identity as constructed, fragmented, and decentered, the product of an array of social, political, and ideological forces. Despite their many obvious differences, the various theoretical and pedagogical discussions in contemporary composition studies have had as one of their primary underlying goals the cultivation of a more complex and sophisticated awareness of how student writers form their own conceptions of identity. Much of what has been thought, said, and done in composition studies over the past forty years has attempted to help students to extend their identities. In fact, we might see the paradigm shift in Hairston's well-known article as a shift toward a better understanding of how discourse and identity are inextricably linked. As Robert Brooke suggests, the "whole call for pedagogical shift is most powerfully a call for a shift in the identity roles offered in the classroom" (105); that is, nearly all of our work has been done in an effort to map exactly what constitutes an individual's identity and how discourse—speaking and writing—is inextricably linked to that constitution.

AN ECOLOGICAL CONCEPTION OF IDENTITY

Writing, then, can be seen as a search for identity. The study of writing can be imagined as an ongoing project that has been progressively realizing exactly how our identities are constituted through discourse. The development of composition studies has enabled students to do more than learn how to construct an error-free essay; it has led to a fuller understanding of who we (and our students) are and how we relate to other human beings in the world. However, what I want to suggest is that our current *conceptions* of identity are *pre-ecological*—we envision identity and selfhood from a strictly human-centered perspective. We have thus far failed to recognize that the construction of identity is subject to influences that are other than human. I'm not suggesting that identity itself is pre-ecological; indeed, our identities already contain an ecological dimension. We orient ourselves to nonhuman others as well as human reference groups; identity and the sense of one's place in the world are fundamentally ecological. The world that we perceive and inhabit, which we commonly forget in favor of the human culture it supports, is always a part of who we are and how we express ourselves. What I am suggesting is that most compositionists do not consider the ecological dimensions of selfhood, nor do they consider the impact of our nonhuman relationships in the construction of identity. When we talk about identity in our journals and in other scholarly conversations, we are almost always referring to a conception of identity that emerges as a product of purely human relationships. I'd like to advance the idea that the individual in society, his or her subjectivity, sense of selfhood, and ways of conceptualizing the world, all have an ecological dimension. Ecologies are about "interaction, flows, fields, systems, as well as the private spaces, worlds, and value systems of individual organisms" (Jagtenberg and Mckie xii). As compositionists interested in identity, we might arrive at a more fruitful understanding of selfhood if we envision ourselves as *ecological selves*. Ecological selves perceive their interconnection with others and comprehend the degree to which their own identities are inseparable from the nonhuman world—a recognition that the material world "out there" is a part of our identity "in here." This recognition accounts for our relationships with locations, material objects, and constructed spaces as well as with the other life-forms and ecosystems that sustain us. As Robin Eckersley suggests, an ecological self is "based on an ecologically informed philosophy of internal relatedness, according to which all organisms are not simply interrelated with their environment but also constituted by those very environmental relationships" (49).

Certainly, much of our identity emerges as a result of our connections with other humans. But, we also experience ourselves as being in relationships with particular environments. We are all essentially grounded in, and bonded to a nonhuman world. Indeed, the nonhuman physical environment is so central to sustainable life that it undermines the very idea of human activity. In recognizing the centrality of spatial environments to human identity, we align ourselves with Frederic Jameson's assertion of the "locus of our new reality [as] space" (quoted in Stephanson 40). We are as influenced by the places we inhabit and our connections with the other organisms that share those sites as we are influenced by human relationships. Certainly, we are all influenced differently, but we are the products of our connections with an array of locations and the inhabitants thereof. We experience this connectedness in various ways—from encounters with the "natural" world to discussions in networked writing environments. But, our experiences and the activities that generate them always depend on shared resources. Our identities are shaped and enriched by our contact with others in specific settings, and the degree to which we maneuver around, beside, and in accord with others has much to do with who we are.

Life and meaning are fundamentally ecological. People worldwide assert the importance of *their* places, *their* homes as integral components in the development of their own unique identities, and many recognize the importance of preserving diverse and thriving habitats—natural and otherwise. The growing interest in environmentalism and green politics attests to this. In the defense and promotion of natural interests, individuals identify with ecological others, assert the importance of diverse habitats and ecosystems, and articulate ecological selves. Obviously, the recognition of an ecological dimension is not limited to academics and theorists. On the contrary, the relatively high visibility of environmental matters in popular culture, especially the media, contrasts sharply with their low profile in academic culture—including composition studies.

And so, it is important that discourse specialists—compositionists in particular—begin to move toward a more ecological understanding of identity. This move—what we might call *a greening of identity*—produces changes in our conceptions of selfhood and alters the way individuals feel about their relationships with others. While a "green" conception of identity doesn't need to focus exclusively on the natural world, individuals who recognize the ecological dimensions of identity often align themselves with environmentalist perspectives, since they are concerned with the preservation and appreciation of all diverse ecological systems. As cultural theorists Tom Jagtenberg and David Mckie suggest, "greening entails a greater identification with nature and the development of an extended self—an eco-self" (123). Identity can now be seen as socially constructed and sustained in community with an enormous number of interconnected others along with their ecologies and habitats. Compositionists would do well to recognize that identity emerges not only from our human relationships, but from the connections we have with other life-forms in an array of habitats.

If we extend our conceptions of community beyond anthropocentric human spheres, we are able to cross a number of significant barriers. The dualisms of nature-culture, masculine-feminine, internal-external are, in theory and in practice, all transgressed by life and nature itself. If we locate our identity outside of, or transcendent to, ecological fields and considerations, we will continue to reproduce alienation and problematic cultural dualisms. Raymond Williams, a pioneer in British cultural studies, suggests that there is a significant parallel between human social relationships and our relationships to nonhuman others. He asserts that the way in which a culture defines nature is often a projection of that culture's human social relationships; for example, Williams notes that in seventeenth-and eighteenth century European thought, the dominant conception of nature was as an object, as a tool to be used, "even at times as a machine" (73). This coincides with the mistreatment and exploitation of peasant workers and the ensuing displacement of rural farmers to factories and work-houses. Both humans and nature, according to many Enlightenment thinkers, were nothing more than commodities to be manipulated by the wealthy. Williams sees our contemporary domination and exploitation of nature—both literally and discursively—as a reflection of problematic re-lations between human beings:

> Out of the ways in which we have interacted with the physical world we have made not only human nature and an altered natu-ral order; we have also made societies. It is very significant that most of the terms we have used in this relationship—the conquest of nature, the exploitation of nature—are derived from real human practices: relations between men and men. (84)

Williams rightly observes that if we continue to alienate the living processes of which we are part, we necessarily alienate ourselves. On the other hand, viewing ourselves as ecoselves locates humanity in an ex-tended community of other life forces and their ecologies. By recognizing our connections to various ecologies, the self becomes extended and inclu-sive. Likewise, by developing ecological relations between ourselves and other humans, we are more likely to transform our relations with other species.

Williams's analysis of the parallel between the domination of nature and patterns of domination in human culture is a line of thinking similar to that of ecofeminists. Briefly stated, ecofeminism critiques the practices and beliefs of patriarchal societies (particularly Western industrial society) that have historically identified women and nature as fundamentally "other" and therefore subject to manipulation, control, and exploitation. While ecofeminists generally focus on *androcentrism, or* male-centered-ness, as the basis for the human exploitation of nature, scholars including Warwick Fox, H. Lewis Ulman, and Roderick Nash suggest that male-centeredness is just one part of a larger problem: *anthropocentrism,* or human-centeredness. Fox suggests that while men have been implicated in the history of ecological destruction far more than women, we must ex-tend this examination to account for the actions and attitudes of all-white, wealthy Westerners, who have been far more implicated in global environmental destruction than precapitalists, blacks, and non-Westerners. He argues that "anthropocentrism has served as the most fundamental kind of legitimation employed by *whatever* powerful class of social actors one wishes to focus on" (22). The work of ecofeminists, environmental ethicists, cultural critics, and ecocompositionists, through their examinations of the discursive practices that enable anthropocentric thought, might begin to extend our sense of community to include nonhuman nature. What makes human beings unique, in Joseph J. Kockelmans's words, is our ability to apprehend the world and our place in it as a "totality of relations" (9). However, without discourse, we stand mute: we can experience our world, but without the ability to articulate ourselves we cannot make the connections between our identities and the world around us fully present to either ourselves or others.

This is why it is so important for compositionists to begin to recognize ecological perspectives of identity. As I've suggested, composition studies has been cultivating a more advanced and sophisticated awareness of how student writers form their own conceptions of identity and selfhood. As discourse specialists, we have come to recognize the degree to which language and writing shape our conceptions of who we are. By incorporating an ecological perspective into our investigations of identity, we might arrive at an even more comprehensive understanding of the connections between individuals and their relationships—both human and nonhuman. Writing is the activity that best allows us to locate ourselves in the enmeshed systems of our world. Theorists like Williams suggest that discourse has been the primary vehicle in the manipulation and domination of the biosphere by human beings. Perhaps ecocompositionists, by addressing the ecological dimensions of identity, can begin to use discourse in more egalitarian, progressive, and democratic ways.

THE GREENING OF COMPOSITION STUDIES

I'm certainly not the first to recognize the connections between ecology, identity, and composition studies. Marilyn Cooper's important article, "The Ecology of Writing" proposes an "ecological model of writing, whose fundamental tenet is that writing is an activity through which a person is continually engaged with a variety of socially constituted systems" (2). In contrast to social constructionist models, Cooper asserts that writing encompasses much more than the individual writer and her immediate context. Her emphasis is on the systems in which writers operate whereas

Bruffee and other social constructionists focused almost exclusively on the writers themselves. While Bruffee's writers find knowledge and construct their identities in apparently immaterial locations, Cooper postulates "dynamic interlocking systems that structure the social activity of writing" (7). This model allows us to see language as a more flexible category. While the structures and contents of a particular discursive moment can be specified, Cooper's ecological model suggests that discourse is constantly in flux. An ecological model accounts for the flexibility of writing and the degree to which each discursive moment is involved in unique circumstances that are themselves subject to rapid change. According to Cooper, the "metaphor for writing suggested by the ecological model is that of a web, in which anything that affects one strand of the web vibrates throughout the whole" (9). Cooper's conception of language use emphasizes the actual medium in which it occurs, while also highlighting how effective language users recognize and adapt their prose to contextual stimuli.

Greg Myers also mentions ecology in his analysis of the social construction of two biologists' proposals. Myers suggests a close relationship between ecology, the science of natural environments and the relationships between its inhabitants, and social constructionist approaches to composition, which see writing as an activity that is negotiated by individuals in discrete locations. Myers argues that there is much that compositionists can learn from the study of ecology, and he concludes by observing that "we should not only observe and categorize the behavior of individuals, we should also consider the evolution of this behavior in its ecological context" (240).

While I agree with Cooper's and Myers's use of ecology as a metaphor, I hope to extend the connections between ecology, discourse, and identity to include more literal purposes as well. Cooper and Myers both work from an understanding of ecology as strictly metaphorical, one that highlights the interaction between language users as well as emphasizing the locations in which this language use takes place. While I agree that these connections are important, I'd like to extend our conceptions of language use—and identity—to include nonhuman living beings in the equation. Both Cooper and Myers work from a conception of language use as dependent primarily—indeed exclusively—upon its human constituents. As I've argued earlier, our identities, and much of what we think, say, and do come about as a result of our relationships with other living beings. Through discourse, we negotiate our relationships with other people, things, and places, and through both internal and external dialogue (writing, speaking, and thinking) we establish who we are and how we fit into the world.

If we are to arrive at a more comprehensive and more ecological understanding of our identities, we might begin by interrogating some of our most basic presumptions regarding language itself. We might begin to recognize, for example, that our very *conceptions* of discourse are human-centered. Nearly all of Western thought tends to construe language as that power that humans possess and that other species do not. We presume that the distinguishing feature of humanity is our ability to think and communicate our thoughts. Since the first Greek *physiologoi,* or "natural philosophers," who named, classified, and ordered the natural world, language has been claimed as the exclusive and distinguishing property of humankind; we have always presumed privileged access to Logos. Our conceptions of discourse, like our conceptions of identity, rest upon a narrowly anthropocentric system of belief.

At least one contemporary linguist has called this system of belief into question. In his book *Language and Nature,* Harvey Sarles argues that the assumption that language is a purely human property provides little more than an ideological justification for the human domination of nature. In fact, Sarles suggests that this narrow conception of language makes it impossible for us to comprehend the nature of our own discourse itself. Our inability to properly contextualize language and to see it as something beyond verbal utterances (or marks on paper or a computer screen) limits our conceptions of how language is created and used. Language is not a strictly human endeavor; only by recognizing that other life-forms communicate in and through their environments will we be able to more adequately theorize our own identities as language users. Sarles asserts that "to define language as uniquely human also tends to define the nature of animal communication so as to preclude the notion that it is comparable to human language" (86). He suggests that language must be understood in much broader terms than it currently is, if we are to fully recognize the importance of discourse in the construction of identity. He writes:

> Each ongoing species has a truth, a logic, a science, knowledge about the world in which it lives. To take man outside of nature, to aggrandize the human mind, is to simplify other species and, I am convinced, to oversimplify ourselves, to constrict our thinking and observation about ourselves into narrow, ancient visions of human nature, constructed for other problems in other times. (20)

Sarles's perspective opens us toward an understanding of the subtle relationships between language, ecologies, and identity. Until we recognize that we hold no monopoly on language, and that our language has an ecological dimension, we will be unable to fully conceptualize identity. David Abram suggests that "as long as humankind continues to use language strictly for our own ends, we will continue to find ourselves estranged from our actions" (97). Adopting a more ecological conception of language, then, can be seen as an integral component in our quest for a more holistic understanding of identity.

The use of ecological and environmental perspectives can be quite valuable in writing courses. Through research and writing assignments that explore how living organisms are mutually dependent upon each other, we might enable our students to more fully understand their own relationships with others—human and nonhuman. For example, in an environmental writing course I taught last year at the University of Tampa, one of the assignments asked students to describe how their identities, and those of their family members, are often shaped by relationships with nonhuman others. One student, whose family had been affected by the recent ban on drift-net fishing, argued that his family identity had been constructed through a "symbiotic relationship with the sea and its inhabitants—the fishes." This student went on to argue that fishing had so saturated nearly every aspect of her family's life that the concepts of "family" and "fishing" were nearly inseparable. Another student argued that her formative years, spent maintaining the family dairy farm, helped her to appreciate the value of hard work and was probably responsible for her success in school and her ability to "balance fun and hard work." A third student suggested that owning two dogs taught him that animals communicate "differently than we [humans] do, but no less effectively."

This is just one simple example of an assignment that assumes an ecological perspective to discourse and identity. There are many other ways in which this perspective can be applicable, in both theory and practice. Many of the other excellent essays in this collection describe useful and innovative assignments that extend our notions of identity in more ecological directions. By exploring local and global ecosystems, student writers may emerge with a greater awareness of their places in the world. Giving students the opportunity to articulate their connections to the world encourages them to reflect on their own authenticity and autonomy. Thinking about the degree to which their identities are the products of particular places and relationships might allow students to see themselves as unique individuals. As a result, their feelings of alienation and otherness might diminish as they learn to recognize their connections to other students. Reinvisioning language to include nonhuman forms might allow students to develop a more holistic, comprehensive conception of exactly what discourse entails. Identity and selfhood, when viewed from an ecological perspective, can be defined as the awareness an individual organism has of its membership in a society. Enabling students to recognize their own memberships to various communities—and the connections these communities have to other groups—is an important goal in many composition classrooms today. At the same time, ecological and environmental perspectives allow students to more fully account for their own unique identities and ways of seeing the world. Recognizing themselves as having both social and biologic imperatives and idiosyncrasies, student writers can make better sense of the contradictory, sometimes chaotic struggles of modern life that often seem inexplicable to maturing adults.

What I hope to emphasize is that ecology and environment, like self and identity, are discursive projects that are realized and experienced in material and symbolic ways. Ecological perspectives are valuable in the writing classroom—both literally and metaphorically. They allow greater access to conceptions of identity, extend our recognition of the connectedness of all life-forms, and enable students to more fully account for issues of diversity, otherness, and difference. Recognizing the degree to which our identities are constructed by our environments—while recognizing how we in turn construct and define those same places—is an important step toward a more complex and holistic conception of the world and our relationships to it. Our notions of community must begin to extend beyond human beings to encompass the earth and all that is in it. While these ideas and those of my colleagues elsewhere in this collection are perhaps new to composition studies, they are hardly original. Aldo Leopold, writing in the late 1940s, suggested that an accurate conception of who we are and how we relate to others must include the land and its inhabitants. In "The Community Concept" portion of "The Land Ethic" he argued that "the land ethic simply enlarges the boundaries of the community to include soils, waters, plants and animals, or collectively: the land"(204).

What I'm trying to suggest here is not so much a pedagogical approach, nor a new set of theoretical tenets, but rather a new way of thinking about how we envision identity. As I've said earlier, our identities are always already ecological; we are who we are as a result of the people, places, things, animals, and plants that have touched our lives. It is only for us to realize these connections and to develop ways to incorporate them into our discourse. As compositionists, we should search for effective techniques to make these ecological connections more apparent to our students. Composition studies has been evolving toward a more holistic conception of identity for decades, through the various personal, social, and political approaches to discourse that I've noted earlier. Perhaps it is time to expand our field, and our field of vision, to include the nonhuman world. If we make efforts toward a greener conception of the relations between identity, ecology, and discourse, we move a step closer toward a more accurate view of who and where we are.

WORKS CITED

Abram, David. "Merleau-Ponty and the Voice of the Earth." *Minding Nature: The Philosophers of Ecology.* Ed. David Macauley. New York: Guilford Press, 1996.

Berlin, James A. *Rhetoric and Reality: Writing Instruction in American Colleges, 1900–1985.* Carbondal; IL: Southern Illinois University Press, 1987.

———. Rhetorics, Poetics, and Cultures: Refiguring College English Studies. Urbana IL: National Council of Teachers of English, 1996.

Brooke, Robert. "Underlife and Writing Instruction." *College Composition and Communication* 38 (1987): 96–107.

Bruffee, Kenneth. "Collaborative Learning and 'The Conversation of Mankind.'" *College English* 46 (1984): 635–52.

———. "Social Construction, Language, and the Authority of Knowledge: A Bibliographical Essay." *College English* 48 (1986): 773–89.

———. "The Way Out." *College English* 33 (1972): 457–70.

Cooper, Marilyn, and Michael Holzman. *Writing as Social Action.* Portsmouth, New Hampshire: Boynton/Cook, 1989.

Eckersley, Robin. *Environmentalism and Political Theory: Towards an Ecocentric Approach.* New York: State University of New York Press, 1992.

Fox, Warwick. "The Deep Ecology—Ecofeminism Debate and Its Parallels." *Environmental Ethics* 11 (1989): 5–25.

Hairston, Maxine. "The Winds of Change: Thomas Kuhn and the Revolution in the Teaching of Writing." *College Composition and Communication* 14 (1982): 76–88.

Halden-Sullivan, Judith. "The Phenomenology of Process." *Into the Field: Sites of Composition Studies.* Ed. Anne Ruggles Gere. New York: Modern Language Association, 1993.

Harris, Joseph. *A Teaching Subject: Composition Since 1966.* Upper Saddle River, NJ: Prentice-Hall, 1997.

Jagtenberg, Tom, and David McKie. *Eco-Impacts and the Greening of Postmodernity: New Maps for Communication Studies, Cultural Studies, and Sociology.* Thousand Oaks, CA: Sage Publications, 1997.

King, Ynestra. "The Ecology of Feminism and the Feminism of Ecology." *Healing the Wounds: The Promise of Ecofeminism.* Ed. Judith Plant. Philadelphia: New Society Publishers, 1989.

Kockelmans, Joseph J. "Language, Meaning, and Ek-sistemce." *On Heidegger and Language.* Ed. and trans. Joseph J. Kockelmans. Evanston, IL: Northwestern University Press, 1972.

Leopold. Aldo. *A Sand County Almanac and Sketches Here and There.* New York: Oxford University Press, 1949.

Miller, Susan. *Textual Carnivals: The Politics of Composition.* Carbondale: Souther Illinois University Press, 1991.

Myers, Greg. "The Social Construction of Two Biologists Proposals." *Written Communication* 2 (1985): 219–45.

North, Stephen M. *The Making of Knowledge in Composition: Portrait of an Emerging Field.* Upper Montclair, NJ: Boynton/Cook, 1987.

Sarles, Harvey. *Language and Human Nature.* Minneapolis: University of Minnesota Press, 1985.

Stephanson, A. "Regarding Postmodernism—A Conversation with Frederic Jameson." *Social Text* 17 (1987): 29–54.

Ulman, H. Lewis. "'Thinking Like a Mountain': Persona, Ethos, and Judgment in American Nature Writing." *Green Culture: Environmental Rhetoric in Contemporary America.* Eds. Carl G. Herndl and Stuart C. Brown. Madison: University of Wisconsin Press, 1996.

Williams, Raymond. *Problems in Materialism and Culture.* London: Verso, 1980.

Great Divides:

Rhetorics of Literacy and Orality

Randall Roorda
University of Missouri-Kansas City
Kansas City, Missouri

The field of literacy studies has developed in parallel, sometimes in tandem, with composition studies. As currently configured, both emerged from events of the early sixties—for composition, the New Rhetoric movement and the Dartmouth conference bringing together learning theorists from England and the United States; for literacy studies, the publication of several crucial works during 1963 (see Havelock 24–29). With both, concern over methods and proprieties of teaching reading and writing have led to concern over the nature of these activities and the terms through which they might be best understood. The two areas are now so closely associated that they are often thought indistinguishable, with the paired expression "composition and literacy studies" becoming more common and the latter term sometimes regarded as subsuming the former. Yet differences in the circumstances of their origins continue to affect their character today, such that their ends and tempers are not identical. The influential works through which literacy studies was first constituted were written mainly by anthropologists and linguists, not by English and communications professors, and did not take education as their point of departure. And their intents were predominantly constrastive: their treatment of writing was couched in terms of the absence of writing, a countervailing condition called "orality."

The general endeavor of contrasting literacy with orality has been termed the *literacy thesis*. In brief, in its broadest forms, the literacy thesis holds that the introduction of writing, whether to an individual, a people, or the course of history, has significant consequences, of sorts that can be generalized about between individuals or across cultures. When differences between cultures are entertained, literacy has been seen as the prime mover in shifts between myth and science, magical and rational thought,

"savage" and "civilized" conditions, and so forth. Differences between individuals have been proposed under the rubric of the "cognitive," with literacy implicated in the growth of high-order instrumental thinking and
success at school-style problem-solving tasks, the sort upon which material
and social progress are thought to hinge. Further distinctions have arisen,
offshoots to the central oral-literate pairing, to account for differences
among sites that writing affects—Walter J. Ong's distinction, for instance,
between "primary" and "secondary" orality, the orality of cultures never
exposed to literacy versus that of unlettered people in societies practicing
writing in some form. In all of its versions, the literacy thesis has been discussed, tested, debated, and adapted to various ends. It has been embraced
by researchers, teachers, and government officials to whom writing's
virtues in promoting economic development, critical thinking, and democratic process have seemed to be evident.

Yet in the decades since it was first articulated, the literacy thesis has
drawn increasing criticism within literacy studies, the discipline it helped
found. Germinal works by such scholars as Ong, Eric A. Havelock, David
W. Olson, and Jack Goody have been regarded alike as positing a "Great
Divide" between written and spoken language. They have been lumped
together as instances of what one prominent critic, Brian V. Street, has
termed an *autonomous model* of literacy, which he counterposes to the
model he prefers, what he calls an "ideological" and others term a *social
model*. Street's charge, echoed by other literacy scholars, is that virtually all
generalizing about literacy and orality, whether framed in historical, social,
or individual terms, treat literacy as an autonomous entity unhinged from
cultural contexts in which it should more properly be seen as embedded.
Writing may have effects upon cultures and individuals, the social model
holds, but these differ so widely from site to site and are so wrapped up in
other aspects of cultural production and expression that no cause-effect relations can be established and no general laws of literacy's consequences
propounded. Features said to characterize written language in some contexts can as readily be discerned in spoken forms in others, so that general
categories must either resist all proof or founder under the weight of evidence and analysis. A model bebutting the literacy thesis is "social" in that
it resists the notion that literacy has set, predictable repercussions upon individuals, rendering them more rational or self-aware or fit to take part in
civilization's putative advance. Explanations of individual thought and
abilities, of cognition, must rather be sought in entire societies, and no society or subgroup, in all its complexity, can serve as a model or precedent
for any other. To Street and his allies, a social view is "ideological" in that
it claims to acknowledge its own interests and biases, believing that any

form of cultural expression is likewise thus ideologically marked. Versions of the literacy thesis, by contrast, are "autonomous" because they speculate about writing as an independent, free-floating variable in human affairs. In so doing, they unwittingly—or worse, disingenuously—promote a suspect ideology of individualism and subjugation of others, for a dualistic model that pairs literacy and orality must necessarily privilege the literate at the expense of its opposite number.

The turn upon the founders that Street exemplifies has occurred in part through the increased dissemination of educationists through literacy studies, as certain "Great Divide" presuppositions, often in oversimplified, stereotyped forms, have proved to be unreliable or counterproductive to those engaged in the teaching of reading and writing. Compositionists especially have embraced these lines of critique, which are echoed and elaborated in a number of influential works (see, e.g., Brandt, Gere, LeFevre, and most recently, Daniell). The "social model" appears to have won the day within composition studies proper, with "autonomous" talk of writing's wide-ranging social and cognitive consequences pretty well displaced by reports of how writing is "embedded" (as Street says) within ideological and discursive formations at various sites, each irreducibly, irremediably "specific." Among literacy professionals, it appears, orality is virtually defunct.

Yet the literacy thesis continues to thrive in other quarters, its appeal and evident explanatory force still widely capitalized upon. This is most strikingly the case in accounts of writing inflected by ecological concerns. I have sat in auditoriums at conferences and heard David Abram, author of *The Spell of the Sensuous,* generalize to rapt crowds about literacy's effects upon environmental sensibilities, emitting pronouncements that would drop the jaws of social model enthusiasts. Abram's book—which unlike most works in literacy studies is widely disseminated as a trade paperback—is attracting readers and exercising a sway well beyond those associated with literacy studies per se. It joins an earlier work—*ABC: The Alphabetization of the Popular Mind,* by Ivan Illich and Barry Sanders— which though less overtly environmentalist is scripted by writers whose ecological predilections are well established, and similarly offers an unabashed brand of "divide" thinking in a form accessible to trade readers. These are serious books, positioned toward an educated readership, yet they reach their conclusions with next to no recourse to the bulk of recent scholarship in this vein.

The problem I wish to take up in this essay concerns the problems that these sites of inquiry might pose for each other were they aware of each other's existence. How might the critique of an "autonomous model" affect the methods and conclusions adopted by those who reflect on literacy, as Abram and Illich and Sanders do, from perspectives that are avowedly or incipiently ecological? And how might ecological perspectives affect the critique that "social model" theorists level against the literacy thesis in its varied forms, mitigating the force of that critique, transforming its terms, or affecting our sense of its methods and objectives? What implications might this cross-referencing of perspectives have for those who teach literate practices and contemplate the continuance of such in a world riven by machine technologies and rife with environmental distress? My intent will be to sketch grounds upon which these disparate camps might agree to disagree, cognizant of points of departure in premises and argumentative procedures.

My procedure, far from comprehensive, will be in effect to argue with everybody, playing both ends against an imagined middle in the rhetorical divide over the "Great Divide." First I will review claims made about literacy by environmentally oriented commentators, especially Abram, and indicate respects in which those claims might be found wanting from the standpoint of many literacy professionals. Then I will turn tables and take on "social view" professionals who dispute the propriety of oral-literate distinctions in essentially any form. I will suggest that in their own zeal over ideology they have been wont to conflate the varied ideologies of those propounding such distinctions, and to fetishize specificity unless generalizations of their own are at issue. Especially, they overlook the fact that the tenor and ends of oral-literate thinking need not conduce to the denigration of nonwriting peoples that they quite reasonably fear, as biocentric formulations of the subject are far from doing. Finally, I will conclude with a qualified defense of "divide" mongering in literacy studies, rhetorically and pragmatically tinged, as a horizon to, not a freeway through, the experiential domains of composition teachers. Rhetorics of literacy and orality, I will contend, can serve as instruments for thinking about instrumentation in thinking—one element in a more generalized critique of technology and culture from which educators cannot be excepted.

As a preamble to this discussion, I'd like to invoke a pair of terms drawn from Jose Ortega y Gasset, which I learned from the linguist, A. L. Becker: *exuberance* and *deficiency*. Remarking on translation, Ortega asserts that every account or interpretation of another's utterance is at once both exuberant and deficient: it says or includes more than the original does, and it falls short of all that the original imparts to a native audience. It does both by virtue of differences in suggestions and reverberations implicit in the prior texts informing utterances in both languages. The pertinence of these terms to translation between languages makes them helpful in the area of literacy studies, which so often involves interpreting the languaging acts of foreign cultures. Yet their implications extend to acts of interpretation generally, meeting up and meshing with the implications of another term: Kenneth Burke's notion of *terministic screens,* the recognition that any perspective, any terminology or description or account, is at once a reflection, a selection, and a deflection of reality (44). It's important to note that there are *always* terministic screens at work in interpretation and that versions of another's utterance are *always* at once both exuberant and deficient. While the task of the critic or philologist is to discern and correct more egregious "deflections," more remarkable surpluses and deficits of meaning, these efforts amount to pragmatic acts of reorientation to circumstances, not positivistic convergences upon some stable preexisting truth. This is because our access to reality is a function of our acts of selection; remarking everything, we could manage to say nothing at all. Our silences, as Becker insists, are as necessary and eloquent as our voicings.

In ethnography, the practice of what Clifford Geertz terms *thick description* has arisen to mitigate exuberances and deficiencies in accounting for the terministic screens of other cultures. Filling in more and more of a culture's prior texts, glossing its nuances and peculiarities, one hones in on an interpretation more adequate to its character. Yet accretion of detail and background is not tantamount to adequacy of interpretation. In acts of translation, such qualities as economy and incisiveness may be effaced or buried under a blizzard of glosses. Nor does degree of detail map onto measures of exuberance or deficiency in any set way. The concise or general can be exuberant, implying too much; yet the "thick" can be deficient, suggesting too little. One's interests, predilections, and ends—one's ideology, if you prefer—can and will constitute screens that authorize dialectial acts, determining what generalities seem admissable and what specificities indispensable.

The books I've mentioned by Abram and by Illich and Sanders are decidedly exuberant—in temper and style, certainly, as in their propensity to generalize. Both propose quite marked distinctions between oral and literate conditions, distinctions of sorts certain to exercise such literacy thesis critics as pay them any attention at all. Focusing largely on twelfth-century Europe but also on other sites including classical Greece—the locus of the shift to literacy as discussed in pivotal works by Eric A. Havelock and by Jack Goody and Jan Watt—Illich and Sanders manage, in the course of not much over a hundred pages, to associate history, memory, epistemology, education, identity, even the notions of a word and of language itself, with the shift from orality to literacy. This tiny tour de force evinces "divide" thinking of a vigorous, unabashed sort, right down to the metaphor the authors select to represent their own posture toward the subjects they discuss. "Standing firmly on the *terra* of literacy, we can see two epistemological chasms," they proclaim. "One of these chasms cuts us off from the domain of orality. The other, which moves like smog to engulf us, equates letters with bits of information, degrading reading and writing" (xi). In part, this prospectus embodies the attitude that the folklorist Ruth Finnegan, a prominent scholar of "oral literature," sees as characterizing divide theories generally "a kind of romantic nostalgia, in 'the world we have lost' tone," giving way to an affirmation "that such losses were worth the sacrifice and that our own fate lies upwards and onwards through literacy" (6). Finnegan renders well the posture of a theorist like Ong, probably the most influential proponent of divide thinking, whose view of literacy includes the notion that while writing separates humans from their natural condition, such separation in the service of "higher" cognitive powers is all to the good, since it is "natural" for humans to be "artificial" (82). But while Illich and Sanders, like Ong and many others, do indeed contemplate a "chasm" separating literates from "the world we have lost," their statement departs from Finnegan's caricature in an important way. While affirming their own literate condition and acknowledging their prejudice in favor of history, they do not represent this "fate" as lying "upward and onward" in any sense. Rather, as a longtime critic of so-called development among indigenous peoples, Illich in particular is profoundly leery of any such pretensions to progress; Sanders, once a collaborator with the environmental anthropologist and philosopher Paul Shepard, can be presumed to agree. Instead of a rising prospect, these oracular coauthors spot a second "chasm" threatening our tenuous literate estate, one that "like smog" is a by-product of advanced technologies. Both the sense of *nostalgia* (if the term will serve for this form of longing) and the jaundiced view of at least some aspects of literacy are worth bearing in mind as we move to consider David Abram.

Abram's *The Spell of the Sensuous* is much read and discussed in environmental circles these days, and Abram himself, as I mentioned, has become a popular figure on the eco-conference circuit—and not just for his skills as a sleight-of-hand magician. His book is intriguing in its accounts of how the "magic" of traditional healers he traveled among in rural Asia serves less a social than an ecological function, reconciling people with the larger prerogatives of their places. It is compelling for its evocations of "animism," of heightened states of involvement in one's surroundings, expressive of what he calls the book's "simple premise": "that we are human only in contact, and conviviality, with what is not human" (ix). (This mention of *conviviality* places him in league with Illich, who in *Tools for Conviviality* takes this as a key term and whom Abram acknowledges in his preface.) Beyond these qualities—and beyond their association with the phenomenology of Husserl and Merleau-Ponty, which Abram, an academically trained philosopher, elaborates at length—the book has attracted attention largely for the claims it makes about literacy. Abram views literacy—alphabetic literacy, more specifically—as the primary instrument of people's separation from place. Alphabetic writing, he asserts, tends to close off the human capacity for participation in place, particularly the capacity to perceive language and voice not as exclusively human but instead as diffused throughout one's experiential horizons. With writing this capacity gets displaced, projected exclusively onto the written text. The text thus magically acquires the ability to voice itself, but in doing so renders the rest of one's environs effectively silent. The separation is less acute, Abram believes, with texts inscribed in pictorial or logographic scripts; but with the alphabet, the characters of the text cease to resemble or evoke any attachment to the tangible phenomenon they figure. The word and the world are thus sundered.

What Abram offers appears as a sort of skeleton key to the nature-culture divide that exercises biocentrism. In the spirit of full disclosure, I can attest to the appeal of this approach, since Abram's case parallels observations I made in a study of oral-literate distinctions a decade ago. I researched especially relations between literacy and views of time, a subject Abram discusses as well, and I did so also from a biocentric perspective, one interested in the achievements of traditional peoples at maintaining sustainable relations with place. My version of the Great Divide sketched large correspondances between orality and such features of indigenous societies as cyclic time, subsistence economies, languages and religions, and so forth. The scheme I came up with excited me, and when I packed myself off for a doctorate at the start of the nineties, I thought I brought a dissertation topic in tow. My first inkling that something might be amiss came when I prevailed upon Becker—philologist, rhetorician, and wilderness canoeist—to read the monograph-length manuscript I'd composed on the subject. Becker did not rebut my grand scheme, exactly, but his cordial, interested response made it clear that he did not think much of it. In the course of continued study on the topic, I began to understand why. I came to realize the extent to which Great Divide theories of literacy and orality have been challenged, rebutted, and in the minds of many researchers, discredited. My nascent professional affiliations chastened me in ways that Abram's have not. Having declined to pursue these perspectives in the face of likely rejection within my field, I find myself now in the position of assessing the import of similar notions as advanced in other quarters.

I would note first that while Abram's conclusions play well to a biocentric crowd, their interpretive exuberance gives behind-the-scenes pause even among some scholars of kindred ideological stripe. When I questioned one well-known environmental philosopher—one among the pantheon Abram lists in his acknowledgments—about Abram's notions of the alphabet, he replied, in effect, that of course it's not so. He did not rebut so much as dismiss the thesis, implying it could not be seriously entertained. Furthermore, sources that Abram relies on in exemplifying his version of a divide cannot be counted upon to support his use of their findings, for instance, Abram reviews at length Keith Basso's work on narrative and landscape among the Western Apache and adduces it in support of an "oral" understanding of place. Yet when I asked Basso, after a talk he gave, whether he would support this linking of Apache storytelling practices with a specifically oral register, he declined to do so. I anticipated that he would respond in this way: as a linguistic anthropologist of a Geertzian, "thick" temperament, Basso is understandably leery of generalizing his findings across the bewildering range of human cultures, even nonwriting ones.

The very idea that one can pronounce upon the condition of "oral" or "literate" people, then, is anathema to many professional students of culture. As someone who, for all his personal expressiveness and anecdotal facility, has aspired "to maintain a high standard of theoretical and scholarly precision" in his writing (x), Abram might be expected to further observe or at least acknowledge and rebut the proprieties prevailing in fields he strays upon. I recognize and appreciate his exuberant, speculative temper and have no desire to fit his work to the procrustean bed of any one disciplinary formation. Yet his failure to come to terms with any but a fraction of the work done on the precise questions he entertains—the character of orality and the implications of literacy—must be counted a problem in his work.

The general opposition to generalization in the study of culture is of course based largely on perceptions among case workers, so to speak, in anthropology, linguistics, and education, that the particular ways of the people they study do not wholly settle into the categories propounded to explain them. Many such points of dissonance might be cited for Abram's generalizations, just as they have for other such cases, but the most important for both Abram and Illich and Sanders concerns the propriety of generalizing about the effects of alphabetic scripts. Both, of course, do so exuberantly, beginning with their titles: *ABC* quite directly, and Abram's title through its pun on "spell," which evokes how alphabetic writing appropriates the animistic voicing that more properly belongs to one's entire experiential domain, such that "oral" people, for instance, might hear a tree speak. Many others—including Havelock, Ong, the early Jack Goody (with Ian Watt) and the literacy historian David Diringer—precede these writers in making claims about how the Greek alphabet's phonetic character, especially its marking of vowel sounds, conduces to special repercussions. The "consequences of literacy" that Goody and Watt so influentially hypothesized were deemed particular to the Greek alphabet, which these writers saw as revolutionary in its effects.

It seems indisputable that alphabetic literacy does make reading and writing at least somewhat easier to learn and thus potentially, though not necessarily, more widespread. And there must certainly be further distinctions to be made between the ways in which alphabetic and other forms of script are taken by, and help to, form readers (see, e.g., Saenger, on differences between reading alphabetic and Chinese logographic scripts). Yet the larger contrasts proposed by Goody and Watt, and yet more exuberantly by Ong, have long been compromised by others working in this area. As long ago as 1968, Kathleen Gough, in a collection edited and introduced by Goody, was carefully qualifying claims for the alphabet's special "consequences," especially as regards Chinese script. In his introduction to that collection as in his subsequent work, Goody has taken note of such objections and been more thorough and circumspect in assessing the import of writing systems of all sorts. More recently, John DeFrancis, a longtime scholar of Chinese, has rebutted widespread misapprehensions about its supposed visual and pictorial character, often adduced as an instance of writing that supposedly can be comprehended directly without the intermediation of speech. Abram, in his exuberant speculations about the residually pictorial and thus putatively less sensorially estranging character of this script, takes none of this work into account.

In this matter of the alphabet, as in so many aspects of literacy, investigators must beware of projecting terms and precepts derived from the very phenomena under study, as the linguist Roy Harris shows. The notion that the alphabet has a distinct and privileged relation to the sounds it's said to represent is, to Harris, a "prestigious bit of cultural mythology" (108), indicative of what he calls "the tyranny of the alphabet"—an attitude that views all other and earlier forms of inscription as somehow striving to become yet falling short of an ideal that was finally realized in fifth-century B.C.E. Greece. In this light, it appears that Abram—and even Illich and Sanders, who restlessly reflect on their own status as writing people—might demonstrate further self-reflexiveness of a sort consonant with their own speculations. I mean, for one thing, that the most interesting thing about the alphabet may not be its ability to analyze and "capture" the sounds of speech, but rather the conviction produced in its users that this is what it is doing. The terms of the inquiry dictate the conclusions, in much the same way that, as Harvey B. Sarles notes, inquiry into the "origins of language" presupposes that there *is* such a thing as "language" (22–39) peculiar to the human estate and constitutive of its superiority.

There are other points where a degree more self-reflexiveness seems called for in Abram. To follow his divide thesis with the "rigor" he claims, he would need to account even further for the ways in which his "story" (as he calls it, avoiding the onus of having an "argument" to make) is itself beholden to the literate ways it expounds upon. He does this in some degree: for instance, he understands myth in indigenous societies as not "literal" since the notion of the literal is itself a product of writing. Yet he still wishes to generalize the import of local tales into broad statements about what "oral" people do—an understandable and even alluring pursuit, but redolent of an abstracting impulse itself decidedly "literate" in character. Furthermore, Abram's preferred mode of what he calls "writing back in" to the places he's been is itself a supremely literate activity. He relies on a sort of profuse, intense physical detail and psychological self-scrutiny that to accomplished readers effectively evokes sensory experience but is nonetheless quite foreign to what paradoxically gets called "oral literature." Illich and Sanders remark on the way in which our categories for understanding past societies depend upon a mode of *description* peculiar to our own, reading society. This mode can be regarded as the sort of contextualizing—filling in elements of an otherwise absent situation—that writing frequently enacts in its push for explicitness. Such writing is novelistic—which means, as per Walter Benjamin, that it's modern, literate, and alienated by machine reproduction—not really an act of "storytelling" at all. In keeping with and extending the terms of his "divide," Abram might acknowledge that whatever the phenomenological import of the "spells" he enters through writing, his activity does not recover a condition of orality, anymore than a jeep can trace an Aboriginal dream line.

The very idea that a "story" can tie together and justify so much over so many disparate contexts can be seen as a quintessentially literate maneuver, in typical literacy thesis terms. It seems to be an exuberant conflating of narrative conventions across cultures to presume that Abram's book or theory as a whole can be styled a "story" in anything like the way Aboriginals tell a story. Rather than elaborate this claim, though, I had better reflexively note some interpretive exuberances of my own. For in the act of tempering some habits and generalities I find in Abram, I have launched off into divide thinking of my own, pronouncing upon what is or is not "literate" in his procedures, implying in circular manner that generalizing about literacy is a very literate thing to do. It's the very circularity of much divide thinking, and thus its resistance to testing and proof, which exercises some of its critics. Yet I confess I find the habit irresistable, in some measure inevitable, and potentially productive for thinkers of biocentric cast. It's in this temper or frame of mind that I wish to consider rhetorics informing debate over oral-literate distinctions within literacy studies—the Great Divide over the Great Divide.

I've been commenting on the interpretive exuberance of the divide thinking of Abram and Illich and Sanders and suggesting that it's this exuberance, this propensity to generalize in oracular manner, which arouses the ire of many in composition and literacy studies today. I now want to consider deficiency, the failure to say as much as might usefully be said: a sort of rhetorical meagerness, at times even bad faith, which I believe characterizes much criticism of the so-called Great Divide.

To apprehend this debate, it may help to think in terms of not one but three sorts of "divide." First is the divide between orality and literacy, and speaking and writing, posited in stronger versions of the literacy thesis. Then there are divides between versions of that thesis—especially between individual or cognitive accounts and sociocultural accounts of oral-literate distinctions, also between historical accounts and the contemporary-educational ones of most interest to compositionists (in which arises the vexed issue of whether an "ontogeny" of individual development recapitulates a historical "phylogeny" of writing). Finally, there is the divide between those who acknowledge the utility and propriety of oral-literate distinctions on some terms or other, and those who refute this—what Street styles the difference between "autonomous" and "ideological" models. Street is a spokesperson for the opposition in this last divide, which means that he discounts any differences associated with the second set of divides, viewing all literacy-thesis versions as anathema alike. This perspective rests on a pair of assumptions. It assumes, first, that oral-literate generalizing of any order must head down a slippery slope toward ideological bias, reifying and privileging writing to the tacit yet ultimately tangible disadvantage of those tagged with "orality." And it assumes, in effect, that a model of literacy that is "ideological" in the sense Street describes—that is, that acknowledges and advertises its biases—will likewise end up eschewing such generalizing.

I have qualms over these assumptions. Undoubtedly much research on literacy has been conducted along the lines critiqued, and many educational endeavors, such as UNESCO-style national literacy campaigns, have presupposed the benefits of letters in ideologically freighted ways. Yet I don't find that the most interesting work on oral-literate distinctions depicts literacy as "autonomous," sundered from cultural contexts. I don't believe it must lapse or sneak into suspect ideological postures. And I don't believe an ideologically interested stance toward literacy must either eschew generalization or end up retrograde. *All* perspectives on literacy are thoroughly rhetorical in the generalizations they admit or refute; none reduce to questions of evidence, though evidence can be produced for all. An ecological or biocentric perspective, I believe, can demonstrate how this is the case.

Of all of the arguments rebutting oral-literate distinctions, some are more likely than others to neglect or exercise a biocentric perspective. Central is the question of technology. It's been a credo to versions of the literacy thesis for decades now that literacy is in important ways a technology and that technologies have consequences. Marshall McLuhan's speculations sprang from this premise; Havelock Ellis's germinal reflections departed from the fact of deforestation for paper in Canada; and Goody thirty years ago termed writing *the technology of the intellect* to emphasize its material, instrumental nature. Since these points of origin, though, it's become suspect in literacy studies to pronounce upon the technological character of literacy. The cautions are in part well-founded. They can be generally classed as forms of opposition to "technological determinism": the discredited notion that certain forms of instrumentation, by their very nature, are bound to issue in certain sorts of outcomes, essentially dictating the actions and mentalities of those employing them. Such an attitude has indeed pervaded the efforts of national literacy campaigns, the organizers and proponents of which have often been abashed when the propitious outcomes projected—the "takeoffs" into "modernity"—did not materialize as forecasted. But here as elsewhere, the reaction to such excesses has issued in a sort of interpretive deficiency. Fearful of the terministic typecasting often involved—the association of speech with unmediated nature and writing with the artifice of culture—critics of divide thinking have as much as proscribed generalizations about writing in relation to technology. In so doing, they have ruled out what may be of most interest to environmentalists.

I'm not claiming that environmentalists ought to espouse technological determinism in any form; what I'm disputing is the assumption that attention to literacy as technology must amount to determinism, and the consequent neglect of technology as prime, perhaps primary, among the factors "embedded" in literacy's cultural milieu. Among critics like Brian V. Street, considerations of technology have gone from central to nearly invisible, with the habitual academic praise of complexity and disdain toward "commonsense" eventuating in notable blind spots and bits of terministic legerdemain. Finnegan, for instance, wary of determinism but finding it hard to dispense with technology altogether, ends up calling *all* modes of languaging "information technologies" or "ITs"—speech included. (One wonders whether she thinks of songbirds as similarly plying technical devices.) Rebutting the emphasis on technology, Street adapts a distinction of Finnegan's at least as spurious as any between speaking and writing: that between "technology" and "use." It's not the technology itself that has consequences, this distinction goes, but rather the use to which it's put in (as always) specific cultural contexts. How technology can exist without use, how use can be contemplated without technology, escapes me; this strikes me as a version of "guns don't kill people; people do," with pens ellided instead of weapons. A researcher like Goody, stereotyped as "autonomous" by Street, is far more instructive on *this* sort of embedding in context, the interplay of instruments and convictions associated with writing. And Abram, for that matter, is far more suggestive, for all his exuberance. Literacy is not *one* technology, of course, and it is not *only* a technology. But neither are forms of agriculture or transportation or warfare, for that matter, which are likewise culturally embedded yet powerful and worth discussing in their own right, and likewise have their influence on cognition, not to mention on dreams. The biocentric rejoinder to the subordination of technology, then, is to insist that technologies are reciprocally implicated with their uses, not determining yet often transforming the contexts they emerge within or are inflicted upon. The instruments of literacy are potent if unpredictable; this has always been the point of most literacy thesis versions.

As for the implications of writing as technology, a primary contention has been that literacy promotes "decontextualization." The likes of Ong and Abram, among many others, agree on writing's tendency to abstract conceptions from circumstances, unmoor understandings from place, and fill in rather than assume a great deal taken as given among nonwriting peoples. Goody suggestively remarks on the universalizing tendencies of "People of the Book," (1986), issuing in religions of conversion and, indeed, the very phenomenon of "ideology" that critics like Street take as universal. Earlier versions of the literacy thesis—of the sort impelling missionary-style literacy programs and Third-World development campaigns—often framed the decontextualization thesis as a matter of the relative presence or absence of "reason"—or "critical distance" or "higher-order cognition" or some other such invidious category—among those who do or don't write. Ong, for one, veers decidedly toward such a stance, with his talk of the "higher consciousness" that the development of writing has conduced to. Critics of the thesis have shown in detail how this notion will not hold, how nonwriting peoples are no more irrational or cognitively challenged than literate ones. A good deal here as elsewhere depends on the definitions of terms. Within the notion of *decontextualization,* abstraction has often been lumped together with generalization and other habits of mind, resulting in a conceptual mish-mosh not difficult to debunk. Yet here again, debunkers have often discarded the kernel with the chaff, undermining the very idea that writing may bear different relations to its context than speaking does. Deborah Brandt, for instance, has insisted that *all* language occurs in a social context and that the notion of decontextualization is invalid for this reason. Her claim is inviolable as far as it goes, if one accepts her manner of defining "context"; but it has the effect of effacing the many and marked differences that led investigators to posit literate decontextualization in the first place. Some of these are amply demonstrated by research of many sorts (summarized in Denny); others are manifest in the maligned realm of "commonsense," in the recognition, especially, that writing goes places that the writer doesn't go. When a Cree girl sends her sister with a note, not to the next village but to the next *room,* requesting money for a pack of cigarettes, she is "saving face"—withholding her face, displacing the terms of an encounter—in a manner that writing allows and in a sense invites (Bennett and Berry 102). A biocentric perspective on "context," of the sort that Abram and Illich and Sanders elaborate, will insist that there are differences worth contemplating in the modes of distance and proximity our technologies promote, and that these are related to our modes of sustaining relations of community in place.

This notion of "face" poses an interesting case in how oral-literate distinctions are posited and rebutted in a manner essentially rhetorical. One aspect of distinctions about context concerns the presence of "extratextual" or "paralinguistic" cues in spoken language: the realm of gestures, facial expressions, and inflections of voice that enliven speech and provide cues to its interpretation but that are largely absent and must be "contextualized," filled in, or compensated for, with writing. Casting doubt on this distinction, Street cites other researchers to the effect that such gestural cues are far from absent in writing, for they exist in such graphic cues as typefaces, paper stocks, page layout, and other graphic elements (1995, 169–71). This is a resourceful point, certainly—such graphic conventions would seem to emulate or in some way stand in for gestural cues in speech, with the tiny typographical sideways smiley faces now popular in e-mail a striking instance of this. But focusing on this area of apparent blurring, one may overlook larger realms of contrast that remain distinct. A biocentric perspective would hold, rather, that written "gestures" are not equivalent to, but are dependant or parasitic upon, responses proper to face-to-face interaction, and that these responses are biologic and evolutionary in character, manifested in the earliest relations of infants to those around them. In fact, they are not confined to that "language" that's posited as an exclusively human construct, as Sarles notes; they are an integral aspect of that "languaging," those acts of interaction that are comparable across species boundaries. Abram does us a service by dramatizing such "synesthesiac" interaction, compensating in his exuberance for the deficiency of models that would conflate cold type with sensual participation in place.

The appeal to biology and evolution would not wash with a critic like Street; this is an angle he would proscribe completely. We see this in his response to the work of M. A. K. Halliday, one of the most eminent of linguists investigating differences between spoken and written language. Street faults Halliday not on the basis of differences he identifies but on broader grounds—the character of the arguments he advances as to why such differences should have come to exist. Halliday argues that spoken and written language developed, or evolved, out of response to different needs. Street responds that both the appeal to evolution and the argument about functions arising from needs are suspect, not just in Halliday's usage but rather in general, wherever they may be found. Explanations from evolution are ideological snares to Street, ipso facto associated with late-nineteenth-century social Darwinism, and arguments evoking needs and functions are necessarily circular to him, in that they assume the terms they claim to derive and are thus unprovable (1995, 4–5). It's true that such arguments have a troubled history and must be used with circumspection. But with evolution a demonstrated fact, and with feedback loops of the sort ecology describes, between needs and adaptations, necessarily and intricately circular, neither can such lines of inquiry be interdicted. A stance that would do so may be enamored of specifics about cultures but has little appetite for specifics of arguments that follow lines or adopt terms it deems tainted.

Biocentrism is an ideological stance as well, of course; it has terms it would prefer to interdict, distinctions it would propound or foreclose. Many of its ends it shares with social model critics—notably, resistance to a unilinear notion of progress effected through literacy. And so it is well advised to air its premises, rendering the implicit more explicit, as Goody observes literate practices tend to do. In concluding this essay, I'd like to switch from a mode of refutation to one of commited speculation, to suggest what rhetorics of literacy and orality might offer to biocentrist ends.

A prime attribute of biocentrism is that it acknowledges and explores our biologic estate while denying that evolution is coterminous with modernity. Our human nature is not simple or set and unchanging, but it is persistent. We're much the same creatures we were before the Neolithic—adapted to the same ends, the same pains and pleasures. No great leap, no punctuated equilibrium is evident from gatherer to farmer, rhapsode to scribe.

Yet there appear to be disjunctures between these conditions of practical sorts, deepseated in history and psyche. They are such that one biocentrist commentator, the ecopsychologist Chellis Glendinning, feels warranted in terming all indigenous cultures of hunter-gatherer economies *nature-based peoples,* and setting them in opposition to all other cultures past and present (9–11). This is indeed a great divide. How is it to be taken? In one sense, it's just a recent outgrowth of the old divide between the savage and civilized, extending from Rousseau through Frazer and Levy-Bruhl to Levi-Strauss. However noble and natural the savage is thought, the distinction must turn out bad for him: this is the line that literacy thesis critics take. This is far from Glendinning's purpose, of course. She believes that civilization as we know it is a form of addiction and maladjustment, a progenitor of myriad other ills, necessitating treatment and recovery. Contemplation and emulation of "nature-based peoples" is for her a form of therapy. The divide she proposes seeks practical consequences but is essentially heuristic in force. In this, it suggests the temper in which divide thinking along biocentric lines might proceed.

What the contemplation of orality can do for us—ironically or contrary to expectations—is to refute the notion that changes in instrumentation, even quite drastic ones, are tantamount to human progress. Such a purpose recovers the expressed purposes of the first few versions of the literacy thesis: namely, to account for observed differences between tribal peoples and "civilized" ones without resorting to a stage model of rival mentalities, by which a "civilized" condition must succeed a "preliterate" one, the way in which the adult succeeds the adolescent. This is what Johannes Fabian calls "the denial of coevalness" in anthropology: the presumption that the "primitive" other does not occupy the same time as the literate investigator but is somehow "behind"—arrested, retarded, delayed, or running in place. Goody and Watt, in their originary paper on "The Consequences of Literacy," were not satisfied to believe that our contemporary condition represented some great leap forward, some pole-vault in capacities from the state of "the savage mind." But neither were they willing to discount observations indicating that contrasts between these conditions were frequently dramatic indeed. This is the "diffuse relativism" they complain of in their article (26), a reluctance to acknowledge disjunctures that to many seem manifest—an attitude rampant in the fixation on the "specific" characterizing critique of their article and of subsequent nuanced works by Goody and others'. "Something really is happening," as Brian Stock insists (9), something *still* happens in the encounter of traditional with writing peoples; this is what the literacy thesis serves best to explain and what to biocentrism most needs explaining. While what happens may not be *one* thing and may not be perfectly predictable, still, the encounter is momentous indeed, and has much to do with instruments of writing.

In the well-known essay "Language Is Sermonic," Richard Weaver hangs a conclusion about rhetoric upon a conditional assertion: "*If* the real progress of man is toward ideal truth. . . ." (1048, my emphasis). The literacy thesis, in appropriately discounted and circular forms, helps us understand this "ideal truth" not as ultimate reality but as an image of the duplicated, "verbatim" text. It helps counter the notion that "real progress" in human affairs is "ideally" accomplished by accretion—by contriving more and more complex instruments and textual artifacts to fill a single big canvas of "truth." This is an end that proponents of an "ideological" model share, though they believe that versions of the literacy thesis are ipso facto deleterious to it. The model or narrative that Abram, Illich and Sanders, and the anthropologist Stanley Diamond among others offer is one of loss through literate capacity. Nonwriting people can do, perceive, and be things that writing people cannot, they insist. Our understanding of what writing can do must be tempered and chastened by such intimations of loss, they suggest—loss that is not total or determined but practical and tangible, not sheerly nostalgiac.

But the literacy thesis so construed need not just counter assumptions about literacy that have authorized the totalizing, ethnocentric efforts of developers and educationists. It can also inform the uses of writing itself—at least I believe that it might, though the circularity of this prospect is dizzying, akin to the "nausea" that Tobin Siebers finds endemic to the hermeneutical enterprise, which obliges one to come to rest in postures one acknowledges as partial and provisional. I mean that reflection on the condition of writing is provoked and transfigured by the sense—a felt sense—that the realm of letters, even more than of language in general, is finally a narrow swath within the entirety of not-only-human experience.

Reflexivity in the exercise of letters can come to terms with without exhausting this recognition, confronting in the process how frustrating and limiting the process of inscription can be, how incommensurate with the circumstances and sensations that lead us to engage in it. In this prospect, reflections on writing process of the sort central to composition come to intersect the outpourings on silence, the emissions on inexpressible conditions, characteristic of mystical traditions. Weaver sees the move to analogy, to similitude, as rhetoric's highest level, one that makes present "a recognition that the unknown may be continuous with the known, so that man is moving about in a world only partly realized, yet real in all its parts" (1049). To me, contemplation of orality as a rhetorical resource, a move at once "literal" and analogical, helps reinforce the partiality of my realizations, while ratifying the irremediable reality of all that writing can only sample.

A biocentric formulation of the literacy thesis, I believe, should restlessly qualify the divides it propounds, yet firmly reject the proposed divide between "autonomous" and "social" models. To identify a divide as a heuristic maneuver does not necessitate the neglect of other distinctions, other divides, both across and beyond the categories of the "oral" and "literate." Social phenomena can be complex, variable, shifting, causally overdetermined, intricately embedded in context, and endlessly specific—and still subject to divides. As a metaphor, consider a single rock, which when closely examined may bear fracture planes in several directions, as well as signs of accretion, interpenetration, warping, and so on. It is irreducibly complex in its causes, analyzable as such. But it can be set back ("distanced") and pointed at: see that big crack *right there.* Smack it there sharply and it falls apart. That's the "divide" in biocentric view: not a rift but a definite fissure, one of many such "divides," but critical and in some cases decisive.

Or if the "great divide" offends, we might speak of the great distinction. Even an "ideological model" of literacy must preserve the terms *oral* and *literate,* penciling in fine disjunctures within its overall picture of determined gray. The divide or distinction is above all terministic—not the weight but the reading of evidence determines its use. Yet it reflects some irreducible facts, that you can do certain things with writing that you can't do with speech—not all of them necessarily worth doing. And the reverse is true and crucial: there are capacities in orality that literacy as we know it cannot approach. It's this recognition that leads Abram to affirm our animism, Pierre Clastres to reflect on how tribal societies resist the literate power of the state, and Johan Galtung to propose a willed withdrawal from literacy as a political act. It is exuberant to suggest that there are endangered species of action and attention in the world—that if something really is happening when writing overcomes a society, this may be part of what is happening. But if something like this were so, and if we failed to address it through as well as despite our terministic screens as writing people, we could find ourselves facing deficiencies of irremediable order—if we are able to *face* them at all.

WORKS CITED

Abram, David. *The Spell of the Sensuous: Perception and Language in a More-than-Human World.* New York: Pantheon, 1996.

Becker, A. L. *Beyond Translation: Essays toward a Modern Philology.* Ann Arbor: University of Michigan Press, 1995.

Benjamin, Walter. *Illuminations.* 1968. Trans. Harry Zohn. Ed. Hannah Arendt. New York: Shocken, 1969.

Bennett, Jo Anne, and John W. Berry. "Cree Literacy in the Syllabic Script." *Literacy and Orality.* Eds. David R. Olson and Nancy Torrance. Cambridge: Cambridge University Press, 1991. 90–104.

Brandt, Deborah. *Literacy as Involvement: The Acts of Writers, Readers, and Texts.* Carbondale: Southern Illinois University Press, 1990.

Burke, Kenneth. *Language as Symbolic Action: Essays on Life, Literature, and Method.* Berkeley: University of California Press, 1966.

Clastres, Pierre. *Society Against the State.* Trans. Robert Hunter in collaboration with Abe Stein. New York: Zone Books, 1989.

Daniell, Beth. "Narratives of Literacy: Connecting Composition to Culture." *College Composition and Communication* 50 (1999): 393–410.

DeFrancis, John. *Visible Speech: The Diverse Oneness of Writing Systems.* Honolulu: University of Hawaii Press, 1989.

Denny, J. Peter. "Rational Thought in Oral Culture and Literate Decontextualization." *Literacy and Orality.* Eds. David R. Olson and Nancy Torrance. Cambridge: Cambridge University Press, 1991. 66–89.

Diamond, Stanley. *In Search of the Primitive: A Critique of Civilization.* New Brunswick, NJ: Transaction, 1974.

Diringer, David. *The Alphabet: A Key to the History of Mankind.* 3rd ed. New York: Funk and Wagnalls, 1948.

Fabian, Johannes. *Time and the Other.* New York: Columbia University Press, 1983.

Finnegan, Ruth. *Literacy and Orality: Studies in the Technology of Communication.* Oxford: Blackwell, 1988.

Galtung, Johan. "Literacy, Education, and Schooling—for What?" *Literacy and Social Development in the West: A Reader.* Ed. Harvey J. Graff. Cambridge: Cambridge University Press, 1981. 271–85.

Gere, Anne Ruggles. *Writing Groups: History, Theory, and Implications.* Carbondale: Southern Illinois University Press, 1987.

Glendinning, Chellis. *My Name Is Chellis and I'm in Recovery from Western Civilization.* Boston: Shambhala, 1994.

Goody, Jack. "Introduction." *Literacy in Traditional Societies.* Ed. Jack Goody. Cambridge: Cambridge University Press, 1968.

———. *The Logic of Writing and the Organization of Society.* Cambridge: Cambridge University Press, 1986.

———. *The Interface Between the Written and the Oral.* Cambridge: Cambridge University Press, 1987.

———. and Ian Watt. "The Consequences of Literacy." 1963. *Perspectives on Literacy.* Eds. Eugene R. Kingen, Barry M. Kroll, and Mike Rose. Carbondale: Southern Illinois University Press, 1988.

Harris, Roy. *The Origin of Writing.* London: Duckworth, 1986.

Havelock, Eric A. *The Muse Learns to Write: Reflections on Orality and Literacy from Antiquity to the Present.* New Haven: Yale University Press, 1986.

Illich, Ivan, and Barry Sanders. *ABC: The Alphabetization of the Popular Mind.* New York: Vintage-Random, 1988.

LeFevre, Karen Burke. *Invention as a Social Act.* Carbondale: Southern Illinois University Press, 1987.

Ong, Walter J. *Orality and Literacy: The Technologizing of the Word.* London: Methuen, 1982.

Ortega y Gasset, Jose. *Man and People.* New York: Norton, 1957.

Saenger, Paul. "The Separation of Words and the Physiology of Reading." *Literacy and Orality.* Eds. David R. Olson and Nancy Torrance. Cambridge: Cambridge University Press, 1991. 198–214.

Sarles, Harvey B. *Language and Human Nature.* 1977. Minneapolis: University of Minnesota Press, 1986.

Siebers, Tobin. *Morals and Stories.* New York: Columbia University Press, 1992.

Stock, Brian. *Listening for the Text.* Baltimore: Johns Hopkins University Press, 1990.

Street, Brian V. "Introduction." *Cross-Cultural Approaches to Literacy.* Ed. Brian V. Street. Cambridge: Cambridge University Press, 1993.

———. *Literacy in Theory and Practice.* Cambridge: Cambridge University Press, 1984.

———. *Social Literacies: Critical Approaches to Literacy in Development, Ethnography and Education.* London: Longman, 1995.

Weaver, Richard. "Language Is Sermonic." 1963. *The Rhetorical Tradition.* Eds. Patricia Bizzell and Bruce Herzberg. Boston: Bedford, 1990. 1044–54.

The Wilderness Strikes Back:

Decolonizing the Imperial Sign in the Borderlands

Stephen G. Brown
University of Tampa
Tampa, Florida

> Our beliefs are rooted deep in our earth, no matter what you
> have done to it and how much of it you have paved over. And if
> you leave all that concrete unwatched for a year or two, our
> plants, the native Indian plants, will pierce that concrete and
> push up through it.
> —John (Fire), *Lame Deer: Seeker of Visions*

John (Fire) Lame Deer's assertion comprises an appropriate point of departure for this discussion insofar as it establishes the conjunction between place, identity, and resistance. Furthermore, it establishes the active, interactive, and reactive nature of "nature." It celebrates the tendency of nature to repossess the land that was seized from it, to recolonize it if you will, to reassert its "title" to the land. As depicted by Lame Deer (whose voice continues to resonate across the landscape of contemporary Native America since the publication of his as-told-to autobiography in 1972) nature is a perfect trope for indigenous resistance. In Alaska, as elsewhere, this resistance is about reclaiming "title" not only to the land, but to many other things besides: ancestral lifeways associated with the land and Native American identity in all of its shifting multiplicity—in short, the Alaskan natives' resistance is about reclaiming "title" to themselves.

In this chapter I want to posit the Alaskan environment as a master trope not only for indigenous identity, but for native resistance as well—resistance to neocolonial imperialism in general, and to its particular manifestation in borderland signifying practices. I want to explore the implications of this tension between signification and a native landscape, between the colonizer's tendency to take possession through naming and the

Alaskan environment's ability to elude linguistic containment. I want to develop as well the implications of foregrounding the environment as a category of critical inquiry in Composition Studies: a category that I believe is as significant as the categories of race, class, and gender that have driven so much of the discourse in the field. I particularly want to develop the usefulness of the environment as a topos of inquiry for actualizing the second, and oft-neglected aspect of Freirean praxis: for translating academic analysis of oppression in its various guises into meaningful social action.

In the course of this discussion I will analyze the manner in which signification functions as a vehicle of cultural domination, deploying as an analytical tool a postcolonial reading of representation in the borderlands across a spectrum of texts: the place-names imposed on an indigenous landscape, the representations of that landscape and of its indigenous peoples by travel writers, and finally the signifying practices embodied in realist novels, such as Jack London's *Call of the Wild* and *White Fang*. Finally, I want to turn a critical gaze not only on the ethics, effects, and implications of these borderland signifying practices, but on the peculiar intimacy between representation and resistance, between our representations of the Other and the Other's resistance to those representations—one of many intimacies that characterize the colonizer-colonized dynamic.

By "borderland signifying practices," I am referring to that matrix of texts in which the written word was used as an instrument of "cross-cultural domination" at the ends of the empire, in those frontier "contact zones" where Euramerican and indigenous cultures collided (and are still colliding): place-names, travel writing, the realist novel, treaties, acts of Congress (and more recently, environmental impact studies, lesson plans, and "settlements" like the ANLCS [1971])—an entire web of words that was flung far and wide in an effort to "capture" not only the Alaskan landscape but its indigenous peoples. The categories "colonial," "postcolonial," and "neocolonial" are embedded with connotations that distinguish them, yet are subject to misinterpretation and therefore misappropriation. For the purposes of this discussion I am using the term *colonialism* as defined by Stephen Slemon: "an economic and political structure of cross-cultural domination" (Scramble 17). It refers to the historic oppression of one people by another through economic and political means. The term *postcolonial* is embedded with connotations that not only distinguish it from "colonialism," but that are subject to widespread misperception arising from the term *post*. Postcolonialism, as Bill Ashcroft, Gerreths Griffiths, and Helen Tiffin assert,

Does not mean "post-independence," or "after colonialism," for this would be to falsely ascribe an end to the colonial process. Post-colonialism, rather, begins from the very first moment of colonial contact. It is the discourse of opposition which colonialism brings into being. (117)

Therefore, a less misleading term might be *anticolonialism* insofar as the term does not connote "after" but "against." The term *post* is misleading in another sense: it connotes an uncontaminated, autonomous temporal existence apart from colonialism, when in reality it is derivative of, and imbricated in, "colonialism." Though sequentially ordered, the "colonial" and the "postcolonial" moments are not sequentially distinct: the two coexist. The term *neocolonialism* attests to this antagonistic, cross-engendering relationship between colonialism and postcolonialism, and refers to the perpetuation of historical, orthodox colonialism through new-historical, unorthodox means: education, the media, transnational corporatism, travel writing, the realist novel, and other cultural apparatuses that were historically not part of the colonial process, but that have come in our own time to be the principal means by which "colonialism" (now "neocolonialism") has perpetuated itself as a structure of "cross-cultural domination."

INFINITY/IMPERIALISM

If there is one thing Alaska possesses in abundance, it is space. And if there is one thing the colonizing impulse requires, it is space: whether it is the unfenced acres of the tundra's open space, the uninhabited regions of outer space, or the unmapped universe of cyberspace. All possess what the cultural imperialist requires: a seemingly infinite space inviting a seemingly infinite appetite to take possession of that space. As noted in a recent edition of *Scientific Frontiers,* "when we colonize outer-space we are building a timeless world on which the sun literally never sets."

Infinity thus becomes a master trope for colonization, as Frederic Jameson observes in "Modernism and Imperialism." Likewise, the "Great North Road" of E. M. Forster's *Howard's End* is the insidious materialization of this imperialistic impulse. The road leading to infinity becomes a trope for imperial penetration of the Edenic. As Jameson writes,

For infinity in this sense, this new grey placelessness, as well as what prepares it, also bears another familiar name. It is in Forster's imperialism, or Empire, to give it its period designation. It is

Empire which stretches the roads out to infinity, beyond the bounds and the borders of the national state. (323)

The road effects the conjunction between the infinite and the imperial, whether figurative or literal, whether it is the electronic "superhighway" or Forster's imperial highway. Upon just such a "Great North Road," I too had ventured into this borderland: the Alkan Highway. It too ventured "beyond the bounds and borders of the national state," traversing Canada and the Yukon Territory, ever wending its way toward its Edenic destination: a serpent intent on corrupting the object of its relentless penetration.

As with Forster's Great North Road, it too transported a tide of colonists northward (as the Chikoot Trail had during the Gold Rush era), though now they traveled in the guise of oil prospectors and missionaries, of recreationists and tourists, of nature photographers, homesteaders, travel writers, and yes—bush teachers.[1] Whether they recognized themselves as such or not, all bore the telltale signs of Forster's imperialist traveler:

> In the motorcar was another type whom nature favors—the Imperial. Healthy, ever in motion, it hopes to inherit the earth. . . . Strong is the temptation to acclaim it as a superyeoman, who carries his country's virtues overseas. But the imperialist is not what he thinks or seems. He is a destroyer. He prepares the way for cosmopolitanism, and though his ambitions may be fulfilled the earth he inherits will be grey. (Jameson 323)

Alaska in the last half of the twentieth century was swarming with these industrious imperial types; I saw them all around me in the guise of loggers, coal miners, geologists, sport fishermen, homesteaders, cultural anthropologists, sociologists, psychologists, nurses, homesteaders, and so forth. All were white, industrious, "ever in motion," and hoping to "inherit" their own piece of a land that once belonged entirely to the native Alaskan. Upon arriving in Alaska they did what settlers do the world over: tried to turn it into the home they left by imposing alien place-names upon it: names usually honoring the imperialistic or historical exploits of white males: Bering, McKinley, and Baranoff.

THE TRAVEL WRITER AS CULTURAL IMPERIALIST

These "superyeomen" were not the only imperial types to prepare the way for the colonization of the indigene's homeland. The myth-making word as disseminated by the travel writer in the name of cultural tourism is every bit as culpable as the buzz saw, the book, and the bible in laying the groundwork for cultural colonization. The romantic images of the native's homeland that the travel writer transmits to the empire's readership also prepare the way for colonization, constructing in the reader's imagination an image that stimulates the settler impulse. Inspired by these romanticized and reductive visions of the Far North, the settler embarks, following the rhetorical roads constructed by a legion of travel writers. Thus, these linguistic constructs open the land of the indigene to "settlement" long before the settler actually sets foot on the native's soil. The work of the travel writer is an engineering feat every bit as stupendous as that of the imperial road builders, of the Army Corps of Engineers who constructed the Alkan Highway, whose place-names are a rhetorical monument to their own industriousness: Soldier's Pass and Contact Creek. The travel writer has similarly engineered a world creation in words, inventing the land of the indigene (if not the natives themselves) in a manner suitable for consumption by the empire's readership, reducing it to bite-size stereotypes that conform to the prejudices and appetites of that readership—in the same manner that the colonizing appetites of the British reader were whetted by what Eduard W. Said terms the *orientalization* of China: by a matrix of stereotypical representations purveyed by travel writers to the Orient.

The travel writer "paves" the road for cultural genocide by constructing the home of the Alaskan native in one of several ways—all of which serve the colonial or neocolonial enterprise. As Mary Louise Pratt observes in *Imperial Eyes,* the empire writer produces "places that could be thought of as barren, empty, undeveloped, inconceivable, needful of European influence and control, ready to serve European industrial, intellectual, and commercial interests" (35). Pratt's observations are significant insofar as they not only establish the more apparent complicity of industrial and commercial enterprises in the process of cultural genocide, but the more often overlooked complicity of intellectual enterprises in the exploitive practices of colonization: the gathering, production, and dissemination of knowledge (by writers, teachers, anthropologists, sociologists, psychologists, historians, and any who "study" the native) has played a ubiquitous role during the neocolonial era of cultural imperialism.

Thus, the travel writer not only misrepresents the Other, but the home of the Other in a manner that invites the colonization of both. Pratt's observations are particularly relevant to Alaska, whose gigantic landscape also seems "barren, empty, undeveloped, inconceivable" and seemingly "needful of European influence and control." The subsequent "development" of this wilderness with the Alkan Highway, the Alaska

Pipeline, the Alaska Railroad, the Alaska Maritime Ferry System, and the "bush" school system show that Alaska too stands ready "to serve Euro-American industrial, intellectual, and commercial interests."

If the land is depicted as "barren" or "untamed" and therefore in need of "settlement" or "development," the native similarly is portrayed as "backward" or "illiterate," and therefore in need of similar development in the form of education or training. The colonizer casts himself in the active, benevolent role of "giver" and the native in the passive and "deficient" role of receiver—and then is outraged or bewildered when the native does not manifest an appropriate appreciation of the "gifts" he or she has received. The native's ingratitude stems from the reality that these "gifts" usually disguise some form of "theft"—usually of their culture. They can only receive the "gifts" of education, capitalism, and Christianity by "paying" with their own lore, language, subsistence lifeways, and pagan beliefs—all as part of a process that Ward Churchill pejoratively calls "genocide with good intentions" (280). In the final analysis, these "words" are the survey markers by which the colonist stakes a claim to the "wilderness"—akin to the red flags tied to trees marked for "harvesting." Signifiers of ownership, possession—and of dispossession. Thus, words are "part of the more general process by which emerging industrial nations took possession of new territory" (Pratt 35).

The place-names the colonizer imposes on the indigene's landscape are therefore just another form of cultural imperialism. They are meant to confer "title" to the land being named. As Paul Carter asserts in "Naming Place," these place-names "do not reflect what is already there: on the contrary, they embody the existential necessity the traveler feels to invent a place he can inhabit. It was the names themselves that brought history into being" (qtd. in Ashcroft 404). Signification thus becomes the initial vehicle for dispossessing the native of title to his or her homeland. The land is repossessed by the colonizer through this linguistic sleight-of-hand. Title is transferred from one culture to the other through the plane of signification. The native's homeland is reinvented rhetorically as a "new world" or as a "last frontier"—as a precondition for transference of ownership from colonized to colonizer. The native's land is given a rhetorical face-lift whose aim is transference of 'title" to the land—an end that signification facilitates by stimulating the settler impulse of the empire's readership.

The indigene's homeland is constructed by the empire's rhetorical road-builders in other ways that also invite the colonization of that land. On the one hand, it is depicted as a second Eden, as a "paradise," a "utopia" offering escape from the ills of civilization, connoting a return to the "garden," to a simpler life foregrounding communion with nature and wanting only an Adam and Eve to "settle" it. On the other hand, it is portrayed as a vast warehouse of natural resources (of timber, salmon, oil, gold, coal, and bauxite) there for the taking. These mythical depictions of Alaska as a barren wilderness, as a second Eden, or as a modern-day mother lode have all prepared the way for its colonization by Russia and America, and for its ongoing neocolonization by a consortium of transnational corporations: Mobil, Exxon, Chevron USA, Placer Amex, Kodiak Lumber Mills, and so forth.

In the last analysis, as much harm as been done to the home of the native Alaskan by the imperial word as by the pickaxe, the sluice-box, the buzz saw, and the skidder. The American realist novel, no less then the representations of the travel writer, has been complicit in this process.

THE GREAT BOOKS AND CULTURAL IMPERIALISM

The oppressive circulation of power through discourse requires an economy of discourses, if not a univocal language; similarly, the circulation of power through culture requires an economy of cultures, if not a monoculture; and finally, the circulation of power through literature requires not only an economy of texts (the Western canon) and of genres (the realist novel), but an economy of subject positions, if not a universal subject that marginalizes and/or subsumes difference. Furthermore, these canonical representations of the indigene effect his or her containment through negative stereotypes that circumscribe native identity as closely as the boundaries that delineated the Athabascan Indian reservation in Alaska on which I taught. The Native American is dehumanized in these texts as either a demonic or a noble savage—is confined to the extreme poles of representation that are then posited as the only "authentic" identities for the indigene—even as she is represented as the promiscuous dusky maiden or as the silent, servile handmaiden of her "brave." Moreover, these textual representations not only reinscribe the native's subjugation in the culture at large, but are partly to blame for it. As Homi K. Bhabha asserts, "the objective of colonial discourse is to construct the colonized as a population of degenerate types on the basis of racial origin, in order to justify conquest and to establish systems of administration and instruction" ("The Other Question" 75). Indigenous identity is reduced to the status of an historical artifact on the pages of the American realist novel, even as the native's beads, moccasins, feathers, and drums are housed in museums as the dismembered, metonymic surrogates for the culture as a whole.

London's *Call of the Wild* and *White Fang* are useful examples of American realist novels that reinscribe stereotypical representations of the land and of its indigenous peoples, preparing the way for the conquest of both. The Far North is depicted as either a realm "red in tooth and claw" and needful of taming, or as a veritable treasury of natural resources, a natural Fort Knox whose reserves of gold lack only a "title" of ownership. London's narratives naturalize this headlong landrush, this "settler impulse" that results in the colonization of the Far North—as the native's subsistence life-style is subsumed in the Euramerican cash-based economy. As Anthony Kwame Appiah observes, the realist text naturalizes the colonization of native lands, and thus functions as "part of the tactics of nationalist legitimization" (quoted in Ashcroft et al Griffith, and Tiffin 120).

The realist text naturalizes the process of cultural genocide by circulating stereotypic representations of the native Alaskan as well. In the penultimate passages of *Wild,* London depicts the Alaskan indigene as a bloodthirsty, demonic savage whose white victim "was lying on his face, feathered with arrows like a porcupine . . . the Yeehats were dancing around the wreckage of the spruce-bough lodge" (97). London's representation of the "Yeehats" as little more than beasts and cave dwellers is further evidenced by the imagery he deploys to describe their destruction by the dominant primordial beast, Buck. They are dragged down by the avenging dog "like deer. . . . It was harder to kill a husky dog than them. They were no match at all were it not for their arrows and spears and clubs" (98). Thus, in London's great chain of being, the Alaskan native is situated somewhere just below the master's pet.

From a pedagogical perspective, offering an appreciative reading of London's *Call* and *Fang* on an Athabascan Indian reservation in Alaska is as grimly ironic as teaching Conrad's *Heart of Darkness* in colonial African universities—a practice that until recently went unchallenged, as Tiffin observes (97). The circulation of such reductive images of the Alaskan native and of his or her homeland through the signifying practices of the colonizer must be resisted insofar as these representations invite the destruction of both the land and its indigenous peoples. Yet, if these very texts function as vehicles of cultural domination, they can also be utilized as instruments for inaugurating counterhegemonic resistance struggle. How and where? By the composition instructor in the Alaskan classroom. These texts not only need to be read, but reread from a subversive, native-friendly perspective—as part of an inquiry that objectifies the process of colonization that has for centuries objectified the Alaskan native: by making the signifying practices embodied in these texts the focus of inquiry. London's tales, thus, still have a vital place in the canon—even for such a situated borderland pedagogy: if used not as vehicles of colonization, but of a decolonizing pedagogy whose aim is to expose the operations of colonization as a first critical step toward intervening against it—toward a liberatory, counterrepresentational pedagogy foregrounding an inquiry into the signifying practices embodied in various colonial and neocolonial, canonical and noncanonical texts (realist novels, travel writing, and environmental impact studies).[2] These texts must become the object of a critical, decolonizing gaze, and must be studied as deadly artifacts of assimilation and deracination, of environmental and cultural exploitation, not as shrines to a transcendent monoculture that subsumes difference. Insofar as London's texts (and other borderland narratives) foreground the Alaskan environment and the bicultural life-style of its residents, they comprise effective vehicles for first engaging the interest of the borderland student (assuming that interest in a function of immediacy and relevancy) as a precondition for a more critical inquiry into the adverse effects of the signifying practices they embody. If the Alaskan natives wish to halt the degradation of their homeland and of the subsistence life-style that is dependent upon it, then it seems useful to expose the signifying practices embodied in these various borderland narratives that inaugurate this environmental and cultural erosion—a tendency that will, if unchecked and unchallenged, result in the catastrophic closure of both the indigenous environment and of the subsistence culture that is inseparable from it. As a critical topos situated at the heart of the native's darkness, in the midst of this colonized and politicized terrain, the borderland composition classroom can play a useful, if not strategic role in the Alaskan native's resistance to cultural colonization, by making the context of colonization in general, and its signifying practices in particular, the "texts" to be read, discussed, researched, written about, and debated.[3] In such a politicized terrain, a pedagogy that does not itself become politicized, is unethical to the extent that it also becomes oppressive—by turning a blind eye to oppression.

Not only might the stereotypical signifying practices of these borderland narratives (in all their unholy diversity) be seized upon as the locus of critical inquiry, as the "texts" to be "studied," but the Alaskan environment itself can be posited as a "sign" that defies signification, as the ultimate transcendent signifier, beyond the bounds of signification, of representation, and of linguistic containment: ineffable, resistant, and free—the ultimate trope for the resistance of the native Alaskan: a fireweed flower sprouting in the frozen subsurface, yielding in the wind without yielding the native earth to which it clings. What qualifies the wilderness of the Far North to be the master trope of indigenous resistance? Its innate ability to resist colonization on both the physical and the linguistic plane. If Alaska's frozen subsurface prevents the great monarchs of the forest from taking root, it also poses a critical barrier to the various forms of colonization, preventing them from taking deep root as well. If its frost heaves buckle the roads by which the colonizer would penetrate, or otherwise "tame" this wilderness, then similarly its undifferentiated oneness eludes linguistic containment. If Alaska's limitless spaces and seemingly infinite resources make it the perfect object for the colonizer's covetous gaze, its ability to resist differentiation enables it to slip the noose of signification. There is a monolithic anonymity, a gray undifferentiated sameness to its seemingly limitless spaces, which subsumes the structures, linguistic or otherwise, the colonizer imposes upon it. The many place-names are themselves subsumed by the vast gaps between them, by the unnamed and unnameable (because undifferentiable) spaces that encompass and ultimately engulf them. Signification is nothing more than a mere outpost in Alaska, a solitary cabin of signs in the midst of an undifferentiated space—which subsumes the very thing that would subsume it. Mountain ranges extend to the horizon without names, reinforcing the sense of "placelessness"—this tyranny of the unnamed. The indigene's homeland resists the colonizer's efforts to name, much less to tame it. It literally defies description—and by so doing, defies capture, preserving something inviolate and forever wild about itself.

The Alaskan wilderness is therefore the perfect trope for indigenous resistance. Could reconnection to such a defiant topos, by reconnecting to the history, lore, customs, and place-names associated with it, do anything but invigorate indigenous resistance and reconstitute indigenous identity (historically inseparable from the land). Indeed, spiritual redemption through reconnection to an ancestral landscape is the central theme of many contemporary Native American narratives (Silko's *Ceremony,* Walsh's *Death of Jim Loney,* and Momaday's *House Made of Dawn*), as Robert M. Nelson observes in *Place and Vision* (99). The recent transformation of Mt. McKinley into Mt. Denali comprises a significant victory in the realm of signification—is a sign that the native's resistance struggle has at last entered the critical arena of signification, where it needs to be waged vigilantly on the many textual fronts where this well-concealed threat appears.

How does the Alaskan wilderness elude linguistic capture? In a realm where boundaries are easily and often blurred in the bicultural ether of hybridity, so too are the boundaries dissolved between the features of the Alaskan landscape: between summit and foothill, mist and snow, and one range and the next: all dissolve into oneness before the colonizing gaze that would have them distinct the better to be named—and would have them named, the better to be possessed. Yet, one cannot name what cannot be differentiated; one cannot impose a chain of discrete signifiers on that which refuses to be differentiated into discrete features, which refuses to surrender its holistic nature: to be compartmentalized, dismembered, and possessed by the colonizer. Thus, the Alaskan wilderness refuses to surrender "title" to itself, is a "claim" that cannot be "staked"—and as such is the perfect master trope for native resistance. If the Alaskan native was to commission a flag of resistance its dominant symbol would be a "frost heave": a sign signifying the eruptive force of the land, the eternal return of the repressed.

The Alaskan wilderness transcends signification insofar as it refuses differentiation. And for a native people whose identity since the mists of time has been undifferentiated from the land, it comprises a useful trope of resistance, freedom, and holistic integrity. Where does the land end and the native begin? There is no answer to this riddle. We cannot speak of one without speaking of the Other. Differentiation is the first, a priori condition of colonization because it makes possible signification, naming, ownership, and title. How to name that which is all the same? In the Alaskan wilderness, the colonizer is confronted by a geographic hegemony that subsumes his or her cultural hegemony—a totalized landscape that defeats his efforts to totalize it with signs. Like Native American identity itself, the Alaskan landscape slips our every effort to name it—a multiple, slippery, shifting signifier that eludes textual capture: a salmon squirting from the hand that would seize it; the shifting skeins of the aurora racing over the rooftops. This, too is why the Alaskan wilderness is a useful, enduring, and apt trope for indigenous identity and resistance: the two are one—and in more ways than one.

Confronted with the undifferentiated, white hegemony of the Alaskan landscape, the white colonizer realizes one thing: that sooner than conquering this land, it would possess him, dragging him off into its undifferentiated limitless spaces—a white whale to whose icy flanks is lashed an utterly possessed and doomed Ahab. As Paul Carter observes, there is for the colonizer "too great a dissonance between language and the land" (quoted in Ashcroft 403). Consequently, the landscape will never be anything more than a "naive reflection of the language available to describe it" (406). The only language available to the colonizer for describing the indigene's homeland is one imported from his own—one that has no connection to the topos being named, which imposes a false signification upon it. As opposed to the native's signifying process, in which the binary between language and land (with regard to ownership) is reversed: it is the native who is possessed by the land. As Linda Hogan states, "land that will always own us, everywhere it is red" (12).

If Alaska's stunted forests might serve as melancholy tropes for native spirits whose growth has been stunted by the harsh realities of acculturation and deracination, by the long winter of their bicultural alienation, then might not the shape-shifting auroras that play upon this vast white realm also comprise a fitting trope for the elusive, shifting, multiple subject positions assumed by the indigenous Other? Similarly, might not the freedom of the land's unconfined spaces serve as a bitterly ironic counterpoint to the rigidity of racial stereotypes that confine the Alaskan native to a reservation of representation? And finally, if the vast silence of the Far North reinscribes the silencing of the native Other, then perhaps it might also serve as the perfect counterpoint to the dissonant noise of native students coming into voice for the first time.

NOTES

1. For a more detailed discussion of the complicity of the borderland teacher in the process of cultural imperialism see my article, " The Bush Teacher as Cultural Imperialist." *Review of Education* 20.1 (Spring 1998): 121–39.

2. See my article, "De-composing the Canon: Alter/Natives and Borderland Pedagogy." *College Literature* (Fall 1998): 30–44, for a more detailed critique of canonical works and for a discussion of useful alternatives for borderland praxis.

3. In my article, "Composing the Eco-Wars: Toward a Literacy of Resistance." *JAC* (April 1999), I critique the signifying practices embodied in an environmental impact study, and their implications for conflict-oriented pedagogy.

˙ WORKS CITED

Appiah, Anthony Kwame. "Is the Post in Postmodernism the Post in Postcolonial?" *Critical Inquiry* 17 (1991): 336–57.

Ashcroft, Bill, Gerreth Griffith, and Helen Tiffin. *The Post-Colonial Studies Reader.* New York: Routledge, 1995.

Bhabha, Homi K. "The Other Question: Difference, Discrimination, and the Discourse of Colonialism." *Out There: Marginalization and Contemporary Cultures* Eds. Russell Ferguson et al. Cambridge: Massachusetts Institute of Technology Press, 1990. 71–87.

Carter, Paul. "Naming Place." *The Road to Botany Bay: An Essay in Spatial History.* London: Faber, 1987.

Churchill, Ward. *Indians R US: Culture and Genocide in Native North America.* Monroe, ME: Common Courage Press, 1994.

Conrad, Joseph. *Heart of Darkness. Heart of Darkness: A Case Study in Contemporary Criticism* Ed. Ross C. Murfin. New York: St. Martin's, 1989. 17–94.

Hogan, Linda. "Who Puts Together." *Studies in American Indian Literature: Critical Essays and Course Designs.* Ed. Paula Gunn Allen. New York: Modern Language Association, 1983.

Jameson, Frederic. "Modernism and Imperialism." *Nationalism, Colonialism, and Literature.* Ed. Seamus Deane. Minneapolis: University of Minnesota Press, 1990. 43–66.

Lame Deer, John (Fire), and Richard Erdoes. *Lame Deer: Seeker of Visions.* New York: Washington Square Press, 1972.

London, Jack. *The Call of the Wild.* New York: Bantam, 1963.

Nelson, Robert M. *Place and Vision: The Function of Landscape in Native American Fiction.* New York: Peter Lang, 1993.

Pratt, Mary Louise. *Imperial Eyes: Travel Writing and Transculturation.* New York: Routledge, 1992.

Said, Edward W. *Orientalization.* New York: Vantage, 1979.

Scientific Frontiers. Nov. 28, 1995.

Slemon, Stephen. "The Scramble for Post-Colonialism." *De-Scribing Empire:* Post-Colonialism and Textuality. Eds. Chris Tiffin and Alan Lawson. London: Routledge, 1994.

Tiffen, Helen. "Post-Colonial Literature and Counter-Discourse." *Kunapipi* 9.3 (1987): 17–34.

Education and Environmental Literacy:

Reflections on Teaching Ecocomposition in Keene State College's Environmental House

Mark C. Long
Keene State College
Keene, New Hampshire

Experience is not what happens to you, it's what you *do* with what happens to you.

—Aldous Huxley

FROM CULTURAL TO ENVIRONMENTAL LITERACY

The correlation between academic and cultural literacy is inspired by the democratic ideal of an informed and involved citizenry. In the words of the philosopher Martha Nussbaum, "building a democratic culture that is truly deliberative and reflective, rather than simply a collision of unexamined preferences," requires rigorous preparation for democratic citizenship" (294). Inspired by the ideals of self-command and cultivated humanity, the citizen of democracy, Nussbaum insists, "must increasingly learn how to understand, respect, and communicate, if our common problems are to be constructively addressed:" Yet for an increasing number of college and university teachers, the common problem in need of constructive address is the impact of human culture on the physical environment. In the humanities in particular, educators have therefore sought to shift emphasis from cultural to environmental literacy. Nevertheless, the problem of cultivating a reciprocal relationship between humanity and habitat, argues David Orr, "cannot be solved by the same kind of education that created the problems" (83). Instead, the study of culture must direct the practices of student reading and writing to habitat, to the cultivation of a "quality of mind able to comprehend its place in the environment," and to "a broad understanding of how people and societies relate to each other and to natural systems"

131

(92). Academic proponents of "ecological sustainablity" would therefore "aim to restore public virtue, a high degree of ecological literacy, and ecological competence throughout the population." Orr concludes, there is little prospect "for building a sustainable society without an active, engaged, informed and competent citizenry" (84).

Pedagogies of cultural as well as environmental literacy are often linked to the Brazilian literacy educator Paulo Freire's concept of "critical consciousness." For Freire, "literacy as a way of changing the world had to be reconceived within a broader understanding of citizenship, democracy and justice that was global and transnational" (Giroux 311). Indeed the ambitious goal of linking academic and ecological literacy hinges, in part, on redefining the term *literacy* and then using it to address the local and global dimensions of environment problems. Definitions of literacy ranges from Allen Bloom's canon of classic texts to E. D. Hirsch's lexicon of cultural literacy to Freire's equation of literacy with the discovery of "critical consciousness." Orr has more recently attempted to redefine this debate by elaborating the term *literacy* in the context of environmental concern. Orr's ambitious book *Ecological Literacy* argues for placing environmental education at the center of a liberal education that seeks to develop whole, balanced persons. He incisively notes that in a traditional education "students learn the lesson of indifference to the ecology of their immediate place. Four years in a place called a campus culminates in no great understanding of the place, or the art of living responsibly in that or any other place" (103). Not only is it surprising, but shocking for Orr, that "students learn practical incompetence is *de rigueur,* since they seldom are required to solve problems that have consequences except for their grade point average" (104). He concludes, "A genuine liberal arts education will foster a sense of connectedness, implicatedness, and ecological citizenship, and will provide the competence to act on such knowledge"(103).

A concern for ecological literacy has emerged within composition studies as a part of this more general motivational shift in the professoriate "from newness, or theoretical elegance, or even coherence" to what William Rueckert has called "a principle of relevance" (72). One recent indicator of this motivational shift is the emergence of ecocomposition. A few short years ago Randall Roorda remarked, "I am [a] peripheral figure: a compositionist specializing in nature writing" (401). Today the evidence from course offerings, conference programs, hiring decisions, and publications suggest an increasing number of environmentally literate writing teachers have moved from the periphery to the contested center of composition studies.[1]

Ecocompositionists have expanded their inquiry beyond specialization in the genre of nature writing; and they have sought to link the intellectual practice of writing to the broader goal of cultivating what I call "environmental literacy." Yet the field of rhetoric and composition has only begun to orient itself toward exploring the connections between writing and environmental literacy. If an increasing number of practitioners in the field of rhetoric and composition seek connections between academic writing and ecological or environmental literacy, then how might the ecocomposition course help us to conceptualize such links? What are the pedagogical strategies and contexts we might use to build these links for our students? And finally, how might practitioners in the field imagine the continuity between the writing students do in the eco-composition course and what they may then go on to do in the world?

TWO VERSIONS OF ECOCOMPOSITION

The emphasis on literacy generates a productive space for the conceptual category of the environment in the context of a liberal education. And yet as Jennifer Beigal reminds us, programs or courses that address environmental issues have been relatively slow to develop in the college and university curriculum. There may be some discussion of environmental topics, but little or no attention to topics of "ecological consciousness, those that deal with the human connection and responsibility to the natural world" (106). The pressing issue, in Beigal's view, is that "as environmental problems become more critical, every thinking human being will have to make both political and life-style decisions that will require a personal environmental ethic." If students are to take this role of civic and environmental responsibility seriously, Beigal continues, "they will have to come to terms with their role in their relation to their environment and how their views and behaviors are an integral part of the current situation." Environmental education, in this definition, seeks to do more than integrate environmental content into the curriculum. Its explicit goal is to encourage students to see the world in certain ways and to consider the moral and political implications of their life-style. The pedagogical outcome would then be students able to make reasoned choices based on an environmental ethic.

A group of recently published theme-based composition readers on the environment draw upon these goals and outcomes for environmental education to justify the use of environmental topics to teach writing.[2] For instance, Chris Anderson and Lex Runciman argue in their prefatory notes to *A Forest of Voices: Reading and Writing the Environment* that the subject of the environment "is a good focus for college reading and writing because it is a complex subject" (v). They point out that reading and writing about the environment requires students to draw upon their subject knowledge in a variety of fields without limiting their inquiry to any one field, encouraging students to think across disciplinary lines. And they explicitly link academic and environmental literacy: "The skills of knowing how to work with complexity and read between the lines are just exactly the skills people need to solve the [environmental] problems overwhelming the planet right now" (vi). Similarly, argues Carolyn Ross, the editor of an ecologically themed reader, "Environmentalism is a subject of real concern in student's lives. They are ready to read, to think critically, to speak and to write about it" (vii). For Ross, there are additional advantages of reading and writing about nature and the environment, and about the related subjects in science and technology. These themes invite students "to relate their personal lives with their academic lives, and their academic lives to their lives as members of both social and ecological communities" (vii).

A genuine desire for students to engage with concrete cases where complex environmental decision making takes place is central to this version of ecocomposition. Importantly, interpretive questions and problems having to do with the environment in the classroom are understood to be analogous to those civic activities of deliberation and decision making in "the real world" beyond school. In the view of Frederick O. Waage, the idea behind such activities is to "increase a student's ability to deal with actual problems of his or her own private and public living"; so that courses that aspire to teach some form of environmental literacy would "provide a context of dialogue, investigation, and self-discovery for students of relations with the non-human world, through experience and the written views of others on this relationship" (xii–xiv).

These pedagogical strategies depend upon the assumption that a more proximate and intimate relation to the environment translates well into more than simply good writing. The hope is that taking students "out there" will facilitate concrete changes in the student's attitudes toward the environment, and potentially lead to more environmentally responsible behavior; and in a similar way, writing from one's experience *in* nature, and reflecting on this process through readings of writers engaged in similar encounters, may in turn develop a critical context for self-interested and economically determined attitudes toward the natural world. This context is most often provided in an "environmentally correct" canon of readings by nature writers, ecocritics, and essayists. The intellectual context into which students would be introduced might include concepts such as biocentrism, or the capacity to acknowledge "that land, animals, waters, mountains, trees, landscapes have inherent value as a human commodity" (Kahn and Weld 166).[3] Students would then ostensibly be in a position to thoughtfully consider, for instance, the relative merits of Aldo Leopold's land ethic, an ethical program for "changing the role of *Homo sapiens* from conquerer of the land community to plain member and citizen of it" (quoted in Kahn and Weld 166). Drawn to "first-person encounters" with nature, this expressivist version of ecocomposition asks students to tap their primary experience of nature as a subject for writing. The pedagogical strategy is simple, if not potentially consequential: the teacher designs activities to get students "out there," in the world, writing about their "primary" experience in the environment, "through experiences lived and intimacy felt" (165). It is through this "primary" experience that personal and ethical transformation is supposed to take place.

Not incidentally, the working definition of environment guiding the field of environmental education conflates the inclusive term *environment* with the exclusive term *nature*. Working within the limited conceptual framework of this definition, the environmental educator understands human beings and their culture as apart from the natural world. In practice, this reductive definition leads environmental educators to lead the ritual pilgrimage of students from the "isolated indoor practices" of the traditional classroom with the intent of reconnecting students to the natural world. It has guided academic experimentation with field-based humanities courses in particular.[4] However with notable exceptions, the ritual of retreat to nature in the writing course simply leads most students nowhere. What students actually find in writing *from* nature is not reconnection but reconfirmation of their existing sense of place in the world. More dangerously, the study of *"the* problem" and *"the* crisis" of the environment leads students to write about issues of enormous complexity that quite frankly, as entry-level students, they are the least equipped to handle. Environmental issues, of course, require subtle forms of thinking. Hence despite the potentially exciting outcomes of such courses, the moral imperative of cultivating environmental awareness has led to simply infusing the theme-based composition course with an environmental subject matter. Furthermore, the urgent rhetoric of crisis coupled with expressivist views of the writing process has led to a version of ecocomposition that is caught between the conflicting goals of teaching writing in the classroom and writing one's way out of the confines of classroom-based writing.

The paradox that this conceptual model presents for ecocomposition is evident: the first-year writing course by definition invites students, first and foremost, to take responsibility for not simply the self-reflexive, interior space of reading and writing but also the rhetorical protocols and self-reflexive habits of mind that shape writing in academic communities. The second version of ecocomposition I wish to propose begins with the observation that the concept of environmental literacy cannot be simply predicated on the ability to think clearly or critically, or on the capacity to imagine the environment in less rigidly homocentric terms. Nor can environmental literacy be cultivated in the writing course by simply getting students in "contact" with the world from which they are presumably separated. Environmental literacy requires the far more difficult capacity to determine when our established habits of observation and principles of understanding do not apply to particular cases, to be able, when the conditions insist, to imagine alternative ways of living in, and learning from, the world. Just as developed and articulated rationales for literacy too often lead to overdetermined, unresponsive, and self-referential interpretive strategies, environmental educators and students of ecological systems know well that the texts and physical systems we study are, if anything, dynamic, and that any constructive engagement with the rich and diverse realm of the environment demands an agile intelligence and responsiveness.

I begin by acknowledging the fact that cultivating this level of intellectual agility and ethical responsiveness can in no way be accomplished in the first-year writing course. Rather the task for ecocomposition, in the second version I wish to propose, is to determine the pedagogical strategies and contexts to set in motion a process students might choose to follow through to these more ambitious ends. This version of ecocomposition invites students to begin thinking about the consequential ways they have already established a working relationship with the discerned features of the environment in which they are currently struggling to find a place, that is, I begin with David Orr's recommendation that we encourage our students to develop a sense of the environment in which they are writing. The curricular contours of ecocomposition thus remain methodologically grounded in the primary function of the course in first-year writing: providing skills for situating one's self in the intellectual community of the academy, and developing the critical and creative process of writing. So that rather than getting students out of the classroom or the college, then, I am advocating placing them in it—intellectually, physically, and spiritually. In twenty years of teaching, mostly in a nonacademic setting, I have come to believe that students benefit from learning how, and why, their relationship to their surroundings has been constructed in particular ways. I have also come to see students take the greatest leaps in problem solving when they learn to imagine practical strategies in order that these connections might be modified, even changed. Student writers, in particular, need to learn strategies for building on their existing ways of learning, and for understanding how language can help to shape a community's interpretive practices and worldview. As initiates into an intellectual community, these students need to take responsibility for their place in the environment of the college or the university.

The identification of the campus as a site for environmental productively unsettles many of the limiting assumptions about what constitutes environmental literacy. Students need to reflect on how relationships to a particular environment has been constructed—and to imagine how that relationship might be changed. But it is only by expanding the term *environment* to encompass more than discerned landscapes, and rather than simply using the term *environment* as a synonym for nature, that more students will begin to find reasons to take their relation to their environment seriously. Not incidentally, this is precisely the kind of conceptual transformation necessary for their success in college.

TEACHING ECOCOMPOSITION IN KEENE STATE COLLEGE'S ENVIRONMENTAL HOUSE

I now want to elaborate on how a theory of ecocomposition, grounded in the location where teaching and learning occur, might enhance the project of teaching writing *and* environmental literacy. I will use as a case study my experience teaching first-year composition to students in Keene State College's "Environmental House" (E-house), a living and learning community centered around a common interest in the environment. The case allows me to elaborate a potential configuration of place and pedagogy for the course in ecocomposition. In what follows, then, I discuss my own attempts to articulate these pedagogical and theoretical connections within a program initiated by the college to integrate academic and student life for first-year students. My goal is to suggest a set of principles to facilitate the process of decision making required for the ecocomposition course.

One of three campuses of the system of the University of New Hampshire, Keene State College (KSC) is a public liberal arts institution. KSC enrolls approximately 3,900 full-time undergraduate students and 1,000 part-time undergraduate and graduate students.[5] Consistent with its commitment to public access, nearly 50 percent of matriculated students at KSC are first-generation college students. The college currently offers students a residential living option supportive of students with an interest in the environment. The "environmental house" helps students help themselves to build continuities between academic and personal life. I see this connection moving from the nexus of residential and academic life to the synergy of academic and postacademic life—to include school major/career, personal/political, vocation/avocation connections. First-year residents of the house enroll in Environmental Studies 101, my section of English 101, and participate in campus activities and community service projects that relate to environmental issues. The "E-house" therefore offers an existing connection among individual students involved in a common set of academic and residential activities.

The advantage of the E-house for me as a teacher of first-year writing is that I can build from a declared student interest in a particular subject. This advantage is not always tangible, but it is discernible to me in the familiarity and trust that class members bring to their shared academic work. Ideally, the E-house experience functions to focus student interest and concern in considering what it is like to live and study and work in a communal environment. The E-house also provides me with students interested in establishing a particular kind of relation to place. However, my task has actually been to help them see how that relationship might be other than what they had considered it to be. I have learned to help them to develop—to borrow a phrase from the writer John McPhee, "a sense of where they are."

I have come to believe that good writing, and good citizenship—respect and personal responsibility, but also purposefulness—follow from awareness; and awareness, in my view, comes from learning to understand how it is we might learn from our experiences. I use the curricular function of the course (critical thinking, college-level reading, and writing), the common point of departure in the course (a declared interest in environmental writing), and physical place (the higher degree of intimacy of a college living-learning community), to develop the kind of awareness and reflectiveness we value in our students at KSC. In the course, negotiating and defining personal and communal values, and learning to explore and articulate reasons for them, is accomplished through rigorous readings that exemplify the process of "coming to terms" with the world and rediscovering one's place in it. Building community requires this kind of thinking.

Specifically designed for residents of the E-house, my course is advertised as having "environmental content for students with an interest in or commitment to environmental concerns." When students show up on the first day of the course, we begin by talking and writing about how they got where they are (college), what they see and do and learn every day in this new environment, and what their aspirations might be for the next four years of their life in school. The common experience is college, after all.

This kind of reflection is personal, collective, *and* environmental. Why are we here? What options are available to us? What do we hope to accomplish? In short, during the first week of the course we discuss the transition into the academic environment the students are experiencing. This environment, I encourage my students to see, needs to be examined.

I explain that as students at Keene State College they will be introduced to conventions of language use and a process of inquiry that includes careful observation, reflective thinking, disciplined research, and purposive writing. The readings for the course compliment this inquiry into the environment to which many of them are struggling to adapt. The readings are designed, then, to help students learn ways that people use certain expectations and assumptions to shape an understanding of an environment. In the matter of writing, I describe to my students how our discussions of the specific motivations, occasions, and values that inform the way individuals make sense of their surroundings will open up the ordinary landscapes in which we define ourselves and carry out our lives. Writing about the ways in which other writers make sense of their surroundings, I also have reason to say, will help them begin to think about their own surroundings, enhancing their capabilities to think creatively and critically about their place in the world.

Hence the course invites students to consider the enterprise of writing as a complex and continuing engagement between the self and the environment. It defines writing as a process of engagement with existing structures of thought, about the past and the present, as well as the future; as a rhetorical and dialogic activity that seeks to connect the thoughts of the individual to the ideas and aspirations of the community, whether academic, disciplinary or cultural; and it encourages a definition of composition as an attentive and disciplined process of engagement with the particular, everyday circumstances of the environment in which any act of writing takes place. However this environmentally based definition of writing requires student writers to work toward more than developing a sense of where they are. It underscores the active process of learning required in an academic setting. And it leads students, finally, to articulate their insights into what Mikhail M. Bakhtin calls the "unfinished, still evolving contemporary reality," the "zone of contact" between the self and "reality in the process of unfolding" (7).

In the second phase of the course I invite students to understand not only the rewards but the difficulties of articulating functional relations to their surroundings. I use the term *relation* as a mode of interaction, or in the philosopher John Dewey's words, "something direct, and active, something dynamic and energetic. It fixes attention on the ways things bear upon one another" (*Art* 134). With the help of Dewey, I want students to see that what "is really *in* their experience extends much further than that which is at any time *known*" (*Experience* 20). The human and philosophical tendency to isolate reflective results from primary experience, writes Dewey, is attributable to three primary causes: "the complete separation of the subject and object . . . the exaggeration of the features of known objects . . . and the exclusive isolation of the results of various types of selective simplification which are undertaken for diverse unavowed purposes" (32). Dewey is helpful for my students in part because of his insistence that these human fallibilities are not wrong but inevitable, and because of his emphasis on how we might come to learn from our own experience as we guide ourselves back to the subject matter of our everyday lives.

In addition to reading Dewey my students study a remarkable essay on the difficulty of adapting to an environment by the poet William Carlos Williams. "The American Background" draws on historical instances of adaptation to what he calls "local conditions." Williams describes how the historical settlers of the North American continent failed to place themselves on the continent because of what he calls a "disenfranchised intelligence" (149). He exemplifies how deep patterns or habits of thought determine the course of the human mind and make it difficult to settle new ground. This condition, Williams writes, makes it all the more difficult to establish "a relation to the immediate conditions" and thereby discern what he calls the "growing edge in every culture" (143). Williams elaborates beautifully the process I wish my students of writing to become a part of, what he describes as the "burning need of every culture" to identify itself in its surroundings:

> It has to be where it arises, or everything related to the life there ceases. It isn't a thing: it's an act. If it stands still, it is dead. It is the realization of the qualities of a place in relation to the life which occupies it; embracing everything involved, climate, geographic position, relative size, history, other cultures—as well as the character of its sands, flowers, minerals and the condition of knowledge within its borders. It is the act of lifting these things into an ordered and utilized whole which is culture. It isn't something left over afterward. (157)

The "embrace," I encourage my students to see, "is the act of lifting these things into an ordered and utilized whole." Williams's conclusion is crucial for students to then understand: "the real and the new, hard to come at are synonymous" (143). The burning need of the culture is its capacity to situate itself in its surroundings; and as Williams documents through-out the essay, the need is for individuals to actively construct sustainable relations "to the life which occupies it."

The remaining readings in the first half of the course seek to develop these insights through the study of theoretical writing on the perception and representation of the environment. Students read and write about John Berger's book *Ways of Seeing,* in which he writes, "The relation be-tween what we see and what we know is never settled" (7). In this segment of the course I emphasize the reciprocal nature of perception, and the con-sequences of these observations for the study of visual and verbal texts. Students read essays on the topic of landscape as well to develop a more re-sponsive and precise terminology for describing the discerned features of the environment, and to learn, in the words of D. W. Meinig, that in any environment, "there can be more and more that meets the eye" (6). Stu-dents use these theoretical readings in the course, first, to write about dis-cerned features of their own environments, including landscapes of home, memory, and history; they also write about the readings, clarifying termi-nology, and concepts so as to be able to use them constructively. Following these activities, students begin reading and writing about authors who put the problem of our relation to the environment in the most primary and direct way. Classic nature writers such as Henry David Thoreau, Aldo Leopold, and Annie Dillard are read, but in dialogue with other genres of writing on perception, cognition and representation by authors such as John Dewey, Mary Ann Caws, Wendy Steiner, and Norman Bryson. Sig-nificantly, these readings are designed to do more than "bring students back into contact" with the natural environment. They enrich and deepen primary student writing about the natural, social, historical, and cultural dimensions of their lived experience in the environment of the school. The goal is for students to see how it is that they live in a world that they are capable of telling themselves is there, a world they have learned to evoke or represent in an intelligible way.

EDUCATION AND ENVIRONMENTAL LITERACY

One goal of this essay has been to argue that the pedagogical effects eco-compositionists imagine are not only describable, but consistent with a de-sire to further both academic and environmental literacy. However, I have demonstrated that calls for shifting our attention from appreciation and in-terpretation to intervention and action, for participation and experience rather than intellectual isolation, often rely on a disabling dichotomy

between thought and action. While understandable, these calls for transformation risk limiting the potential of environmental literacy by demanding that students assume and act upon a set of values that may not be their
own. As with many other academic activist agendas, ambitions for the ecocomposition course are too often guided by a belief in the continuity between what students do in the classroom and what we imagine them doing
once their coursework comes to an end. In fact the greatest risk for a course
in ecocomposition is to determine the continuity between coursework and
the work of life in advance. For if we simply model "correct" relations with
the environment, and demonstrate the value of these relations in terms of
civic action, we miss the fact that these models and relations are inspiring
precisely because they are creative *attempts* to formulate and develop a plan
for action.

Teaching in Keene State College's Environmental House has allowed
me to broaden my own definitions for the terms *literacy* and *environment.*
It has helped me to understand more specifically how preparing students
for academic life can also prepare them for the complex literacy required
to live responsibly and responsively in the environment. It has enabled me
to see how most of us teach with one eye on what a student is doing, and
the other eye on what a student might do when the class comes to an end;
how most of us seek to share with our students the endeavor of seeking
new questions, defining problems, and organizing models for inquiry; and
how most of us have committed ourselves to help our students become active learners, offering them complex situations that require their best creative and critical faculties.

Reflecting on my experience teaching ecocomposition in the Environmental House has also led me to learn a number of lessons. As a teacher of
reading and writing and as a human being who aspires toward a more responsible and responsive relation to my environment, I have learned to
appreciate the elusiveness of the ecological and human systems we ask our
students to better understand. Similarly, I have learned that the literacies
of environmental writers and activists are, at their very best, fundamentally speculative. And I have learned to humbly acknowledge that even the
best versions of the human relationship to the environment, and the most
important and consequential solutions to problems of environmental concern, have been the product of thinking beyond a set of assumptions
about what should or should not be done.

For instance, in the kind of course I am suggesting here, I make it possible for students to understand Aldo Leopold's land ethic as anthropocentric in its breathtakingly precise and far-reaching extension of human
ethics. *Biocentrism,* students then come to see, is not a turn away from the

human. It is rather a powerful descriptive term, an ethically enabled rendering of the environment as a community inclusive of, but not limited to, the desires and needs of the human species. Yes, I have affirmed why we need to move our students outside the single idea that human beings are the center of all things; but I have been reminded why we need to help them understand, again and again, how the human center gives meaning and value to the world in radically specific, and consequential ways.

NOTES

1. Donald A. McAndrew's descriptive characterization of ecofeminism points to the theoretical and pedagogical potential of the environment as a critical category. By suggesting the links between literacy theory and the emancipatory claims of ecofeminism, McAndrew intends "to widen our circle of concerns to include—in addition to our continuing concerns about race, class and gender—a concern for the environment" (368). He goes on to suggest that "this widening of perspective might be accomplished in a way that will simultaneously promote what we recommend in the teaching of literacy and what ecofeminists recommend to save the natural world."

2. Available readers and rhetorics for the composition classroom include Sarah Morgan and Dennis Okerstrom, eds., *The Endangered Earth: Readings for Writers* (Boston: Allyn, 1992); Scott Slovic and Terrell Dixon, eds., *Being in the World: An Environmental Reader for Writers* (New York: MacMillan, 1994); Melissa Walker, ed., *Reading the Environment* (New York: Norton: 1994); Walter Levy and Christopher Hallowell, eds., *Green Perspectives: Thinking and Writing about Nature and the Environment* (New York: Harper Collins, 1994); Chris Anderson and Lex Runciman, eds., *A Forest of Voices: Reading and Writing the Environment* (Mountain View, CA: Mayfield, 1995); Carolyn Ross, *Writing Nature: An Ecological Reader for Writers* (New York: St. Martin's, 1995); Carol J. Verburg, ed., *The Environmental Predicament: Four Issues for Critical Analysis* (Boston: Bedford, 1995); and Lorraine Anderson, John P. O'Grady, and Scott Slovic, eds., *Literature and the Environment: A Reader on Nature and Culture* (Addison Wesley Longman, 1998).

3. In "Environmental Education: Toward an Intimacy with Nature," Peter H. Kahn and Ashley Weld suggest that "environmental education should seek to place scientific and social learning about environmental issues within . . . an overarching context of intimacy with nature" (166). This discussion of environmental education for elementary age children is interesting in the present context because its grounding assumptions underlie college and university classes that seek to link academic and ecological literacy. My interest is not to question or devalue such an approach, as primary experience in nature, in its varied forms, does appear to instill in children the ethical elements of love, respect, and admiration Aldo Leopold claimed necessary for a sustainable shift from human domination over land to an intimate living relationship with it. Nevertheless, I will argue that the term *environment* can prove useful for its inclusiveness. It can be contrasted with the more exclusive and fundamentally relational terms such as *place, landscape,* and *nature,* all of which suggest a discerned part of the environment.

4. For an especially thoughtful rationale for teaching environmental literature in the field see Walter J. Clark's "What Teaching Environmental Literature Might Be" in Frederick O. Waage's *Teaching Environmental Literature: Materials, Methods, Resources,* 4–8.

5. Keene State College, first organized as a normal school in 1909, is a Carnegie Foundation Master's I institution, and a founding member of the Council of Public Liberal Arts Colleges. Member colleges are predominately undergraduate public institutions, of moderate size, with strong liberal arts offerings, and offer at least half of their degrees in liberal arts fields.

WORKS CITED

Anderson, Chris, and Lex Runciman. *A Forest of Voices: Reading and Writing the Environment.* Mountain View, CA: Mayfield, 1995.

Bakhtin, Mikhail M. *The Dialogic Imagination.* Trans. Caryl Emerson and Michael Holquist. Austin: University of Texas Press, 1981.

Beigel, Jennifer. "Literature and the Living World: Environmental Education in the English Classroom." *ISLE: Interdisciplinary Studies in Literature and the Environment* 2.2 (Winter 1996): 105–18.

Berger, John. *Ways of Seeing.* New York: Penguin, 1972.

Dewey, John. *Art as Experience.* New York: Perigree, 1934

———. *Experience and Nature.* New York: Dover, 1958.

Giroux, Henry A. "Remembering Paulo Freire." *JAC: A Journal of Composition Theory* 17.3 (1997): 310–13.

Kahn, Peter H., and Ashley Weld. "Environmental Education: Toward an Intimacy with Nature." *ISLE: Interdisciplinary Studies in Literature and the Environment* 3.2 (Fall 1996): 165–68.

Leopold, Aldo. *A Sand County Almanac.* New York: Oxford University Press, 1949.

McAndrew, Donald A. "Ecofeminism and the Teaching of Literacy." *College Composition and Communication* 47.3 (October 1996): 367–82.

Meinig, D. W., ed. *The Interpretation of Ordinary Landscapes: Geographical Essays.* New York: Oxford University Press, 1979.

Nussbaum, Martha. *Cultivating Humanity: A Classical Defense of Reform in Liberal Education.* Cambridge: Harvard University Press, 1997.

Orr, David. W. *Ecological Literacy: Education and the Transition to a Postmodern World.* Albany: State University of New York Press, 1992.

Roorda, Randall. "Nature/Writing: Literature, Ecology, and Composition." *JAC: A Journal of Composition Theory* 17.3 (1997): 401–14.

Ross, Carolyn. *Writing Nature: An Ecological Reader for Writers.* New York: St. Martin's, 1995.

Rueckert, William. "Literature and Ecology: an Experiment in Ecocriticism." *Iowa Review* 9.1 (Winter 1998): 71–86. Repeated in Eds. Cheryl Glotfelty and Harold Fromm. Athens: University of Georgia Press, 1996.

The Ecocriticism Reader: Landmarks in Literary Ecology. University of Georgia Press, 1996.

Waage, Frederick O. *Teaching Environmental Literature: Materials, Methods, Resources.* New York: Modern Language Aassociation, 1985.

Williams, William Carlos. *Selected Essays.* New York: New Directions, 1954.

The Liberatory Positioning of Place in Ecocomposition:

Reconsidering Paulo Freire

Arlene Plevin
University of Washington
Seattle, Washington

. . . nature was my comfort and my "mother" if you will. . . . She was my refuge. My place to go to be totally immersed in something "other." . . . The sky never argued with the clouds and the earth never argued with the sky. They agreed as to their purpose and didn't try to take each other's places.
   —Student in Intermediate Expository Writing, English 281, University of Washington

In a writing class, I begin with and center the class around my students' words, whether they are in reaction to an essay, each others' work, or student experiences. While many composition teachers start with students' works—supporting the concept of student writing as text suitable for evolving critical thinking, writing, and reading skills—I have found that students' own desire to write about location also argues for place, making it a productive site. But, as this essay will argue, it is productive in ways that categories of race, gender, and class have not been, and it offers an opportunity to revisit Paulo Freire, extending his educational concepts and theories of teaching interaction. For many writing students, place becomes an integral part of what I will call an "ecocomposition course," one that evolves naturally from their own writing, their own concerns. It is also a category that is intrinsically part of their awareness of the world beyond the human.

As this epigraph suggests, my writing students' own language invites the category of place into the composition classroom. From their first informal writing responses to later revisions, their words explore their relationship with place and what it means to them. Place, as this student's words reveal, suggests a complex view of nature or the environment, along with human interactions with that challenging "category." It is the physicality of sky,

147

clouds, and earth; an actual location seemingly the opposite of culture; a desired and valued "other"; and a parent who by not displaying the very human characteristic of arguing, for example, functions ideally as a never-ending source of comfort. There is even a sense of boundaries: neither the sky nor the earth "try to take each other's places." This suggests a belief in "proper" place, one defined by purpose and respect. Crucially, it is one that desires nonhuman otherness thereby preparing for difference being more than human.

For my students and me, the category of place in composition studies embraces and extends from what this student suggests. Place's very complexity reinvigorates composition studies by offering the additional potential for political engagement—environmental activism—a kind of activism that can be, as Freire writes in *Pedagogy of the Oppressed*, "not pseudo-participation, but committed involvement" (51). An environmentally oriented "committed involvement" is what Jonathan Collett and Stephen Karakashian indirectly argue for in the February 1996 the *Chronicle of Higher Education*, noting "Human behavior is responsible for our planet's current predicament, and only a change in the ways we think and act can begin to repair the damage and avoid future depredations. These sobering realities are gaining increased attention among academics. . . ." (B1). It is a "sobering" reality attended to by many students: their environmental concern already motivates support for "green" products and for campus organizations lobbying on behalf of environmental legislation. Importantly, my students' passions for something other than themselves signify a readiness to consider other paradigms and prompts the integration of place into composition studies.

However, integrating place into the classroom and creating an eco-composition course is more than smuggling in an essay about trees—or even discussing the powerful pull of students' favorite places. It is arguably a more radical move, one capable of continuing a postmodern teacher's desire to diffuse his or her authority, in decentering the classroom. It is move that is able to reduce, even critically disrupt, the archetypal binaries of culture/nature, male/female, and even human/nonhuman. A composition course that goes "green" extends its boundaries to invite activism, a connection with the world beyond the writing classroom. The attempt to define the category of place helps students hone critical thinking skills while inserting place itself prompts interrogating anthropocentrism and considering that human-centered perspective a form of oppression. All of these moves further Freire's project of liberatory politics and consciousness about what teachers do in the classroom. As Ann E. Berthoff so eloquently notes in "Paulo Freire's Liberation Pedagogy,"

Paulo Friere teaches us to look—and to look again—at our theory and our practice and at the method which we can derive from the dialectic of their relationship. Nothing in the field of literary theory is more important than looking and looking again at the role of an awareness of awareness, of thinking about thinking, of interpreting our interpretations. (62–63)

Although Freire's work does not look beyond the realm of the human, I believe his concept of conscientization argues for the kind of critical consciousness that implacing place can achieve. An ecocomposition course can help students grow from functioning as objects into subjects. In turn, it can enable them to recognize their role in oppressively positioning others as objects while broadening their notion of what an "other" can be. Critically, in recognizing the "domesticating" power of oppression, they can strive "[t]o no longer be prey to its force" (*Pedagogy of the Oppressed* 33). While many writing teachers endeavor to create a classroom in which students recognize discourse hegemonies, how this kind of recognition is accomplished is particularly important to Freire: "This," he writes, "can be done only by means of the praxis: reflection and action upon the world in order to transform it" (33). At its core—yes, a word that signifies a very unpostmodern stability—an ecocomposition course can be commensurate with Freire's lifelong belief in the inseparability of practice and theory.

CONSCIENTIZATION, STUDENT DESIRE, AND PLACE

In his introduction to Freire's book *The Politics of Education*, Henry Giroux writes that

Education is that terrain where power and politics are given a fundamental expression, since it is where meaning, desire, language, and values engage and respond to the deeper beliefs about the very nature of what it means to be human, to dream, and to name and struggle for a particular future and way of life. As a referent for change, education represents a form of action that emerges from a joining of the languages of critique and possibility. It represents the need for a passionate commitment by educators to make the political more pedagogical, that is, to make critical reflection and action a fundamental part of a social project that not only engages forms of oppression but also develops a deep and abiding faith in the struggle to humanize life itself. (xiv)

Interestingly, education itself becomes "terrain," the *place* where questions of human power and politics meet. However, Giroux's focus highlights how many educators have come to know Freire's work: as being that which not only requires "a passionate commitment" on their part but that which is also a struggle for deed-oriented critical reflection on the nature of oppression. By interrogating their own positionality, Freire's work has set up educators' own roles in perpetuating oppression for critical reflection. For many, Freire's emphasis on having those who are usually unacknowledged—the oppressed—learn to use education to not only read but to further self-awareness thereby preempting further exploitation, and Freire's orientation toward liberation with an eye for whether it was "reproducing and legitimating capitalist ideologies," is essential to students developing critical thinking skills (xv). These critical skills take as their subject the student and his or her life. This is intrinsic to Freire's pedagogy: "illiterate learners must see the need for another learning process: that of "writing" about one's life, "reading" about one's reality" (10). It is, in some respects, the learner as subject, once, of course, the learner can read and then position herself in such a way that self-reflection is possible. As Freire writes, "they are questioning the very validity of their state of *asentamiento,* a state in which they must overcome their previous role as objects and assume the new role of subjects" (32).

This questioning begins the process of conscientization, which is more than awareness. It is not a stable state, but a participatory one, an ongoing self-reflexivity that recognizes oneself and the world. Leaving little doubt as to what conscientization is not, Moacir Gadotti writes in *Pedagogy of Praxis,* "It is not enough to be conscious" (180). While consciousness is certainly worthy, it lacks the understanding that one may be an object, not functioning as a "knowing subject." In *The Politics of Education,* Freire explains, "conscientization refers to the process in which men, not as recipients, but as knowing subjects achieve a deepening awareness both of the sociocultural reality that shapes their lives and of their capacity to transform that reality" (93). Bertoff, her words emphasizing conscientization's dynamic intent, writes,

> Knowing THAT you know is what Freire means by conscientization. It is the process by which one becomes the subject of what one learns, a subject with a purpose which can be represented, assessed, modified, directed, changed. Conscientization means

discovering yourself as a subject, but it is not SELF-conscious-ness; it is "consciousness of consciousness, intent upon the world." (365)

This consciousness, this process of conscientization, begins in the eco-composition course with students' words about place and their often un-examined attitudes about a nonhuman other moving to the foreground.[1] Positioning students' language as the text initiates self-reflexivity and helps them progress toward becoming the subject of the class. This is, of course, a pedagogically sound strategy regardless of any course's focus. In *The Politics of Education*, Freire's words valorize an educator's inclination to use student writing and to question even his own perspective: "I am inviting my readers to act as subjects and thus to reject the idea of merely accepting my analysis" (100). By examining their own writing, students begin to move from objects to subjects. Knowledge isn't, in Freire's well-known metaphor, "banked" in their brains: "'filled' by the educators' words (101). Instead of passively accepting codified knowledge, the students become the subjects of their own learning. Such a setting supports Freire's belief that students are not "empty," that they bring knowledge to the class: "Almost never do they realize that they, too, 'know things'" he writes in *Pedagogy of the Oppressed*, that "they have learned in their relations with the world and with other women and men" (45). An educator who recognizes that will most likely be one who seeks to enable conscientization, shaping a class where teachers and students interact in a liberatory dialogue. Both are subjects, despite their positions and positionality. Crucial to Freire's concept is the following, excerpted from *Pedagogy of the Oppressed*:

> A revolutionary leadership must accordingly practice *co-inten-tional* education. Teachers and students (leadership and people), co-intent on reality, are both Subjects, not only in the task of un-veiling that reality, and thereby coming to know it critically, but in the task of re-creating that knowledge. As they attain this knowledge of reality through common reflection and action, they discover themselves as its permanent re-creators. In this way, the presence of the oppressed in the struggle for their liberation will be what it should be: not pseudo-participation, but committed involvement. (51)

Here Freire joins both teacher and student, reflection and action. In a liberatory classroom, a setting where students can move from being merely an object—for teaching, for the "deposit" of "knowledge"—the students make their own knowledge. In an ecocomposition course, the process of conscientization continues with what Freire does not include: the other who is not human. It is an other who enters through students' own words on place, with what is not overtly constructed by people (much as the students may initially overlook the usual signs of human presence). Importantly, this nonhuman other enters easily, does not require any bidding. When asked to create an introductory freewriting on something important to them, students readily write about a place. Reflecting on their language and others, they see their desire for habitats long gone, for a respite away from humans. It may even be a location that due to a lack of people verges on "paradise," for example, the place-world the following student describes suggests ecoperfection. There are the human signifiers of environmental health—green trees, clear water, and fish—and there is the nondestructive human, able to hear "little creatures," those harmless, conveniently small and innocuous other nonhumans. The writer is not intruding, and indeed, is a happy onlooker to this somewhat Edenic view of place. Many of the senses are satiated; the writer arguably enraptured by the "wonderful, pure, clean signs of life":

> I can see all of the green of the trees, shrubs, and ground covering the water is nice and clear and sometimes I can see a little fish swim by. I can hear frogs and crickets in the distance. I see flowers blossoming, I hear little creatures in the shrubs near by. And when I see all of these wonderful, pure, clean signs of life, I can relate them all to one word . . . nature. (Student at the University of Washington, English 281 class)

It is a place organized by human perception yet one that is apparently unaffected by it. Repeatedly, my students in English 281, an intermediate expository writing class taken by non-English majors and English majors alike, return to this image of a secure and unaffected place. It is both the subject of their writing and, at this point of the class, an object: a kind of plateau of stability. Interestingly, this favorite place, while described longingly, is often one where certain kinds of desire are absent. While enjoying the surroundings, the physical body does not hamper (within reason) a pastorallike communion with place. Of her favorite place, one English 281 student writes,

> It is slightly chilly. Cold enough so that my nose is a little colder than the rest of my body but I am not uncomfortable at all (not wanting another jacket or *anything*). (my emphasis)

The student's rhetoric reveals this place as a location where even slight physical discomfort is mitigated by beauty, solitude, and the comfort of just being there. One does not want "anything" or for "anything." (Even desire is parenthetical.) This hiatus in desire is quite striking to the students, who note how the usual consumer cravings seem quieted by place. It is place as other—still as object, however—and their words as text that prompt these inklings of other voices. As students build on their awareness of how their words are positioning place, they simultaneously reconsider place as being very "out there." The boundary between self and place blurs, and place becomes less of an object. Because student language and perceptions about place are the text, the students themselves are less likely to remain as objects. Instead, they become the subjects as their growing awareness of others (both others and other) also reinscribes that position. Such a move reduces the "thingness" of place and helps students and teachers become more conscious that how they have viewed place, how they have viewed others of all kinds, might begin to be considered another form of oppression.

While Freire writes of the oppression of people, his words can extend to heretofore unconsidered otherness without diminishing the importance of freeing humans from an object position. In *Pedagogy of the Oppressed,* he notes; "An act is oppressive only when it prevents people from being more fully human" (38–39). Fully human can be extended to include awareness, respect, and consciousness for nonhuman, an awareness of Western ideas of anthropocentrism. Positioning anyone or anything as an object, as merely that to be acted upon, can affect all interactions. In fact, Freire's words emphasize the fact that oppression can subjugate more than humans: "The oppressor consciousness tends to transform everything surrounding it into an object of its domination. The earth, property, production, the creations of people, people themselves, time—everything is reduced to the status of objects at its disposal" (40). This objectifying can continue the subjugation, preventing the oppressor's connection with the object, maintaining its object/oppressed status. The objectifying continues the oppression, reducing even the earth to something the oppressor can dispose. And yet, it is that upon which the oppressor lives, that which he, she, or it must be part of to endure. Would maintaining it as something to be disposed, as Freire's words suggest, not be the ultimate act of oppression, preventing "people from being more fully human"(38–39)?

Because student reflections about place come quite easily to them, because they all have stories that mix yearning for, and delight in, those sites, place begins to escape its usually unexamined "boundaries." It begins to escape its situation of object, even as object, which in Freire's words is transformed by an "oppressor consciousness" into something for their "disposal." It's a repositioning prompted by the students' own placeness, their valuing of where they have come from, the other that offers them a respite from themselves as totalizing subject, oppressive subject.

The students valuing (and oftentimes romanticizing) of place in nature initially falls neatly into a binary of subject/object. Often their language valorizes so-called native intelligence, the wisdom of place knowledge: knowledge outside of humans. For some, it is their first "taste" of considering the other, of reflecting on how they may have positioned that which is not them. "When I think of being 'in nature," writes one English 281 student, "I think of being silent, of forgetting about book-intelligence and gaining natural intelligence (as Wordsworth would say)." Book knowledge resides between the covers of human-constructed information. It is not tracked the way "natural" intelligence is nor is it the ability to read nature or to merely be in it, silent in its knowledgeable presence. Of course, this student's words suggest that her silence will enable nature, her natural place, to speak and disclose what insights can be found in the world beyond books. It prompts students to consider the fact that there may be voices beyond them that they do indeed seek and listen to, but that they have never classified as voices, or even as others. In fact, their language often positions themselves as wistful outsiders, visitors to a "promised" land, one where they are not the only determinant of meaning.

FREIRE AND ALDO LEOPOLD'S "LAND ETHIC": THEORY AND PEDAGOGY IN PLACE

All of the students I've worked with are comfortable reflecting on their writing about place. In addition to having a place easily accessible to them, writing about place positions them as experts; who can dispute the existence and details of *their* place? Initially, their response to reading or hearing their writing on place, and how it seems to turn effortlessly to an Edenic-like nature—gorgeous, fruitful, and without human sin—focuses on the pleasure of being in this special location. Each of them tends to react enthusiastically to the descriptive writing, remembering the time it evoked. They are also respectful of differences while enjoying similarities. Many immediately segue into disappointment that this place has changed: the water is no longer clear or there's been some kind of development, changing the possibilities it offered for refuge from that very human activity. This disappointment is a dissonance that creates a productive tension:

they look more closely at what they have done, or perhaps inadvertently been a part of, which has made that site into an object. It's a disappointment that creates a site of heretofore unexamined meaning, and it prepares them for Aldo Leopold, one of the class' first readings, and his way of including place, the land, into the community. In fact, Leopold's "The Land Ethic," anthologized in numerous recent collections, startles them, offering an opportunity to work more overtly with Freire's educational philosophies and practices and continue extending them to the nonhuman community.

Leopold's "Land Ethic" suggests the notion of ethics and of according status to nonhumans. Leopold historicizes ethics and their progression, noting that initially Odysseus' slave girls were not considered human and were killed without remorse. Students extrapolate from that, discussing how things have changed, while continuing to reflect on Leopold's next move of positioning the land. As Leopold explains, "Land, like Odysseus' slave girls, is still property" (196) indicating a relationship between land and people that is strictly economic. Introducing land as being valued only economically so close to a discussion about the emotional importance of place makes for some provocative writing: "Why," many students wonder, "shouldn't land be considered equal?" For many, it's one of the first moments a dominant paradigm is questioned. Why, indeed, should land be merely that which we walk upon, they often write. Contemplating a nonhuman aspect of their world heretofore unconsidered in this fashion, in an ethical light, creates strategic pauses, productive tensions. How to juggle positioning humans as the makers of meaning, the determinant of all that is valuable, in light of their love of place and Leopold? As Leopold defines an ethic as a "mode of guidance for meeting ecological situations," their writing struggles with how this might manifest itself (197). What would, for example, their part of the world look like if their favorite place had possessed a "voice," not just theirs in praise or protection, but a systematic, worldwide (or region-wide) guidance, an ethic, to govern its care? Why not extend the kind of ethical growth not killing slaves represents to how we view the land? What challenges and excites them most is what many consider the core of Leopold's land ethic, that a "land ethic simply enlarges the boundary of community . . . [and] . . . a land ethic affirms right to continued existence" (197).

With students' own places achieving importance, and with Leopold's work suggesting the previously unconsidered notion of land having a "voice," ecocomposition students can also see the rights of others to their voices. They also consider the fact that "others" can be Leopold's land community, the site of previously unconsidered relations of domination.

For Freire, "Equally important is the insight that domination is more than the simple imposition of arbitrary power by one group over another" (*Politics of Education* xi). The idea that land and place can be dominated in a way that people can and have, coupled with students' belief in the "sanctity" of their place, suggests to them other ways of viewing human/place relations and human/human relations. For many of the students I've worked with, privileged and in possession of the potential to be heard without much of a struggle when they choose to, it can be liberating to consider the nature of domination, the nature of struggle, and to consider struggling for others. Certainly many teachers know what Michael McDowell acknowledges in "Talking about Trees in Stumptown: Pedagogical Problems in Teaching EcoComp," that "it's usually easier for students to question the assumptions of those with whom they disagree than it is for them to question their own assumptions" (23). Freire, speaking with Donaldo P. Macado in "A Dialogue: Culture, Language, and Race," specifies that which would have students question. For Freire, educators must work for student conscientization, not avoid that process for fear of "intervening." Freire writes, "by not intervening so as not to impose, the teacher commits an ethical error. I think it is an ethical duty for educators to intervene in challenging students to critically engage with their world so they can act upon it and on it" (391).

The students' desire for place, their beginning belief in overtly honoring it, and then their envisioning their part in oppressing it, provides educators with a position from which to enable critical thinking. Place implaces people and can provide a commonality and critical juncture. It recognizes the body; indeed a good deal of how we position ourselves. As student writing notes, we tend to be place-beings. We ask questions about places, weather, and getting from one point to another: about moving our bodies. We identify ourselves as being from places: from the city, the country, the East Coast, the Midwest, Indianapolis, Ontario,—sharing specific locales that become a code for that which shapes us, which makes us, in part, who we are. Edward L. Casey's work, *Getting Back into Place: Toward a Renewed Understanding of the Place-World,* argues for and affirms the importance of place:

> I shall accord to place a position of renewed respect by specifying its power to direct and stabilize us, to memorialize and identify us, to tell us who and what we are in terms of *where we are* (as well as where we are *not*). To be in the world, to be situated at all, is to be in place. (xv)

For Casey, place is a point of origin, a positionality that encourages honoring all that "places" one, including the environment and "nature." Place allows the reclamation of the body, and bodily knowledge, but does not necessarily make both the center of the universe. It is a reclaiming of the ground beneath our feet, the physicality of the body. It is that which can be available to all. Casey writes of the

> "power" *(dynamis)* of place. This power is considerable. It is much more considerable than we are willing to grant as modernists— and now as postmodernists—whose obsession with time and space has blinded us to the forgotten but formidable presence of place in our lives. (21)

This "formidable presence" is more than the ground on which we stand; it is an embrace of our tangible nature and others. When limited, or confined to being merely concrete, its potential to be fully dimensional is violated. It becomes, like almost anything reduced to one trait, an example of essentialism. Casey's work reveals his understanding of this pitfall, writing, "When place has been subjected to simple location, it becomes what I shall call "site." Site is place reduced to being "just there" (66). Consequently, place does not have to mean an exclusionary position. In fact, *position* itself is too site-bound a word, suggesting an anchor, a stable point of reference that if too unmovable or static can obstruct permeability and a desired openness to diverse voices, to paradigms other than those that have been historically dominant.

When students have begun this process, have written about themselves as subjects, for example, as those capable of recognizing a special place and preserving it, they are participating in an aspect of Freire's project and, indeed, move closer to his idea of subject. In *The Politics of Education,* Freire notes,

> But it is also true that action upon an object must be critically analyzed in order to understand both the object itself and the understanding one has of it. The act of knowing involves a dialectical movement that goes from action to reflection and from reflection upon action to a new action (51).

By considering land as a place as deserving of equality, students and teachers are also troubling their own idea of anthropocentrism, arguably a paradigm more dominant than any form of colonializing. While Freire did not overtly embrace the land as a member of the community, his words encourage rethinking this human strategy of domination. As Freire explains, "The cognitive dimensions of the literacy process must include the relationships of men with their world" (50). In this case, the world is enlarged by self-reflection to embrace placeness and all places. While it is language, literacy, on which Freire dwells—that *speaking the word* really means: a human act implying reflection and action"—he is also concerned with the change that must come from that reflective act (50):

> the literacy process must relate *speaking the word* to transforming reality and to man's role in this transformation. Perceiving the significance of that relationship is indispensable for those learning to read and write if we are really committed to liberation. Such a perception will lead the learners to recognize a much greater right than that of being literate. They will ultimately recognize that, as men, they have the right to have a voice. (51)

OTHER NATIONS AND OTHER VOICES

This understanding of a "right to have a voice" evolves as students hear others' ideas about place and write about their own particular place. Many include the sounds of place, the wind through long grass and, of course, birds of no particular identity. There is something about the nonhuman voices that satisfies, and there is something about considering nonhuman voices that suggests the need to protect and construct them as worthy as human voices. That these nonhuman voices are tangible, are a part of the daily life, lends credence to this move for students. Nature and place becomes more than inert. The land grows beyond being, as Josephine Donovan notes, "an absent referent" (74). The students' eagerness to write about place underscores the importance, indeed, the "naturalness" of considering place, their environment, as a pivotal paradigm. Easily, they evoke images of trees, real or imagined; the plot of land they had access to as a child or the location they now return to, often for quiet or to get away from others. They don't necessarily conceive of what other voices might mean, even after their work with Leopold has disrupted their human centrism. However, place opens up to suggest more than Leopold's idea of land as member of the community, leading to the possibility of reconceptualizing animals, the nonhuman. In some classes, I have shared the following words from *The Outermost House*, Henry Beston's work, which suggests what including place as a paradigm can contribute as it ruptures the binary of human/nonhuman:

We need another and a wiser and perhaps a more mystical concept of animals. Remote from universal nature, and living by
complicated artifice, man in civilization surveys the creature
through the glass of his knowledge and sees thereby a feather
magnified and the whole image in distortion. We patronize them
for their incompleteness, for their tragic fate of having taken form
so far below ourselves. And therein we err, and greatly err. For the
animal shall not be measured by man. In a world older and more
complete than ours they move finished and complete, gifted with
extensions of the senses we have lost or never attained, living by
voices we shall never hear. They are not brethren, they are not un-
derlings; they are other nations, caught with ourselves in the net
of life and time, fellow prisoners of the splendor and travail of the
earth. (25)

Beston's words, taken from his book about living a year on the Great
Beach of Cape Cod, reconsiders Western culture's history of placing nonhuman as beneath humans, as being incomplete, of "having taken form so
far below ourselves." Such a positioning is arguably another form of oppression, one that even considering it might exist offers liberating possibilities, spaces beyond the current "cultural patterns" of which Freire spoke
with Macado. Conversing about the individual as being "the subject of
history," Freire explains:

I see history exactly as do the liberation theologians, among
whom I feel very good. . . . For me, history represents a time of
possibilities and not determinism . . . we need to view history as
possibility so we can both liberate and save ourselves. This is possible only through a historical perspective in which men and
women are capable of assuming themselves, as both objects and
subjects of history, capable of reinventing the world in an ethical
and aesthetic mold beyond the cultural patterns that exist. (397)

As Beston's words suggest, seeking "a wiser and perhaps more mystical
concept of animals" and encountering—in two English 281 students'
words—that area where one does not "want for anything" and is capable of
"gaining natural intelligence," disrupts "cultural patterns." Students review
their perspective, consider that they even have a perspective and positionality.
It is critical consciousness writ about the nonhuman world, valuing humans
and nonhumans' place in the environment. It breaks with how most students
have seen themselves positioned, and it furthers Freire's liberatory process.

In *Education, Cultural Myths, and the Ecological Crisis,* C. A. Bowers argues that students study for years with textbooks that position "humans . . . [as] . . . the reference point for making sense of the world," a perspective which, along with "cultural myth," is "further reinforced in thinking that humans are separate from nature" (123). Any text that provides a window on this division helps break down what many believe to be a predominately Western myth. Although the more astute student readers of Leopold's "Land Ethic" argue that he places his beliefs in economic terms—somewhat undercutting his suggestion that we position land as an equal member of the community—they recognize what kind of overall move Leopold advocates. Considering place in the composition classroom suggests another kind of Other, what Bowers notes that all students encounter: "The Western myth that humans have a privileged status among the forms of life that make up the biotic community is one of the central cultural messages students encounter in schools" (123). It is the first place the students can, in Beston's words, move closer to the idea that "we are fellow prisoners of the splendor and travail of the earth" (25). Their own language about place, and their growing consideration of their place in the world, helps them reconsider human's positions. Who do we hear, they ask.

This constructively enlarges the circle, something Christopher Manes emphasizes, writing, "For human societies of all kinds, moral consideration seems to fall only within a circle of speakers in communication with one another" (44). Consequently, my students' interest in place, their confidence that they have something to write about, helps them consider what species centrism might be and if it burdens us, thwarting an environmentalism that is less use-oriented and more cognizant of the rights and values of all things. The ecocomposition class suggests there is a responsibility, a timeliness, to address place as paradigm. It is an opening of ethics beyond humans, as well as valuing the knowing bodies and embodied knowledge the writing students have. Place becomes a valid—and necessary inclusion—in thinking about ourselves and our whereabouts in the world at large. In a writing class, place can value the body that knows, that lives in itself. Yet place can power moving beyond humanism and anthropocentrism, but is not necessarily exclusionary. To move place more forward in our studies, to add it to race, gender, and class, is to recognize more fully that place is not just about environmental destruction, but is, in part, how we live in relation to other cultures, discourses, and species. In many respects, this move releases the environment from the background and expands it: it is no longer merely setting. Critically, it is a move with crucial ethical implications for thinking about *who* we are, how we interact, and how we behave, which echoes many of my students' desire for place, an important position from which to begin. Freire's own words nudge in this direction. In *Pedagogy of the Oppressed,* he writes, "World and human beings do not exist apart from each other, they exist in constant interaction" (32). The students themselves, leaping from their initial nostalgia about place, disrupt this hegemony and even human-centrism in general. It is a new subject-position for students and teachers alike.

NOTES

1. It is not that they haven't thought about environmental issues or been involved in some capacity with one of the many environmentally oriented groups that they encounter, but most of them haven't considered the binary of human/nonhuman from which they usually operate. For the most part, they are very aware of aspects of environmental issues, even if they may not have investigated the many sides one issue (e.g., jobs vs. the environment) may contain.

WORKS CITED

Bertoff, Ann E. "Paulo Freire's Liberation Pedagogy." *Language Arts* 67 (April 1990): 362–69.

Beston, Henry. *The Outermost House.* 1928. England: Penguin Books, 1956.

Bowers, C. A. *Education, Cultural Myths, and the Ecological Crisis.* Albany: State University of New York Press, 1993.

Casey, Edward L. *Getting Back into Place: Toward a Renewed Understanding of the Place-World.* Bloomington and Indianapolis: Indiana University Press, 1993.

Collett, Jonathan, and Stephen Karakashian. "Turning Curricula Green." *Chronicle of Higher Education,* 23 February 1996. B1–2.

Donovan, Josephine. "Ecofeminist Literary Criticism: Reading the Orange." *Ecofeminist Literary Criticism: Theory, Interpretation, Pedagogy.* Eds. Greta Gaard and Patrick D. Murphy. Urbana and Champaign: University of Illinois Press, 1998. 74–96.

Freire, Paulo. *Pedagogy of the Oppressed.* 1970. Trans. Myra Bergman Ramos. New York: Continuum Publishing Company, 1997.

———. *The Politics of Education.* Trans. Donaldo Macedo. South Hadley, MA: Bergin & Garvey Publishers, 1985.

———, and Donaldo P. Macedo. "A Dialogue: Culture, Language, and Race." *Harvard Educational Review.* Vol. 65 (Fall 1995): 377–402.

Gadoti, Moacir. *A Pedagogy of Praxis: A Dialectical Philosophy of Education.* Trans. John Milton. Albany: State University of New York Press, 1996.

Leopold, Aldo. "The Land Ethic." Eds. Walter Levy and Christopher Hallowell. *Green Perspectives: Thinking and Writing about Nature and the Environment*. New York.: HarperCollins, 1994. 195–210.

Manes, Christopher. "Nature and Silence." *Postmodern Environmental Ethics*. Ed. Max Olschlaeger. Albany: State University of New York Press, 1995. 43–56.

McDowell, Michael. "Talking about Trees in Stumptown: Pedagogical Problems in Teaching EcoComp." *Reading the Earth: New Directions in the Study of Literature and the Environment*. Eds. Michael P. Branch et. al. Moscow: University of Idaho Press, 1998. 19–28.

Ecofeminism and Ecocomposition:

Pedagogies, Perspectives, and Intersections

Greta Gaard
Western Washington University, Fairhaven College
Bellingham, Washington

For those teachers committed to using their classrooms as a vehicle for educating students about issues of social justice and environmental politics, ecocomposition has much to offer. Although ecocomposition courses will vary in practice—shaped by each teacher's own composition pedagogy, educational philosophy, and environmental ethics—at its most inclusive, ecocomposition has the potential to address social issues such as feminism, environmental ethics, multiculturalism, politics, and economics, all by examining matters of form and style, audience and argumentation, and reliable sources and supporting documentation. My own interest in ecocomposition came at a time when my primary teaching assignment was in Composition, but my primary research and activism was in ecofeminism. After listening to an exciting presentation about the potentials for ecocomposition (see McDowell), I wanted to find out what intersections were possible between ecofeminism and ecocomposition, and how ecofeminist perspectives might be introduced in a composition classroom. Through the process of teaching an ecocomposition course, I am persuaded that ecocomposition and ecofeminism share many features of both process and perspective, and that ecocomposition offers a new and valuable approach to teaching not only writing but environmental ethics and social justice as well.

PEDAGOGIES AND PERSPECTIVES

Perhaps the easiest explanation for this compatibility has to do with the common historical roots of not only ecofeminism, but of certain composition pedagogies and educational philosophies as well. In 1980 (the year I began teaching Composition), process-based writing instruction was the newest, most innovative composition pedagogy, and novice writing teachers absorbed its tenets like tofu soaking up curry sauce. The theories and texts of Peter Elbow, Linda Flower (1979, 1981), Donald Murray, and Maxine C. Hairston provided the foundation for a composition pedagogy I still use today. This approach rests on the fundamental assumption that good writing skills develop not by memorizing the rules of grammar, but by exploring the process of writing itself. By postponing the emphasis on the writing product, teachers can foster a writing process that is free to become more spontaneous, creative, dynamic, and inventive; more possibilities can be discovered the more writers are encouraged to explore ideas in ways that are messy and nonlinear, rather than to capture and control ideas in tightly constructed essays. Heuristics popular since the early 1980s include "rushwriting" or "freewriting," a practice of writing whose only stipulation is that the pen must not stop moving; generating lists about specific topics using a variety of perspectives originally called "particle," "wave," and "field";[1] and planning essays in a way that emphasizes the organic connections between ideas ("treeing") rather than the linear development characteristic of a more formal approach (i.e., Roman numeral outlines).

Process-based pedagogies also emphasize the writing context and the writing community. Peer review groups of four or five students read and discuss every rough draft in class. Because this technique is so effective in revealing the interdependence of an essay's form and content, I continue to ask my writing students to analyze the communication context for every essay they read or write, describing that essay's intended audience as well as the writer's persona, purpose, and message (see Hairston). These strategies for teaching writing initially were shaped in response to a social context where concepts of authority and objectivity were being challenged as instruments legitimating a hierarchical social structure. The search for more participatory, democratic structures for communication and decision-making extended from the countercultural movements of the sixties into the classrooms of the seventies and eighties.

At the same time that process-based and student-centered pedagogies were gaining popularity in Composition, the liberatory pedagogy of Paolo Freire and feminist ideals about equalizing power and authority in the classroom began influencing teaching strategies in the fields of Literature and Women's Studies, as well as some of the Social Sciences (Bunch and Pollack and Culley and Portugues).[2] These pedagogies stress the belief that students already know what it is they need to learn, and for this reason, they should be encouraged to participate at every level of course planning, from topics and textbook selection, to class discussions, assignments, and evaluations. Democratizing knowledge and education means decentering authority, sharing it equally among students and teacher(s); this strategy is often made visible through the rearrangement of chairs in a classroom, from a single lecturer addressing rows of students, to a circle of chairs that encourages face-to-face discussion among students and teacher alike.[3] Radical pedagogies also emphasize the belief that knowledge is socially produced, and can be constructed in the classroom discourse community, found in the library, and discovered through interviews or service-learning projects with agencies and organizations outside the university. The learning process, the classroom, and the college campus are also seen as part of the curriculum, and students are encouraged to critique the course syllabus, the composition of the student body within that particular classroom, as well as the structure, policies, practices, and funding of the academic institution itself. Instead of (or in addition to) letter grades, feminist and democratic classrooms tend to shift emphasis in evaluation away from standardized testing to essays, performances, art pieces, and student-led discussions or even direct action demonstrations. Moreover, students are encouraged to participate in the construction of learning criteria and in their own self-evaluations.

While radical and feminist pedagogies were being introduced in the academy, ecofeminist activism and theory was being articulated through such community events as the Women's Pentagon Actions of 1980 and 1981, the founding of Feminists for Animal Rights in 1982, and the publication of the first ecofeminist anthology, Léonie Caldecott and Stephanie Leland's *Reclaim the Earth* in 1983. Growing out of the conviction that the peace, feminist, and environmental movements were converging into a more inclusive ecofeminist movement, activists at the 1980 Women's Pentagon Action demanded an end to "male violence in all its forms (warfare, poverty, educational deprivation and distortion, battering, rape, pornography, reproductive control, heterosexism, racism, and nuclear power), an end to oppression, an end to warfare" (Gaard 1998;19). Ecofeminism's earliest analysis linked the structures of militarism and corporatism, and called for a transformed cultural, political, and economic order as the only lasting strategy for achieving women's liberation and for ensuring ecological health. Radical ecofeminism's critique of speciesism, along with social ecofeminism's critique of hierarchy and domination, inspired later explorations of the ways in which the various oppressive structures (racism, sexism, classism, speciesism, and heterosexism) are interconnected and mutually reinforcing (Plumwood 1993, Gaard 1997). Most recently, ecofeminists have explored the intersections of ecofeminism and democracy (Plumwood 1995; Sandilands 1995, 1997; Gaard 1998), explorations that are thoroughly compatible with the feminist and liberatory pedagogies for creating a democratic classroom, and with process-based writing pedagogies that emphasize the value of fostering community and collaboration throughout the writing process.

Clearly, the roots of these various liberatory movements—in composition, in education, and in ecofeminism—can be traced to the same era, articulating diverse activist and intellectual responses to a specific historic, ecological, and economic context. In the past twenty years since their inception, composition and radical pedagogies have continued their parallel development, while ecofeminism has developed more in the areas of social action and environmental theory than it has in classroom pedagogy. But with the recent developments in ecofeminist literary criticism (P. D. Murphy and Gaard and P. D. Murphy), ecofeminist approaches to teaching ecocomposition cannot be far behind. Like the theory and practice of ecofeminism, ecofeminist pedagogies are still in the process of discovery and articulation, since a basic tenet of feminism and ecofeminism is that theory grows out of practice. As more courses are taught using the frameworks and perspectives of ecofeminism, more teachers will contribute to the articulation of ecofeminist pedagogies. For me, this was certainly the case: in order to theorize the potential intersections between ecofeminism and ecocomposition, I first had to experience teaching an ecocomposition course.

ECOFEMINIST IN THE ECOCOMPOSITION CLASSROOM

The composition, feminist, and liberatory pedagogies just described were what offered the strongest guidance in designing my first ecocomposition course. For a course reader, I chose Chris Anderson and Lex Runciman text, *A Forest of Voices,* both for its selection of readings and for its introductory chapters on composition. Though I never assigned the introductory chapters to the class as a whole, those sections were available to students who needed further instruction beyond the class discussions. My particular method of teaching introductory composition does not require a composition textbook, but rather makes textbooks out of everything— class discussions, newspaper articles, student writing, and texts from other courses students are taking—so the seventy or so pages on writing in the Anderson and Runciman reader fit my approach nicely.

Ecofeminist analyses of the links between social and environmental justice, the "interidentity" of humans (of all genders) as part of both culture and nature (see P. D. Murphy), and the necessary unity of theory and practice also influenced my selection of readings and the progression of writing assignments. In conjunction with selected articles from the Anderson and Runciman reader, I assigned a series of seven essays over a ten-week quarter, arranging the essays in order of increasing complexity. These assignments encouraged student writers to think about their individual relation to place (essay no. 1), to undertake a comparison of places in terms of the classic culture/nature dualism (essay no. 2), to classify several viewpoints about place (essay #3), and to develop a research paper on some topic that arose in essay nos. 1–3. Essay nos. 4–7 were linked to the research paper: the research proposal (essay no. 4), a report on an article for the research paper (essay no. 5), a comparison and contrast paper involving three sources for the research paper (essay no. 6), and the research paper itself (essay no. 7). The "final exam" (with the question given in advance) asked the students to write an essay explaining their own environmental ethics to an audience they selected.

The combination of composition and feminist pedagogies guided me to choose a deductive approach to teaching the course: that is, the students' education would depend largely on their own discovery of effective prose styles, research techniques, and organizational methods in the essays we were reading, as well as the their own reflection and discovery of the beliefs they held (or had inherited) about culture, nature, and their place in relation to these. The readings and assignments were arranged in such a way that students were invited to ask larger and larger questions about themselves in relation to their own homeland (essay no. 1), about the economies of culture and nature, and who is present or absent in each of these economies (essay no. 2), and what the rationalizations are for those relationships, economies, and the absence, presence, or ranking of people therein (essay no. 3). Along the way, as their questions emerged, I was able to present students with an overview of anthropocentric, ecocentric, and radical environmental theories, and to help them classify their readings in relation to those theories.

Because my ecocomposition course was intended to serve as an alternate to first-year expository composition, I was somewhat restricted in the types of writing I could choose as models for analysis. Certainly ecofeminist critics have deplored the unitary association between nature writing and the nature essay, not only for the restrictiveness of its form and for the types of writers (in terms of their race, class, gender, and sexuality) it foregrounds as "nature writers," but also for the very "Western" manner in which this form defines what counts as "nature" (P. D. Murphy). Anderson and Runciman seem to have held some of these considerations in mind as they selected readings for this text: though the essay predominates in this anthology, these essays range in style from the persuasive essay (the research or philosophical essay) and even the "list" essay to the various forms of creative nonfiction—the personal essay or memoir, science writing, travel writing, and of course, "nature" writing. But the editors also include a few short stories (I counted three, though some quibbling could occur about the features of extended anecdote in what I counted as essays rather than short stories), and at least twelve "nature" poems. Clearly, this diversity of genres is taking us in the right direction, but I would still ask, what definition of "nature" is a work in selecting examples from these various forms of writing? How is the way in which Western culture has traditionally defined nature come to be part of the problem we face today and how can shifting our very definition of "nature" help us in addressing and resolving those problems? Again, because of the limitations around my ecocomposition course, I selected only persuasive and creative nonfiction essays, and this requirement emphasized how restrictive these forms really are: two essays by black women, one essay by a Native American man, and a memoir by a wealthy white woman do not constitute *diversity* in any sense of the word. Where was the history and perspective of Asian Americans or Chicanos in writing about "nature" and the "environment"? How do nonheterosexuals write about such topics as place and identity? These were questions that the selections in the reader did not encourage me to raise.

Nonetheless, the Anderson and Runciman reader allowed me to address environmental politics and composition through a strong selection of culturally "Western" essays. For the students' first essay on their relation to homeplace, we read and discussed Gretel Ehrlich's "Solace of Open Spaces," an essay about her chosen home in Wyoming, and N. Scott Momaday's "Sacred and Ancestral Ground," about the Kiowa's sense of self and sacred places such as the Black Hills, Medicine Wheel, and Devil's Tower (or "Rock Tree"). These essays raised culturally contextualized questions of how place shapes identity, not just how people shape the land; in turn, students were encouraged to ask such questions about identity in relation to their own homeplaces and cultures. Kathleen Norris's essay about the Dakotas and David Guterson's essay on the Mall of America gave us excellent departure points for writing the comparison essay exploring the economies of culture and of nature, particularly because most of my students were familiar with both places. Bill McKibbin's "Daybreak," an essay comparing television with nature's informational "broadcast," gave us an opportunity to explore ways of organizing comparative essays. For the classification essay, we examined the problem of organizing urban life in ways that respected both humans and nature, using such essays as David Seideman's "Trouble in Mill City" about the collapsed economy in a logging town, Cynthia Hamilton's "Women, Home, and Community" about women and environmental justice, and Marc Reisner's "Semidesert with a Desert Heart" about water struggles in the West. The combination of these readings and essays introduced questions of ecology and economics, and democracy and diversity, so that students were able to choose their own research topics to pursue.

After the research proposal, we explored the problem of choosing reliable sources and structuring argumentation through essays developing a single line of argument, such as Stephen Jay Gould's "Nonmoral Nature," and by pairing essays such as Dixie Lee Ray's "Greenhouse Earth" and Samuel W. Matthews's "Under the Sun," which both address global warming and the greenhouse effect but make very different arguments. The project of comparing and contrasting viewpoints was continued in the sixth essay, for which we read Gifford Pinchot's "Prosperity," John Muir's "Hetch Hetchy Valley," Marsden Manson's "Statement of San Francisco's Side of the Hetch-Hetchy Reservoir Matter," and Ron Arnold's "Rethinking Environmentalism." At this point, students wanted to know more about the differences among these culturally similar views on nature, and in response, I offered them information on white Western environmentalism—conservation and preservation—as well as the "wise use" backlash, and encouraged students to explore the strengths and limitations of these perspectives in various contexts. Our readings concluded with selections from radical environmentalists, including Paul Watson's "Shepherds of the Labrador Front," Dave Foreman's "Earth First!" Wangari Maathai's "Foresters without Diplomas," Terry Tempest Williams's "Clan of One-Breasted Women," and Edward Abbey's "Great American Desert." Of course, students observed that these perspectives differed considerably from Pinchot and Muir, and in response to their interest I introduced them to the anthropocentric/ecocentric distinction, along with an overview of radical environmentalisms such as bioregionalism, deep ecology, ecofeminisms, and social ecology, and the environmental justice movement. All of these discussions prepared the students for naming and supporting their own environmental ethic (the task of their final exam), along with giving them (through the readings) sample essays for treeing, and thereby breaking down and analyzing the structure of various arguments, their use of facts and supporting data, and the ways in which the essays were organized to appeal to different audiences. Of course, these discussions also raised more questions than we could possibly address in a single ecocomposition course, and created a curiosity and interest in the students that may lead them to a deeper exploration of environmental politics.

The beauty of this process was that it allowed me to "teach" environmental ethics as an adjunct to teaching writing. It kept me from having to battle "for" or "against" any particular viewpoint, and simply allowed the students to map out the conflicts and explore these struggles through writing. Teaching ecocomposition allowed me to reconfigure my teaching identity, backgrounding my identity as "ecofeminist scholar/activist" and foregrounding my role as "writing instructor." Consequently, the students' teacher-pleasing behavior was structured around their writing processes and styles, and the logic of their arguments, but not the actual content of their beliefs. This shift was liberating for both students and teacher alike. Ecocomposition offered me a tangible means for sharing authority with students, and for encouraging students to develop their own authority and beliefs in the area of environmental ethics, in a way that is not always possible when I teach other subjects, such as environmental politics, radical environmental philosophies, or ecofeminisms. In those classes, students accurately perceive me as an invested player, and I worry that this perception alters and influences what they are willing to say and write in class; perhaps the imperative for faculty to "come out" and thereby eschew falsely "objective," artifically neutral positions for more authentic subject positions has a few limitations after all. In a nondominative or "heterarchical" classroom, the teacher's authority needs to be established in such a way that it makes room for, even requires, the development of students' authority as well (P. D. Murphy); ecocomposition offered me this opportunity.

Developing students' own authority also involved a different approach to grading. Because there are definite skills to be taught and learned in first-year composition, the grading process had to be anchored to each student's progress in demonstrating competency with those skills; as in any class, the students' own environmental ethics were never graded, but the rubric of "Ecocomposition" rather than "Environmental Studies" gave students an added sense of freedom to develop their own environmental perspectives. At the start of the term, I distributed a sheet listing all of the writing skills to be introduced, practiced, and mastered over the course of the quarter, describing the progressive development of writing skills and their relation to each of the seven assignments. Each essay was to be evaluated in reference to the skills introduced up to that point, with essay no. 7 and the final exam weighing most heavily in assessing the student's final grade. On the grade sheet and in class, I explained that only their reasoning, their strategies for structuring an argument, their use of reliable sources, and their effectiveness in addressing a noncompliant audience were components for evaluation. Before collecting each final essay, I asked students to evaluate their essays in terms of the writing skills for that essay, as well as their own satisfaction with the articulation of their ideas. Any teacher who has tried this method will not be surprised to find that these evaluations are usually frank and honest. Students can easily learn to be their own best critics. In the cases when my evaluation differed from the student's, I invited the student to meet for a conference so that we could hear each other's views and address that student's particular writing competencies and challenges. This method, like any democratic teaching method, was more time-consuming than traditional letter grades, and much more satisfying to the students and teacher alike.

STUDENT WRITINGS AND ASSESSMENTS

The outcomes for this class were varied: out of seventeen students, there were only two C grades, with the others B's and A's. In short, the composition aspect of the course was very successful. As indicated in the research papers and final essay exams, the environmental ethics that developed among these students ranged from two ecofeminists, a few conservationists, a couple of environmental justice advocates, several bioregionalists, and other students who didn't explicitly name their environmental theories but used words like *respect* and *cultural and ecological diversity* and *interdependence*. The introductory paragraph of one student's final essay exam exemplifies this view:

> When I think of the land and the environmental ethics that I believe in, I recall one important passage from one of the best sources ever printed: "The land shall not be sold forever: for the land is mine, for ye are strangers and sojourners with me" (Lev. 25:23). This bible verse describes being strangers with each other but sharing a common goal and place in the land. Respect is the key word which brings us together: respect for our community, respect for our economy, and respect for our ecology. The process is a circle of decisions that deals with responsibility. Without the respect for these three things, respect cannot be gained for ourselves or our neighbors.

Unlike some teachers, perhaps, I choose not to prevent students from expressing deeply held religious views; however, I do point out the way these

views may selectively focus the audience for their essays, and by emphasizing the difference between rant and argument, I encourage students to
choose verifiable data as the basis for the body of their arguments. The
context of ecocomposition (rather than, say, women's studies or environmental ethics) freed me from any obligation to review the theories that patriarchal religions have historically functioned to obstruct social justice
and to legitimate environmental degradation: teaching ecocomposition allowed me to focus primarily on writing skills, with environmental studies
as a lens through which we examined essays. This focus allowed for a
much greater range of perspectives, both philosophical and religious, to
flourish among the students. Of course, diversity was present in the ex-
tremes: for example, there was even one student whose research paper concluded—despite my best efforts for interrogating the reliability of
sources—that "the use of nuclear power has been efficient and will continue to be so." At the other end of environmentalisms, the evolution of
"Nicole's" writing is a statement of ecocomposition's radical potential,
when taught with an ecofeminist pedagogical approach.

    In her introductory essay, Nicole explained that she was from a tiny
farming community in rural western Minnesota, where the primary crops
were wheat, soybeans, and sugar beets. Her first essay on place and identity
painted an idyllic picture of her family's farmhouse, the crops, the sense of
community in her home town, and that community's connections to the
land. For essay no. 2, when we raised questions about the economies of culture and nature, along with who is present or absent in these economies,
Nicole became more aware of the farmworkers in her community. From
this point forward, Nicole undertook a dangerous and compelling investigation that revealed her own community's complicity in exploitative labor
practices, the use of toxic chemicals, the construction of substandard housing, the differential treatment of whites and Mexicans in public recreation
and education, and the profits and costs that structured and mediated her
relationships with other residents and the land itself. For her research paper,
Nicole traced the history of Eastern European immigration, the poor treatment of those immigrants, their later rise to land ownership, and their subsequent treatment of the next wave of immigrants, the Mexican farmworkers. Though she explored the economics of sugar beet production and the
workers' wages, substandard housing, and education, I was most strongly
impressed by her use of anecdotal data in argumentation:

    In a community that is predominantly white, migrants and com-
    munity members always experience tension. Some community
    members can't seem to accept what the migrants add to the com-

munity. They provide hard labor for low wages, and live in housing that no white people would accept. It's frustrating to see how
community members react when the migrants arrive during the
summer. For example, I work at the local swimming pool and
many swimmers leave when the migrant school comes. The community tends to blame everything on the migrants: whether it's a
stolen bicycle or vandalism, the migrants were behind it. While
it's true that some migrants have been caught stealing bicycles and
other items of value, it's equally true of some local white residents.
It's no coincidence that we treat migrant workers like dirt.

Through her writing in class, Nicole reflected on various incidents from
her experiences as a lifeguard at the public pool, where white children regularly left the water as soon as Mexican children entered the pool. Nicole
also remembered the crop duster plane flying over her childhood home,
and her mother complaining about how the wet laundry on the laundry
line might have been sprayed; Nicole's mother would rewash the clothes,
but the workers who were sprayed in her family's fields could not stop to
bathe. As Nicole's final essay concluded, "Just like migrant workers don't
want to be abused or taken for granted, neither should our environment
be abused or taken for granted."

ECOFEMINIST INTERSECTIONS WITH ECOCOMPOSITION

The composition, feminist, and liberatory pedagogies that guided my ecocomposition course were inherently student-centered. From the start, the
writing classroom became a writing community. Working together, students explored the shape of ideas over time and in comparison with other
ideas, through the heuristic of particle, wave, and field lists. They analyzed
the complementarity of form and content in effective writing, and the relations between text and context for every essay they read or wrote. These
features of my ecocomposition course clearly intersect with some of the
central characteristics of ecofeminist thought: the emphasis on centering
previously marginalized perspectives; the concept of human identity as
fundamentally interconnected with other humans and animals as well as
the land itself; the emphasis on attentive listening; the necessary unity of
theory and practice; and the importance of context in ethical decision-
making. These intersections were not apparent to me, however, until my
initial experience in teaching ecocomposition.

Consistent with feminist and ecofeminist strategies for theory-building, the strategies I used in teaching ecocomposition allowed students to build their own environmental ethics through a process of exploration that included reading, discussion, analysis, and reflective writing. Rather than a "top-down" or "teacher-centered" authoritative approach to teaching environmental theories that is so often used in traditional environmental studies courses, my ecocomposition course foregrounded the structure of writing through which those theories were articulated, and encouraged student questions to lead our exploration and analysis. The ecofeminist emphasis on foregrounding previously marginalized perspectives (Warren) fits well with a student-centered approach to teaching, since for too long in traditional classrooms it is the students' own voices that are marginalized. With encouragement to analyze environmental theories in terms of each writer's audience, purpose, message, use of reliable sources, and structure of argumentation, and then to compare and contrast those analyses with the analyses for other essays, students were able to discover the political and ecological implications of various environmentalisms for themselves. This student-centered process of analysis and discovery seems inherently more democratic, and may also be more effective: people aren't radicalized by being fed the "correct" line, but by discovering radical insights for themselves.

Ecofeminist insights also influenced the sequence of essays and readings, developing from the individual writer's relation to place and moving outward to the economics of culture and nature, and the varying historical and contemporary perspectives on culture and nature within that homeground. In most cases, this strategy served to foreground human differences of race, class, and gender, and articulated ecofeminist ideas about the interconnected self as "political animal" (Sandilands 1997), an identity shaped through relationships with people, place, and other animals. In turn, the idea of the writer/self as interconnected is fundamentally compatible with notions of the classroom as a writing community, and with the emphasis on peer review groups.

Ecofeminism and ecocomposition alike have emphasized the importance of attentiveness to details, to looking carefully and seeing the thing in itself with loving attention, or "thou-ness" (Donovan). This attentiveness to detail and to strategies of perception can be taught through such heuristics as the particle, wave, and field listings. It can also be taught through field trips, community-based research, and experiential learning, all of which are well suited to the ecocomposition classroom. Breaking down dichotomies between academy and comunity or between theory and practice has been central to the work of ecofeminists, and is also practically a requisite component of ecocomposition.

The necessary unity of theory and practice in ecofeminism is echoed in the composition heuristic of treeing: students took apart polished essays by professional writers to uncover each essay's underlying "tree" structure of organization, and used treeing to organize their own essays as well. Used in conjunction with the analysis sheet, treeing allowed me to emphasize the ways that form, content, and context were interconnected in effective writing—just as theory and practice are interconnected in the best of ecofeminism. Ecofeminist theories have also emphasized the importance of context in addressing environmental problems and in responding to ethical problems. Marti Kheel's notion of the "truncated narrative" suggests that in order to understand and respond to environmental problems more effectively, ecofeminists should look for the whole ethical story, and the context in which a seeming environmental crisis may have occurred. This emphasis on context is compatible with composition theories that encourage analysis of the writing context for every essay, including a description of the writer's audience, purpose, persona, and message. According to the writing theorist Dona Hickey, According to writing theorist Dona Hickey, "If ideas and feelings give rise to particular forms, it can also be said that forms give rise to particular ways of thinking" (79).

This emphasis on the interconnection of structure and content in ecocomposition is analogous to the ecofeminist critique of oppression and its emphasis on the structures of oppression (Warren's "logic of domination") and the ways in which those structures are mutually reinforcing. While we know quite a bit about the ways in which sexism, racism, classism, speciesism, and heterosexism are interconnected and reinforcing in Western ideologies of domination, we know much less about the ways that the nature essay, for example, as a structure shapes writers' and readers' perspectives on human identity, on culture/nature relations, and on whose voices are authorized knowers. Ecocomposition has the potential to explore questions of structure and content, not just in the essay, but in other genres and genre hybrids as well. In this way, ecocomposition studies have the potential to contribute to an ecofeminist understanding of writing and writing pedagogies. How else might ecofeminist perspectives be articulated, other than the academic essay or the nature essay? Early ecofeminist anthologies, Léonie Caldecott and Stephanie Leland and Judith Plant, included not only the essay but the short story, poem, and art image, a diversity of form recently revived in Noël Sturgeon's guest-edited special edition of *Frontiers* magazine. But these are anthologies, where diversity of form may be achieved through simple accumulation: What kinds of diversity are possible within a single text? What diverse kinds of texts are suitable models for use in teaching ecocomposition? And how can the texts we choose for ecocomposition help to interrogate and inform our understanding of "nature"?

Drawing on the observation that diversity characterizes a healthy ecosystem, ecofeminists and other radical environmentalists have noted the similarities between biodiversity and cultural diversity. In a democratic, ecofeminist classroom, one of the measures of teaching success will be the flourishing of diverse environmental perspectives. And from the perspective of liberatory pedagogy, democracy in the classroom is a necessary precedent to democracy in the community. Where else will students be able to develop and to practice the skills of democratic citizenship? Consider the social systems in which their first eighteen or more years of life are spent: the family (usually though not always heterosexual, patriarchal, and monoracial); the synagogue, church, temple, or mosque (all predominantly hierarchical); and the schools and colleges (again, predominantly hierarchical). Hierarchical authoritative systems and institutions teach obedience to authority, define whose identity will be seen as authoritative, and define free choice as the selection among predetermined and restricted alternatives (Coke or Pepsi and Democrat or Republican). Freedom and democracy mean much larger things, such as questioning the shape of choices, the structure and distribution of power and authority, the participatory process of decision making. These skills can and must be practiced in the classroom if they are to be used in the larger society. Developing an ecological, economic, and political citizenship can be encouraged through ecofeminist pedagogies that examine the construction of essays as well as identities, the economies of course evaluation as well as of culture and nature, the social construction and multiple locations of knowledge, and the shape of power and decision making in the classroom.

An ecofeminist pedagogical approach to teaching ecocomposition has the potential to encourage a healthy diversity of environmentalisms in the classroom, and to teach students an appreciation for diversity that can prepare educated citizens to shape and participate in a multicultural, democratic, and ecological society. It is this potential, I believe, that is ecocomposition's strongest appeal.

NOTES

1. Ostensibly inspired by the new physics of light, these lists examine a topic or object in itself ("particle"), the topic and its development over time ("wave"), and the topic in comparison to others like it ("field").

2. For more current developments in feminist pedagogy, see bell hooks, *Teaching to Transgress* and Frances A. Maher and Mary Kay Thompson Tetreault, *The Feminist Classroom.*

3. This strategy has been trivialized in the backlash against feminism, but the effects of rearranging the tangible shape of power as articulated through seating arrangements should not be underestimated. Recently, I asked for such a rearrangement in seating at a local Forest Practices Board meeting, with excellent results: placing the citizens face-to-face with representatives from industry and county government encouraged more citizen participation than at the three preceding meetings, and led to discussions and decisions that reflected citizen requests for more environmentally and economically sustainable forest practices.

WORKS CITED

Anderson, Chris, and Lex Runciman, eds. *A Forest of Voices: Reading and Writing the Environment.* Mountain View, CA: Mayfield, 1995.

Bunch, Charlotte, and Sandra Pollack, eds. *Learning Our Way: Essays in Feminist Education.* New York: Crossing Press, 1983.

Caldecott, Léonie, and Stephanie Leland, eds. *Reclaim the Earth: Women Speak Out for Life on Earth.* London: Women's Press, 1983.

Culley, Margo, and Catherine Portuges, eds. *Gendered Subjects: The Dynamics of Feminist Teaching.* Boston: Routledge, 1985.

Donovan, Josephine. "Ecofeminist Literary Criticism: Reading the Orange." In Gaard and Murphy. 74–96.

Elbow, Peter. *Writing Without Teachers.* New York: Oxford University Press, 1973.

Flower, Linda. *Problem-Solving Strategies for Writing.* Ft. Worth, TX: Harcourt, 1981; Repr. 1993.

———. "Writer-Based Prose: A Cognitive Basis for Problems in Writing." *College English* 41 (1979):19–37.

Freire, Paolo. *Pedagogy of the Oppressed.* Trans. Myra Bergman Ramos. New York: Continuum, 1970.

Gaard, Greta. *Ecological Politics: Ecofeminists and the Greens.* Philadelphia: Temple University Press, 1998.

———. "Toward a Queer Ecofeminism." *Hypatia* 12:1 (Winter 1997):114–37.

———, and Patrick D. Murphy, eds. *Ecofeminist Literary Criticism: Theory, Interpretation, Pedagogy.* Urbana; University of Illinois Press, 1998.

Hairston, Maxine C. *Successful Writing: A Rhetoric for Advanced Composition.* New York: Norton, 1981.

Hickey, Dona J. *Developing a Written Voice.* Mountain View, CA: Mayfield Publishing Company, 1993.

hooks, bell. *Teaching to Transgress.* New York: Routledge, 1994.

Kheel, Marti. "From Heroic to Holistic Ethics: The Ecofeminist Challenge." *Ecofeminism: Women, Animals, Nature.* Ed. Greta Gaard. Philadelphia: Temple University Press, 1993. 243–71.

Maher, Frances A., and Mary Kay Thompson Tetreault. *The Feminist Classroom.* New York: Basic, 1994.

McDowell, Michael. "Talking about Trees in Stumptown: Pedagogical Problems in Teaching EcoComp." Paper Presentation at ASLE's First Biennial Conference, Colorado State University, Ft. Collins. June 1995.

Murphy, Patrick D. *Literature, Nature, and Other: Ecofeminist Critiques.* Albany: State University New York Press, 1995.

Murray, Donald. "Writing as Process: How Writing Finds Its Own Meaning." *Eight Approaches to Teaching Composition.* Eds. Rimothy R. Donovan and Ben W. McClelland. Urbana, IL: NCTE, 1980. 3–20.

Plant, Judith, ed. *Healing the Wounds: The Promise of Ecofeminism.* Philadelphia: New Society Press, 1989.

Plumwood, Val. *Feminism and the Mastery of Nature.* New York: Routledge, 1993.

———. "Has Democracy Failed Ecology? An Ecofeminist Perspective." *Environmental Politics* 4 (Winter 1995):134–68.

Sandilands, Catriona. "From Natural Identity to Radical Democracy." *Environmental Ethics* 17 (Spring 1995):75–91.

———. "Wild Democracy: Ecofeminism, Politics, and the Desire Beyond." *Frontiers* 18:2 (1997):135–56.

Sturgeon, Noël. Guest ed. "Special Issue: Intersections of Feminisms and Environmentalisms." *Frontiers* 18:2 (1997).

Warren, Karen J. "The Power and The Promise of Ecological Feminism." *Environmental Ethics* 12(Summer 1990):125–46.

Ecology and Composition Studies:

A Feminist Perspective on Living Relationships[1]

Colleen Connolly
University of South Florida
Tampa, Florida

In recent years *difference* has become a key concept in composition studies.[2] Writing teachers have introduced into the classroom discussions of, and writings about, issues of race, class, gender, sexuality, physical ability, age, and so forth to interrogate the social nature of producing and communicating knowledge. Such epistemological projects are not meant to focus on the foreign, the remote, and the exotic; instead, they work to develop strategies that examine students' meaningful, probable, and various encounters with others.[3] Though this kind of curriculum has been called into question by Julie Drew who claims that "it is fast becoming a dominant discourse," Wendy Hesford argues that multicultural education is neither about initiating students into the logic of dominant discourses nor about simply celebrating diversity. Rather, it is about teaching students how to investigate official and unofficial discourses and the power structures that they enact. For Hesford, multicultural curricula should not be based on appeals to an uncritical mass of differences. On the contrary, they should "seek to enable students to recognize the limits of their self-positioning and worldviews, to practice critical citizenship, and to develop critical awareness of the power of discourse instead of being subsumed by it" (138).

Providing students with opportunities to question the many ways in which their differences affect and are affected by both the material and the symbolic realities of their lives, Min-Zhan Lu, for example, often bases her pedagogy on sequenced reading and writing assignments that examine the "political uses and abuses of personal experience" (239). For Lu, it is imperative that composition teachers identify the many ways in which differences define us, not to privilege particular positions or experiences but rather to teach students to reflect on the connections between various systems of oppression in order to imagine ways of altering those systems of oppression. Because I support and often draw on the work of composition scholars such as Lu and Hesford, I would like to extend a logic present in their pedagogies: the need and value of teaching and communicating a diverse humanity. More specifically, since *diversity* is an important and critical term for the way in which we think about and act in the world, I want to suggest that composition studies expands its notion of diversity—of society as an immensely complex global system, in which power, matter, and ideas interact—to include the natural world, that is, when composition teachers ask students to think and write critically about their and others' relation to the social world, we should also ask them to examine their and others' relation to, and understanding of, the natural world.[4]

Asking composition studies to draw on ecological theories in addition to a wide range of language and cultural theories and practices, I want to suggest that we consider a writing curriculum that examines how our relationship to the natural world, like our relationship to each other and to the social world, is based on the values, discourses, and institutional practices that shape and maintain our realities. Such a curriculum seeks to educate an awareness that we have reached an age of environmental limits, a time when the consequences of human actions are damaging the planet's basic life support systems. Toxic waste, pesticides, and herbicides seep into groundwater, marshes, bays, and oceans, polluting the earth's circulatory system. Tropical rainforests and woodland forests are cut down at alarming rates, altering air quality, atmospheric temperatures, and ozone layers. Entire species of plants and animals become extinct each day. Indeed, we are approaching a moment in history when the survival and extinction of species may well delimit our future. As the earth's burgeoning human population strives for a steadily rising technological standard of living, the natural world is being brutalized to build a dizzying blend of artificial environments—villages, housing developments, parking lots, roads, factories, shopping malls, schools, parks, gardens, golf courses, and croplands. Most people living in North America, however, give little thought to the natural world because we are increasingly estranged from the workings of the ecology.[5] Nearly half of us live in urban settings, and that figure continues to grow.[6] Tucked away in our homes and offices, removed from the natural world by beautifully manicured lawns and asphalt pavements, nourished on bottled water and shrink-wrapped foods, and blanketed under the progressive promise of a future that will improve the quality of our lives, it is very easy (if not necessary) to lose sight of our reliance on plants, animals, insects, and microbes, as well as on the cyclic processes they drive. Without a more informed and direct relation to the workings of the natural world, perceptions of nature are often lessened to "the world outdoors." As Yvonne Baskins observes, "Nature in a city can too quickly be reduced to ranks of imported trees lining our boulevards, pets, exotic zoo animals, and gardens of wondrous flowers assembled at whim into unlikely 'communities' plucked from every continent—African daisies nestling at the foot of South American bougainvilleas and Australian eucalyptus" (9). Therefore, it is necessary for humans to forge a relationship to the earth, to point the way to the possibility of an ecologically way of life.

If we follow the advice of ecological arguments that tell us to change our ways of being in the world or face global desolation, we must realize that current environmental problems are largely of our own making, are the consequences of our life-styles and by-products of culture, and thereby alterable constructs. To understand how we might teach ourselves and students to question the many ways in which our lives affect and are affected by the ecology, I want to examine how the natural world functions as both a biospheric event and as a discursive category in the next section of this essay. From there, I offer an ecofeminist pedagogy that aims to examine and think about the discursive and cultural practices that define the relations among individuals, society, and nature—providing students with opportunities to write environmentally conscious essays that locate a diverse humanness within an extended community of other life forces and ecologies.[7] Ultimately, my efforts here can be read as an attempt to work effectively to integrate the natural world and composition studies, for the emerging paradigm makes possible an understanding of ecological perspectives on living relationships, a sense that each item in a web of connections is necessary for the viability of existence.

ECOLOGY: BIOSPHERIC EVENT AND DISCURSIVE PRACTICE

Most of those attempting to understand the ecology crisis, like those attempting to understand the workings of postmodern society, see Western civilization—with its assumptions of progress in knowledge, reason, technology, the arts and the economy—as oppressive. Postmodern theorists such as Heidegger, Foucault, Haraway, Derrida, and Lyotard, for example, call into question the destructive tendencies of an idea of progress, providing considerable insight into the workings of power in language. What they make clear is that ideology produces and in turn is produced by the economic and political arrangements in a given society. Foucault's *Madness and Civilization,* for instance, illustrates the way in which Western society has thought about and treated mental illness. Madness, he demonstrates, from the Middle Ages on, has been defined by its opposition to what society deems reasonable. With this kind of argument, Foucault examines what might once have seemed to be an unproblematic concept into something that is both thoroughly historical and political. In addition, his work illustrates how concepts draw on the ideas and norms of the society into which they are born, socialized, and educated. People living in a given period construct a term in ways that give meaning to their own lives.

Though Foucault may not have been thinking about the workings of the natural world in his writings, his ideas help us understand how, as a discursive category, *nature* becomes meaningful within a logic of structures by which social relations are made intelligible. To talk of nature, then, is to invoke complex frameworks of concepts based on metaphors negotiated and sustained by a large number of social institutions, which are in turn sustained by political and economical institutions and processes at different local, national, and global levels. As Raymond Williams' "Ideas of Nature" makes explicit, contemporary treatment of, and relationship to, the workings of the natural world has been shaped by a Western European ideology. His essay, which is written as a conventional historical narrative, notes that early cultures initially thought of nature in terms of spirits or gods who embody or direct the wind or the sea or the forest or the moon. In these images, nature is a multitude of forces that act upon human inhabitants of the earth. According to Williams, at some point, though, the idea of nature becomes a monotheistic creation narrative that illustrates an all-powerful and loving God who brings into being light and darkness, the universe's heavenly bodies, and the earth with all its plants, animals, birds, and fish. In this narrative, God also creates Adam and, as an afterthought, Eve to keep man from being lonely. Furthermore, since man is made in God's image and works to advance God's word, he becomes the caretaker and supreme being of the earth and all that the earth is meant to represent.

Although Williams does not say it, the message of this creation story becomes the foundation from which a Western, anthropocentric, progressive logic sees life in either/or, self/other, mind/body dualisms. Within this logic, the human world is constructed over and against the natural world as well as women's lives. More importantly, man's "God-given rights" guarantee him the power of "mastery," the destruction of nature, and the domination of women in Western rationalistic, scientific, and industrial societies. As Carolyn Merchant's *Death of Nature* argues, between the sixteenth and seventeenth centuries the image of a God-created earth gave way to a mechanistic worldview in which nature was reinvisioned as dead and passive, to be dominated and controlled by man. The scientific revolution of the sixteenth and seventeenth centuries, according to Merchant, reconceptualized reality as a machine rather than as a living organism, which accelerated both the exploitation of human resources and women. In addition, the scientific revolution brought about an idea that science can reflect and explain the world. Gone is the teleological explanation, replaced by man's ability to think and rationalize in an autonomous human-centered form of objective consciousness. What is important to note about this change in thought is nothing else in existence possesses mind; the mind becomes disembodied and the body/nature becomes mindless: the natural world—including other animate life—is seen as an inert object to be analyzed, controlled, and manipulated. Furthermore, this line of thinking, which gives primacy to the mind and rejects the body, condemns women, who are identified by their association with the body.

As Merchant's work illustrates, the ideas that emerge during the scientific revolution of the sixteenth and seventeenth centuries provide the underpinnings of our contemporary concepts of the natural world and women. What I want to do in the next section of this essay, then, is consider an ecofeminist pedagogy that addresses the underlying phallocentrism of nature, especially ideas of mastery and destruction. My goal is modest but suggestive: I want to consider theoretical points of intervention among ecofeminism and composition studies in the interest of developing classroom discussions and writing assignments that make explicit the relationship between the exploitation of nature and the domination of women. Donald A. McAndrew's "Ecofeminism and the Teaching of Literacy" attempts to develop such a curriculum. Based on the premise that the exploitation of people is linked to the exploitation of nature and that the ending of the former is a precondition for the ending of the latter, McAndrew wants to advance a literacy about the ecology that critically examines the ways in which patriarchal paradigms dominate nature and our place within it. Though I agree with and endorse such a curriculum, I think that in order to realize the potential of McAndrew's claims, we need to understand the natural world both as a potentially catastrophic biospheric event and as a discursive category. As Julie Drew's article in this volume illustrates, social issues of domination and a strategy for change are particularly significant in the ecological feminist movement where life-style politics are linked to fundamental questions about the future viability of the planet. In order to make the necessary changes to sustain our lives, critiques of the ecology must be feminist because if they are anything less, we risk the same destructive patters of our current patriarchal-hierarchical system in which certain things and people are valued over others (i.e., men over women, First World over Third, north over south, white over black, humans over nonhumans, and society over nature).[8] If we take seriously—and I think that we should—Judith Plant's idea that making connections between feminism and ecology "enables us to step outside the dualistic, separated world into which we were all born" (5), then teaching students to read ecological concerns through a feminist lens has the potential to make visible how our relations with each other are reflected in our relations with the natural world. This realization is a necessary step in changing not only the conditions of our material lives but also the environment in which we live. More importantly, it offers composition studies a theory to teach students to think differently about the living process of transforming the relations among individuals, society, and nature.

A FEMINIST PERSPECTIVE ON LIVING RELATIONSHIPS

As a methodological stance, ecofeminism has shown ways in which ecology, understood in its broadest terms, is a feminist issue. Susan Griffin, for instance, contends that there are perceived similarities between woman and nature—such as passivity and life-giving qualities—that make them equally vulnerable to male domination. Ynestra King, with a different line of reasoning, proclaims that women's association with nature gives women a special stake in healing the alienation between humanity and nature, and eventually, in solving today's global environmental crisis. The difference of opinions notwithstanding, ecofeminist critiques of oppression do not merely focus on the binding relations between the oppression of women and the oppression of nature. Rather, they emphasize how the operation of one form of oppression is intimately interrelated with other forms of oppression. Sheila Collins observes that "racism, sexism, class exploitation, and ecological destruction are four interlocking pillars upon which the structure of patriarchy rests" (51). In a similar vein, Rosemary Radford Ruether claims that an examination of ideologies that support sexism must not overlook "the interrelationship of sexism with other structures of oppression, such as race, class, and technological power" (xi). In short, taking nature and women as its subject matter, ecofeminism aims to educate us to the idea that systems of oppression are intimately connected and mutually reinforcing.

In addition, the ideology of ecofeminism demands critical attention of, and opposition to, forms of dominance in which any part of the world, human or nonhuman, exists solely for the use and pleasure of any other part. This assertion may sound simple, but it challenges the tradition of Western civilization that places man's superiority over nature. Ecofeminists take as their starting point this relation of power, not as a means to urge us to be responsible for nature but rather to change the power dynamics that maintain dominance. Here ecofeminists draw on the better aspects of ecological science to emphasize the value of diversity, interdependence, sustainability, cooperation, and renewal. As many ecofeminists argue, *ecology* is a multidimensional concept that works both to sustain the differences in our lives and to recognize the interdependence of biodiverse environments.[9] Biodiversity, defined by Yvonne Baskin, is "an intricately linked web of living things whose activities work in concert to make the earth a uniquely habitable planet" (3). It constitutes a living ecosystem, which may be as small as a rotting log or as large as a redwood forest or mountain lake, which interacts with the physical environment in a specific geographic location. Species, of course, are the critical components in this system. If too many species from a forest are lost—the trees, the truffle-forming fungi on their roots, the insects that prey on tree-destroying pests, and the beavers that create ponds and meadows amid the woods—at some point the forest will cease to work like a forest (Baskin 8). Practically speaking, this means learning to live with all of the differences that are inherent and indeed necessary for humanity's survival and for healthy and stable ecosystems. For in the natural world, good health is sustained by a tolerance of diversity, and stability is a result of ongoing mutual aid between and among species. Ecofeminism, then, is not only about nature but rather about contexutality, about understanding our lives and our struggles in their broadest terms and forms. It is about reclaiming and reconstructing reality.

So how does one "do" ecofeminism in a composition classroom? Ecofeminism in the composition classroom works as a conceptual framework, an analytic methodology that is constantly aware of relationships—between humans, between humans and nonhumans—and the workings of power within and between these relationships. In this way, it becomes a means for action, asking important and tough questions about our environment and our relationship to it. The answers, however, may not be in agreement, which suggests, to me, a process that respects differences and encourages discussions of a range of praxis. Diversity of experience, like diversity of life-forms, is a necessary goal of ecofeminism. As Linda Vance notes, "There can be no single set of answers, no one portal through which to enter. To insist on a single ideology, or a single praxis, is to deny the tremendous complexity of the problems that centuries of patriarchy have created" (135). This diversity and complexity implies that ecofeminism, rather than being constituted through the practice of a single movement, depends on a series of alliances among and across a spectrum of differences.[10] By building common ground, ecofeminists build coalitions that begin to create a community in which differences work together for the common well-being of both people and place: "For if one thing is certain," writes Greta Gaard, "it is that women alone cannot 'save the earth'—we need the efforts of men as well" (5). To educate people to these ideas—the need for responsible cooperation with the land—composition teachers can implement a curriculum that examines simultaneously various ecological concerns, for instance, one may ask students to document the effects of environmental pollution and degradation on the lives of women and animals. Many ecofeminist writers note that toxic pesticides, chemical wastes, acid rain, radiation, and other pollutants take their toll on women, women's reproductive systems, and children.[11] At the same time, students may be asked to read how hazardous chemicals are often initially tested on laboratory animals to determine levels of toxicity. Juxtaposing these two practices may illustrate the ways in which women and whatever is associated with women (emotions, animals, nature, the body, and children) have been conceptualized historically in Western thought. In addition, composition teachers may ask students to document the racism and classism inherent in First World development strategies that have resulted in tremendous hardships for women, who are frequently the major providers of food, fuel, and water in developing countries.[12] Asking students to examine the poor quality of life for women, children, and people in the Third World, provides a means to demonstrate how systems of oppression are mutually reinforcing on a global scale.

Another ecofeminist pedagogy might include a historical approach to understanding our relationship to the environment. Carolyn Merchant formulates an ecofeminist framework for understanding how change over time is a function of complex interactions between the ecology of a place, human production and reproduction, and human consciousness. She proposes a conceptual model that consists of three nesting spheres. In the center sphere lies the ecological core, which constitutes the relations between humans, animals, plants, and physical objects and forces of a particular habitat at a particular moment in history. Interacting directly with the ecological core is human production (i.e., extraction or processing of "natural resources"). Surrounding these two cores is a sphere of biologic and social reproduction. This outer sphere represents human consciousness and ideology. The space between each core, what Merchant calls a "semipermeable membrane," allows for a passable interaction between them.

Merchant herself uses this model to describe environmental changes in New England from the precolonial period to the industrial/capitalist revolution of the mid-1800s. In the same way, it could be just as useful for composition studies to understand the so-called green revolution of this century, a scheme imposed by Europeans and Euramericans on the developing world, which significantly altered ecological balances, disrupted traditional social patterns, and led to sharp ideological conflicts. Nonetheless, an ecological/environmental approach to history could illustrate the affect of social and political changes on an ecosystem, emphasizing shifts in consciousness and/or in modes of production.

Yet another teaching strategy might study nature writing and environmental psychology to heighten our awareness of our relationship to the natural world. Nature writers such as Annie Dillard, Leslie Marmon-Silko, and Paula Gunn Allen are constantly probing, traumatizing, thrilling, and soothing their minds—and by extension those of their readers—in search of a natural consciousness. Both nature and writing for these authors require and contribute to their awareness of self and nonself. By confronting "face-to-face" the separate realm of nature, by becoming aware of their "otherness," each writer implicitly becomes more deeply aware of her own dimensions, limitations of form and understanding, and processes of grappling with the unknown. The verbalization of observations and reactions of the written word makes these authors (and others who write about the environment) acutely aware of the ecology. Dillard describes her process thus; "Seeing is of course very much a matter of verbalization. Unless I call my attention to what passes before my eyes, I simply won't see it" (30). As Dillard's quote suggests, putting observations into language helps people see better. Although I recognize that several of these authors have political agendas that deserve greater attention, my use of their works has been to offer a quick overview of the possibilities of using their writing to elevate a consciousness that may lead to behavioral and political changes. In this way, I prefer to view their works as epistemological, the human process of becoming conscious of the nonhuman environment—an implicit desire to know the truth about the world and a belief that we need this awareness.

The ecofeminist project of learning to live with our infinite differences is particularly useful in questioning Western civilization's destructive ways of being, strong fear of difference, and desperate need to control the world. Incorporating such a project into composition studies, students are exposed to the ways in which concepts of ecosystems, of natural processes, are central to our relationship to nature. As I have tried to suggest, concepts of nature are numerous and have been used to justify the degradation of nature and oppression of women. Learning to recognize the ideological assumptions and the hierarchical structures of power and domination that together that determine our relationship to each other and to the natural world can help us find ways to build alliances that will create a sustainable way of life for all inhabitants on earth.

NOTES

1. I am aware of the fact that the phrase "living relations" often carries a negative connotation within feminism. In psychoanalysis, for instance, it implies that the separation of the individual from the mother is a violent yet necessary development. Though the mother-child relationship has been traditionally viewed as "natural," we know that this relationship is the result of social formations. In *Patriarchy and Accumulation on a World Scale,* Maria Mies sees the logic of reciprocity (symbiosis) as basic to the reproductive economy: it is women's labor that most often produces something new, whereas the tools of modern instrumentalism are not necessarily productive for they have the power to appropriate "the abundance of nature" to coerce the complex productive capacities of women and other colonized peoples. In fact, Mies claims that men's relation to nature has most often been one of destroying life.

    Using the phrase here, then, I want to suggest that living relations also holds men accountable for life. In addition, and more importantly, it signifies the necessary living and life-sustaining interrelatedness of life on earth, at both the personal and social levels.

2. As Lynn Worsham reminds us, we are at a particular moment in history in which writing and teaching "must make difference its by-word" (330). In a similar vein, Min-Zhan Lu argues that composition teachers must develop curricula in which "differences can and must engage one another" (251).

3. For a discussion on postmodern ethics vis-à-vis encounters with the Other, see Gary A. Olson.

4. When I evoke the description "natural world" I am speaking about an array of biodiverse organisms that not only sustain but are also sustained by an intricately linked web of living things whose activities work together to make the earth a habitable planet. See Yvonne Baskin (4–5) and Carolyn Merchant (xxiii–xxiv).

5. I realize that concepts like North and West posit a false geographic privilege, for there are wealthy societies in the South (Australia and New Zealand) and in the East (Japan). Such a geographic distinction also ignores the inequities within particular societies: not everyone in rich countries is rich nor is everyone living in a poor country poor. Following Mary Mellor, I will generally use the term *West* to represent European culture and *North* to represent the global capitalist economy and internationally dominant nation-states.

6. North America and Europe were more than half urban by midcentury, and the shift of people from the countryside into the cities is increasing across Asia, Africa, and Latin America. By the year 2025, it is estimated that 60 percent of the world's population will reside in cities, increasingly removed from the natural settings that sustain us. See Baskin (13).

7. When I evoke the idea of thinking differently, I am drawing on Rosi Braidotti's efforts to imagine the activity of thinking differently. For Braidotti, thinking is an active state that opens up unsuspected possibilities of life and action. It is a way of being in the world that is committed to the task of subverting conventional views and representations of human subjectivity, especially female.

8. In the vernacular, "patriarchy" refers to the male-dominated system of social relations and values, and should be distinguished from "hierarchy," which refers to relationships of command and obedience enforced by (patriarchal) social structures and institutions. For a discussion of these different meanings, see Gerda Lerner and Mies.

9. It is an ecological axiom that stability in an ecosystem is a function of diversity in that ecosystem. See Andrea Dobson (25). See also Mies and Vandana Shiva who write;

> Within a limited planet, there can be no escape from necessity. To find freedom does not involve subjugating or transcending the "realm of necessity," but rather focusing on developing a vision of freedom, happiness, the "good life" within the limits of necessity, of nature. We call this vision the subsistence perspective, because to "transcend" nature can no longer be justified, instead, nature's subsistence potential in all its dimensions and manifestations must be nurtured and conserved. Freedom *within* the realm of necessity can be universalized to all; freedom *from* necessity can be available to only a few (8).

10. For useful explorations of alliance building and commitments from women to work together across differences see Childers and hooks, Hirsch and Keller, Jakobsen, Reagon, and Worsham.

11. See Petra and Timberlake and Thomas.

12. See Mies.

WORKS CITED

Baskin, Yvonne. *The Work of Nature: How the Diversity of Life Sustains Us.* Washington, DC: Island Press, 1997.

Birkeland, Janis. "Ecofeminism: Linking Theory and Practice." *Ecofeminism: Women, Animals, Nature.* Ed. Greta Gaard. Philadelphia: Temple University Press, 1993. 13–59.

Braidotti, Rosi. *Nomadic Subjects: Embodiment and Sexual Difference in Contemporary Feminist Thought.* New York: Columbia University Press, 1994.

Childers, Mary, and bell hooks. "A Conversation about Race and Class." *Conflicts in Feminism.* Eds. Marianne Hirsch and Evelyn Fox Keller. New York: Routledge, 1990. 60–81.

Dillard, Annie. *Pilgrim at Tinker Creek.* New York: Harper Perennial, 1974.

Dobson, Andrew. *Green Political Thought.* 2nd. ed. New York: Routledge, 1995.

Drew, Julie. "Re-Envisioning Composition's Radical Scholarship: Ideology, Disciplinarity, and Feminist Standpoint Theory." Ph. D. diss., University of South Florida, 1997.

Foucault, Michel. *Madness and Civilization: A History of Insanity in the Age of Reason.* Trans. Richard Howard. New York: Vintage, 1988.

Gaard, Greta. "Living Interconnections with Animals and Nature." *Ecofeminism: Women, Animals, Nature.* Ed. Greta Gaard. Temple: Temple University Press, 1993. 1–12.

Griffin, Susan. *Women and Nature: The Roaring Inside Her.* San Francisco: Harper, 1978.

Hesford, Wendy. "Writing Identities: The Essence of Difference in Multicultural Classrooms." *Writing in Multicultural Settings.* Eds. Carol Severino, Juan C. Guerra, and Johnella E. Butler. New York: Modern Language Association, 1997. 113–49.

Hirsch, Marianne, and Evelyn Fox Keller, eds. *Conflicts in Feminism.* New York: Routledge, 1990.

Jakobson, Janet R. *Working Alliances and the Politics of Difference.* Bloomington: Indiana University Press, 1998.

King, Ynestra. "The Ecology of Feminism and the Feminism of Ecology." *Healing the Wounds: The Promise of Ecofeminism.* Ed. Judith Plant. Philadelphia: Between the Lines, 1989. 18–28.

Lerner, Gerda. *The Creation of Patriarchy.* Oxford: Oxford University Press, 1986.

Lu, Min-Zhan. "Reading and Writing Difference: The Problematic of Experience." *Feminism and Composition Studies: In Other Words.* Eds. Susan C. Jarratt and Lynn Worsham. New York: Modern Language Association, 1998. 239–51.

McAndrew, Donald A. "Ecofeminism and the Teaching of Literacy." *CCC* 47 (1996): 367–82.

Mellor, Mary. *Feminism and Ecology.* New York: New York University Press, 1997.

Merchant, Carolyn. *The Death of Nature: Women, Ecology, and the Scientific Revolution.* San Francisco: HarperCollins, 1979.

———.*Ecological Revolutions: Nature, Gender, and Science in New England.* Chapel Hill: University of North Carolina Press, 1989.

Mies, Maria. *Patriarchy and Accumulation on a World Scale: Women in the International Division of Labour.* London: Zed Books, 1986.

———, and Vandana Shiva. *Ecofeminism.* London: Zed Books, 1993.

Olson, Gary A. "Encountering the Other: Postcolonial Theory and Composition Scholarship." *JAC: A Journal of Composition Theory* 18 (1988): 45–55.

Petra, Kelly. "Women and Global Green Politics: A Call for the Formation of a New Political Party in the United States." *Woman of Power* 20 (1991): 24–25.

Plant, Judith, ed. *Healing the Wounds: The Promise of Ecofeminism.* Toronto: Between the Lines, 1989.

Reagon, Bernice Johnson. "Coalition Politics: Turing the Century." *Home Girls: A Black Feminist Anthology.* Ed. Barbara Smith. New York: Kitchen Table, Women of Color Press, 1983. 356–68.

Ruether, Rosemary Radford. *New Woman/New Earth: Sexist Ideologies and Human Liberation.* New York: Seabury Press, 1975.

Timberlake, Lloyd, and Laura Thomas. *When the Bough Breaks . . . Our Children, Our Environment*. London: Earthscan Publications, 1990.

Vance, Linda. "Ecofeminism and the Politics of Reality." *Ecofeminism: Women, Animals, Nature*. Ed. Greta Gaard. Philadelphia: Temple University Press, 1993. 118–45.

Williams, Raymond. *Problems in Materialism and Culture*. London: Verso, 1980.

Worsham, Lynn. "After Words: A Choice of Words Remains." *Feminism and Composition Studies: In Other Words*. Eds. Susan C. Jarratt and Lynn Worsham. New York: Modern Language Association, 1998. 329–56.

The Ecology of Writerly Voice

Authorship, Ethos, and Persona

Christopher J. Keller
University of Florida
Gainesville, Florida

ECOCOMPOSITION: A DESCRIPTION

Ecocomposition will, no doubt, become a term of contention in rhetoric and composition studies—held up for productive debate by some while entirely dismissed and misunderstood by others. Although little agreement exists about the meaning and implications of *ecocomposition,* most who make use of this term concur, at least in a broad sense, that we should take the "eco" quite literally in its reference to "ecology." This is to say, ecocomposition investigates *ecologically* the relationships between discourses and places, or, as Sidney I. Dobrin clarifies (in this collection), the relationships between "individual writers and their surrounding environments, between writers and texts, between texts and culture, between ideology and discourse, between language and the world" (11). Thus, the benefits that teachers and scholars of writing gain from such theories and pedagogies arise not only from ecocomposition as an *ecological* approach alone, but also from ecocomposition as it embraces and cultivates numerous *other* areas of critical inquiry. To quote Dobrin again, ecocomposition "is encouraged by not just ecology and composition, but by ecocriticism, cultural studies, ecofeminism, environmental justice, conservation, service learning, race and ecoracism, public intellectualism, and a host of other critical areas of study" (13). However, despite this methodological diversity, ecocomposition is primarily informed by rhetoric and composition studies, which itself thrives tremendously on interdisciplinarity.

At first glance, ecocomposition may look like an attempt by composition teachers and scholars to incorporate studies of the natural world into the writing classroom. This may be true in some cases but is, for the most part, a glaring oversimplification. In her essay (in this collection), Julie

Drew concentrates on ecocomposition's concern for *all* places in order to debunk perceptions that ecocomposition must always make *nature* part of its subject matter. She notes:

> We [compositionists] don't have to go far—indeed, we don't have to go anywhere at all—to think about the ways in which *place* plays a role in producing texts, and how such relationships affect the discursive work that writers attempt from within the university. In fact, the very idea of nature, or natural environment, in the composition classroom might arguably be subsumed within a larger notion of place that certainly includes, but is not limited to nature (57).

I agree completely with Drew that we must divest ourselves of the notion that ecocomposition *necessarily* deals with nature, but *this* essay, nevertheless, does examine relationships between students of writing and the natural world. However, that nature is involved here is, to some degree, coincidental, that is, nature is only *one* possible place from which to understand ecocomposition's interests and tactics, but it is a place I investigate, nonetheless, because of the outcome of a particular pedagogical endeavor in which I asked students to write an essay about nature. And from this pedagogical assignment and its outcome I shall consider *ecologically* useful ways to think about *voice,* a concept of great importance to teachers and scholars of writing. This essay, then, does not attempt to define an extensive or general theory of ecocomposition. Thus, my ideas about ecocomposition cannot and will not serve here as a grand theory. Instead, I analyze a specific cultural and rhetorical situation that shall provide a new way of understanding—and hopefully teaching—the ecology of the writerly voice in the composition classroom.

STUDENT WRITERS AND NATURE WRITING

A few semesters ago I designed for beginning writers an assignment that asked them to write about nature in the form of a "retreat narrative." According to Randall Roorda, retreat narratives

> exist at the larger genre's core [nature writing's], where observed nature borders on observing self. That this core is fluid, this border far from hard and fast, with trade between information, experience, and philosophizing free and open across it, is a recognition such writing exists in large part to explore. If an element of retreat

from what's human does indeed thread through and tie together the genre's disparate types, such retreat might best be figured as an encounter rather than an escape, conducted at this (shifting, or imagined, or negotiable) border of observed and observer. (5)

In addition, Sharon Cameron suggests that "to write about nature is to write about how the mind sees nature, and sometimes about how the mind sees itself" (351).[1] My retreat narrative assignment grew in large part from Cameron's and Roorda's ideas that writing about nature as well as "retreating" to nature offer students a way to explore and observe themselves in addition to the world outside, but the assignment also stemmed from my frustration that students too often see writing as something done in isolation—a task completed far away from social, political, institutional, and cultural forces. The retreat narrative, then, was also supposed to function as a way to help students understand that writing—no matter where it is *physically* composed—is always motivated by such forces and embedded in specific historical contexts.

Students were asked to visit a place they considered "natural" and, in the spirit of Henry David Thoreau and Annie Dillard, students were supposed to write their own narratives of retreat. However, because I did not want to *force* students to visit natural environments, I offered them the option to write instead a more research-oriented essay about a contemporary environmental problem.[2] This was a new pedagogical experiment, so I had no idea what to expect when the students handed in their essays. When I read through all of the completed assignments I was surprised not so much by their content but, instead, by which students wrote the retreat narrative and which chose the more traditional research essay. Thirty students were enrolled in two sections of the same freshman writing course. Almost half of these students (fourteen of them) were African American, while all the others were white. Fourteen students decided to write a retreat narrative—to experience nature up-close and personally—but of these fourteen *none* were African American. I wondered why most of the white students decided to write narratives of retreat while, on the other hand, *all* the African-American students chose the assignment that let them stay away from nature and write instead about the politics of an environmental issue.[3]

NATURE AND EXCLUSION

I first believed the African-American students' lack of interest in writing a retreat narrative stemmed from the scarcity of minority authors within the genre, and, in turn, that these students felt excluded from nature because of this. The students had all read minority writers such as Elizabeth Martinez, Robert Bullard, and Alice Walker in order to understand better the disparate racial and cultural attitudes about environmental issues, but the only two retreat narratives they studied—as just defined—were written by white authors: excerpts from Thoreau's *Maine Woods* and Annie Dillard's *Pilgrim at Tinker Creek*. A closer look at these is in order.

Thoreau is one of the most canonized American (nature) writers. Sections of *The Maine Woods* and *Walden* are present in numerous anthologies of American literature, great essays, and nature writing. In "Ktaadn," a travel essay from *The Maine Woods*, a simple pattern exists: Thoreau wants to lose the human and reach a pure and raw state of nature. Thoreau and his companions journeyed through the woods in order to "retreat" from civilization.[4] He writes:

> Nature was here something savage and awful, though beautiful I trod on, to see what the Powers had made there, the form and fashion and material of their work. This was that Earth of which we have heard, made out of Chaos and Old Night. Here was no man's garden, but the unhandselled globe. . . . There was there felt the presence of a force not bound to be kind to man. (69–70)

Thoreau was inspired by what he saw in this place, but he was astonished by more than the savagery and beauty of this realm. He was also bewildered by somehow having been transported *back* through time. This place was primeval, and it appeared to him as the original matter—"chaos" and "night"—from which God made the world. Thoreau, in addition, wrote in "Ktaadn": "Can you well go further back in history than this?" (79). As Thoreau moved across the earth, crossing the imaginary division that separates culture from nature—as he sees it—he felt as if he had moved into an earlier temporal space—a prehistorical, precivilized space.

When I read these passages in Thoreau's "Ktaadn," I am reminded of a recent television commercial for a sport utility vehicle (SUV), an advertisement that might help clarify these perceptions of the natural world. In the commercial a white man in a business suit walks up to the vehicle and while he stares at it, his suit slowly transforms into a pair of blue jeans and a flannel shirt, and his face becomes covered with a large, bushy beard. But before he climbs into the sport utility vehicle—before he goes off to conquer nature with this recent piece of technology—he throws his cellular telephone into a garbage can. Like Thoreau who was taken back to an earlier time by staring at the "primeval" wilderness, this man is taken back by simply staring at Japan's newest four-wheel drive. (I cannot help but wonder if the makers of the commercial see the paradox of their rhetorical appeal: escape the civilized world by jumping into a new SUV where one can experience nature by driving over it.) Nature, then, in Thoreau's essay and in the commercial is constructed as prior to civilization, a place where hairy mountain men live (in their all-terrain vehicles). In white discourse and imagination, this return appears safe; it may be "savage" at times, but Thoreau's essay (and the commercial) suggests that nature is awesome, thrilling, and even comforting—represented as a time and place away from the burdens of "civilization." Thoreau asks: "Who shall describe the inexpressible tenderness and immortal life of the grim forest, where Nature, though it be mid-winter, is ever in her spring, where the moss-grown and decaying trees are not old, but seem to enjoy a perpetual youth; and blissful, innocent Nature, like a serene infant, is too happy to make a noise, except by a few tinkling, lisping birds and trickling rills?" (81). Here nature is "innocent" and "serene," and it is blissful and peaceful. Because white people have always controlled structures and discourses of power in the United States, such returns to the past may seem to be innocent and pleasurable for them—perhaps like awe-inspiring, nostalgic vacations to visit ancestors. Such returns, however, even in discursive realms, may not be safe or pleasant for African Americans but troublesome and difficult instead.

Evelyn C. White's essay, "Black Women and the Wilderness," provides more information about African Americans' experiences with nature:

> I was certain that if I ventured outside to admire a meadow or to feel the cool ripples in a stream, I'd be taunted, attacked, raped, maybe even murdered because of the color of my skin. . . . My genetic memory of ancestors hunted down and preyed upon in rural settings counters my fervent hopes of finding peace in the wilderness. Instead of the solace and comfort I seek, I imagine myself in the country as my forebears were—exposed, vulnerable, and unprotected—a target of cruelty and hate. (317–18)

If some retreat narratives take readers to the past, we cannot assume that they will provide feelings of protection for everyone. It is necessary at times for all of us to come into contact with the past, with history—to know how we construct it and are constructed by it—but this does not make history, and nature, any less dangerous. When white people make a return to nature—a return to a more "simple," more "innocent" time and place—they may divest themselves of modern life, just as the man in the commercial grinned when he threw his cellular phone in the garbage. But as White demonstrates, African Americans do not necessarily divest themselves of anything when they make this return; instead, they may take on the terror of their history and feel excluded from natural places.

When *anyone* goes to the natural world, however, safety is always an issue. Many people—regardless of race, class, or gender—just do not want to face the discomforts that await us in forests, lakes, and even parks. Thus, I do not intend to essentialize the experiences of the fourteen African-American students in my composition classrooms by suggesting that, for some reason or other, they were all fearful of the assignment because a trek to "nature" would evoke some kind of cultural, historical, or genetic terror. Fear in some sense may have been part of this issue but cannot be the only explanation. That *none* of the African-American students chose the retreat narrative assignment does raise a curious situation that warrants further investigation.

NATURE AND SILENCE

Other than the occasional natural disaster that rips, roars, and screams, nature is often viewed as a "silent" place. For many people, on the other hand, cities and streets bustle and move and speak; they have characteristics and traits in and of themselves. Certain cities, for instance, are even thought to have individual "personalities"—The Big Apple, The Windy City, The City of Angels, and The Big Easy. Nature, though, is unified—undifferentiated—in the minds of most. Thus, nature often becomes merely that generic place outside of cities and towns, whose only voice speaks through pesky insects and dangerous animals.

Christopher Manes proposes that "Nature *is* silent in our culture (and in literate societies in general) in the sense that the status of being a speaking subject is jealously guarded as an exclusively human prerogative. The language we speak today, the idiom of Renaissance and Enlightenment humanism, veils the processes of nature with its own cultural obsessions, directionalities, and motifs that have no analogues in the natural world" (15). If nature itself is a silenced realm—other than a few well-voiced political debates about how nature should be *used*—then nature may well prove to be an unattractive place for African-American students who themselves already feel silenced and wish to be heard, those who want to position themselves better as writers, students, and persons. This is to say, because our society tends to silence nature, many students—especially African-American students—may see nature as an impractical, unimportant place where retreat narratives will only further silence or marginalize their already excluded voices.

Richard White's ideas about "nature and work" shed more light on the lack of credibility that retreat narratives receive in society and in the academy. He writes:

> Work once bore the burden of connecting us with nature. In shifting much of this burden onto the various forms of play that take us back into nature, Americans have shifted the burden to leisure. And play cannot bear the weight. Work entails an embodiment, an interaction with the world, that is far more intense than play. We work to live. We cannot stop. But play, which can be as sensuous as work, does not so fully submerge us in the world. At play we can stop and start. A game unfinished ultimately means nothing. There is nothing essential lost when recreation is broken off or forgone. Work left unfinished has consequences. (174)

Because narratives of retreat often focus attention on direct contact with nature—often constructed as that place where white people play—they too are viewed as a "leisurely" form of discourse. Annie Dillard, for instance, writes in *Pilgrim at Tinker Creek* (from which the class read excerpts): "A couple of summers ago I was walking along the edge of an island to see what I could see in the water, and mainly to scare frogs. Frogs have an inelegant way of taking off from invisible positions on the bank just ahead of your feet, in dire panic, emitting a froggy "Yike!" and splashing into the water" (7). Even though Dillard is making an important commentary about the way we see (and don't see), such writing easily lends itself to criticism that it is playful and frivolous, especially in relation to the "larger" social and political problems that face us all. Dillard says that for nature writers, "Your life is literature. It's all hard, conscious, terribly frustrating work. But this never occurs to people. They think it happens in a dream, that you just sit on a tree stump and take dictation from a chipmunk" (Trimble 32). Writing is, of course, work—a lot of work. Narratives of retreat may be "playful" at times—this gives them some of their greatest appeal—but this should not necessarily separate them from "work" as White sees it: as "an embodiment, an interaction with the world that is far more intense than play." Narratives of retreat are not mere trifles with language and nature, but they are works—writings—that toil within an intricately entangled web of important social, political, historical, and cultural relations.

Thomas Fox discusses "authentication" as a focal point in any consideration of African-American students' writing. It is "the means by which African American writers guarantee the 'credibility' of their text. . . . A central strategy of African American writers is to seek authorial control and legitimacy in the face of an audience that seeks to deny the very literacy that African American authors demonstrate. Demonstrating literacy, in this context, is an act of liberation" (107). If African-American students wish to authenticate their texts—to prove their texts' legitimacy as well as their own credibility as writers and students—then it is unlikely that they would have chosen the retreat narrative as the rhetorical form or genre most suited to evoke these feelings of authorial control and authentication, that is, because nature itself is in constant need of authentication and credibility in our capitalistic—and anthropocentric—world, writers who seek more authorial confidence and control will not likely write within a genre that appears to marginalize or silence their voices from the outset, a genre that is often not taken seriously by anyone, regardless of race.

The African-American students who didn't write the narrative of retreat, most likely, did not actually fear nature itself or feel uncomfortable by merely going there. I believe the fact that none of these students composed retreat narratives manifests, instead, the difficulties they had constructing the necessary *voice* to compose comfortably a "credible" or "authentic" essay for an audience they imagined as (mostly) white. However, the complicated and problematic nature of the term *voice* in composition studies deems that I describe more closely what I mean by this assertion, and, in particular, why ecocomposition should become part of this concern.

THE ECOLOGY OF WRITTEN VOICE

Debates surrounding the meaning (and even existence) of voice in rhetoric and composition studies are long and complex, and a detailed sketch of this history is beyond the scope of this chapter (see Elbow). I will, however, offer a model of voice that is closely aligned with notions of selfhood. Such a model, I argue, falls between the Western liberal humanist tradition that regards one's voice/self as stable, unified, and transcendent and the poststructuralist belief that sees voice/self as a collision of discursive forces, contingently positioned in language by various historical, economic, cultural, social, and political discourses—in short, voice/self as a heteroglossic vessel that contains no real essence or agency. This is to say, an individual's voice/self is never entirely fixed and stable, determined completely by the will of the individual herself, but one's voice/self is not, on the other hand, entirely *subject* to the effects of all its discursive encounters. Marshall Alcorn suggests, "The self is stable enough to resist change and changeable enough to admit rhetorical manipulation but no so changeable as to constantly respond, chameleonlike, to each and every social force. Rhetoric therefore needs a theory of the self that is sufficiently complex to conceptualize these features. A theory of rhetoric needs an understanding of the self that appreciates the relative stability of self-structure" (17). I agree with Alcorn that one's self—and, in turn, one's voice—is a fragmented and protean structure, but it must be, to some degree, coherent and stable in order for rhetoric to function in the first place, and, in addition, for one to construct any lasting beliefs. This notion of voice/self also implies that people have recourse, at times, to agency—some ability, that is, to resist discourses that attempt to impose change and oppression. This is all to say, I believe we can often, though not always, understand the relationship between texts and (actual) writers. Or, to put it another way, that we can to some extent examine the presence of (actual) writers and other textual voices in written discourse.

Nevertheless, to say that one's voice/self is at various times both changeable *and* resistant to change is not enough. Voice may also be broken down into three interrelated components: (1) the "actual" or "historical" author, (2) ethos, and (3) persona. I will sketch each one briefly. First, an actual or historical author means, simply, the person to whom we attribute authorship. Such an idea, of course, contradicts announcements of the author's death. Michel Foucault, for instance, claims that

> we find the link between writing and death manifested in the total effacement of the individual characteristics of the writer; the quibbling and confrontations that a writer generates between himself and his text cancel out the signs of his particular individuality. If we wish to know the writer in our day, it will be through the singularity of his absence and in his link to death, which has transformed him into a victim of his own writing. (117)

I do not wish to suggest, however, that the author is the one true "authority" in a written text, and that we have unmediated access to this person but, instead, I believe that the author is not entirely *dead* or even moribund; he or she may never be in complete control of texts but is, nonetheless, aworking and necessary component of textual voice—one that is partially detectable.

Ethos refers to the credibility that an author tries to achieve by appealing to his or her audience in certain ways. Ethos is often delineated into smaller characteristics: most notably, *phronesis* (practical wisdom), arête (virtue), and *eunoia* (goodwill toward the audience). But for the purposes of this essay, I would like to use ethos more generally as credibility constructed by the interchanges among author, discourse, and audience.

Persona refers "originally to a device of transformation and concealment on the theatrical stage" (Elliot 21). The term, though, has come to mean, more generally, the roles people play not dramaturgically but socially, politically, culturally, and discursively—most importantly though, the roles or masks people take on when they compose written discourse. This, of course, is closely related to the trope *prosopopoiia,* deriving from the Greek *prosopon,* which means "mask" or "visage" (see Mauss). Very few doubt the notion that writers wear certain *masks* when they write, however, the debate about such a term centers on whether we can ever get beneath the mask to an actual author's voice or whether we can only peel away the mask and find an endless number of other masks. These three components—actual author, ethos, and *persona*—help raise questions about how directly a text can provide access to an author's voice, how writers attempt and achieve self-presentation in their texts, and, more generally, how writers construct texts in the first place.

However, no matter how much one details these components of voices, they are not determined solely by, or self-contained within, the author; thus, by themselves they can never fully answer these questions, that is, voice is also contingent upon other factors: namely, audience and place. Audience, though, can never be taken too literally. D. B. Park notes that "However real the readers are outside the text, the writer writing must represent an audience to consciousness in some fashion; and the results of that 'fiction' appear in what the text appears to assume about the knowledge and attitudes of its readers and about their relationship to the writer and the subject matter" (249). The idea of a fictional or imagined audience is, of course, relevant to our understanding of how the students in my classes composed their essays, as well as how and why they chose their writing assignments, that is, the audience that all of these students "imagined" played some role in their decision to write or not write a narrative of retreat.

In addition, *place* is rarely looked at as an effect on how writerly behavior, unless the place from which the writer writes is somehow exotic or out of the ordinary. Occasionally one might note, for instance, how the prison cell affected Antonio Gramsci, how specific natural places inspired Wordsworth, or how the teeming streets of London influenced Dickens, but rarely do we look at, for instance, the effects and implications of writing within the university, the business world, or the laboratory—all of which seem like neutral places that have little bearing on writers. However, all places reflect and construct certain institutional, cultural, economic, political, and social power structures. Perhaps, this is the most important sites of investigation for ecocomposition, but it raises certain questions which, unfortunately, can never be answered completely, that is, place affects individual writers in different ways in relation to history, race, class, gender, and, a host of other forces. Thus, as ecocompositionists, we can never assume that a writer's habits will be consistent across all places nor can we assume that one place will affect all writers in the same way, but instead, we can only investigate the effects of a specific place in a specific rhetorical situation.

STUDENT VOICES

I would like to spend a moment relating some of the actual spoken voices of my students—both white and black—as they offered their opinions about this assignment, this rhetorical situation. I held conferences with my students after the assignment was completed, and I cite here five students (two white and three black) who I believe are most representative of the class as a whole. First, two white students, Mark and Stacy, gave responses about why they chose to write the narrative of retreat.

Mark admitted that he thought the assignment would be "easier" than the other because it seemed that the authors of retreat narratives "just went to nature and wrote about what inspired them"—as if nature acts as a muse for those with writer's block. He believed, in short, that this assignment—and its insistence on a first-person narrator—seemed "unacademic" and would probably prove to be less difficult than anything else he'd ever written because there is "no right or wrong answer in this kind of writing." He equated retreat narratives with merely *seeing* outward instead of *thinking, feeling,* and *observing* inward. Despite Mark's misunderstanding of the assignment's seriousness and relevance to the course, he always showed great enthusiasm and interest in the class readings and writings, and he wrote an interesting retreat narrative that described his encounters with alligators and their habitat around a local pond; he lamented that the alligators had been reduced solely to the status of university mascot and that most students could see them as nothing more. This led him to understand better the harmful racist stereotypes that occur when school and team mascots are named after Native American groups.

Stacy wrote her retreat narrative about birds and other animals she observed in a local park and contrasted them with animals she saw in a zoo. She reduced part of the essay to clichéd statements about animal rights, but Stacy's ability to show great care and concern for zoo animals demonstrated a maturity not often found in freshmen students. The introduction to her essay narrated an account of a tiger moved from its natural habitat to a zoo, but it is recounted through the tiger's eyes and voice; the rest of the essay, however, returns to the first-person singular. Stacy chose the retreat narrative because she saw the assignment as "a chance to do something different." She believed that there would be plenty of other opportunities to write "traditional essays" in her college career, and it would be "fun and exciting" to try the retreat narrative. She also admitted that the retreat narrative seemed to be "less serious" than the other assignment because the topic appeared so "open-ended and unstructured," and because she had to "rely on my own instincts and experiences." Mark and Stacy both admitted that they had previously spent little time in "nature," but both expressed that they enjoyed the assignment even though it proved more difficult than they first imagined.

I also spoke at some length with three African-American students—Sheila, Karen, and Michael—who chose *not* to write the retreat narrative. Sheila preferred instead to write about ecoracism, which, in general, refers to the practices of corporations that tend to dump waste products on, and pollute, communities whose inhabitants are primarily people of color. She found an article that gave statistics about the unfair dumping practices on small, predominantly African-American communities in Alabama, Louisiana, and Texas. She mentioned that the retreat narrative "didn't seem very practical," and that she was thinking in terms of her audience (which I had stressed in class) because she "wanted to write something that would interest a larger group of people. The retreat narrative was too personal, and no one would want to read about my personal response to nature." Others, she thought, would likely be more interested in a "larger, more important issue like eco-racism."

Karen wrote an essay about a local debate that centered on the University of Florida's desire to relocate an already thriving bat house in order to make room for a new dormitory. Coincidentally, the bat house was located within a hundred yards or so of the pond that Mark visited to write about alligators, but Karen used local newspaper articles about the issue to formulate her essay, rather than visiting the actual location. She told me that she wrote this essay because she was "truly interested in the subject more than anything else that would fit the assignment," but she also expressed that "coming from Miami" she had some reservations about "going into nature." Because she never actually visited the bat house, I don't think she even realized it was right next to one of the main roads running through campus.

Michael wrote about Americans' tendency to overconsume and waste certain foods. He was raised in a family of avid fishermen and discussed problems with the decline of Florida's fish population, which led him into other issues such as the large number of tourists and the rapidly expanding population in Florida. Ultimately, he contended that Florida needs to enact and enforce stricter game laws. Even though Michael had spent a lot of time outdoors, he asserted that "the narrative of retreat just seemed too strange, and it was not what I expected in a college-writing course." He believed his writing skills would improve if he wrote this essay instead of the retreat narrative because it was "more normal and more like the kind of writing I'll do as a journalism major." He too, in short, chose the assignment that came across as more practical, or pragmatic.

CONCLUSION

These student responses should help us understand better the kinds of voices they were trying to construct. In "When I Was a Young Soldier for the Revolution," bell hooks writes that "Appropriation of the marginal voice threatens the very core of self-determination and free self-expression for exploited and oppressed peoples. If the identified audience, those spoken to, is determined solely by ruling groups who control production and distribution, then it is easy for the marginal voice striving for a hearing to allow what is said to be overdetermined by the needs of that majority group who appear to be listening, to be tuned in" (55). The African-American students in my class must have felt, to some degree, that writing a retreat narrative would mean taking on a marginal "voice," the consequences of which would appear particularly detrimental and threatening to those whose voices already are marginalized in most situations. On the other hand, the white students—all but the two who didn't write a narrative of retreat—must have felt particularly comfortably writing such an assignment. Despite these differences, it appears that each group would have imagined the same audience, one primarily comprised of white readers. And, if both groups of students fictionalized a white audience then we may better understand how they attempted to voice themselves, and more specifically, how they tried to achieve credibility in their texts.

Every writer, in varying degrees, employs all three elements of voice—actual author, ethos, and persona. The degree to which a writer tries to invoke his or her own, actual self will vary according to the rhetorical situation. In addition, the kind of persona or mask an author takes on will also vary according to such contexts. However, we might assume that all writers are, in some fashion, always trying to appear credible, for instance, even a student who purposely tries to do poorly in his or her writing assignments may be attempting to construct credibility by appearing like a rebel, an archetype our culture often values. Nevertheless, the white students in my class appeared comfortable using the first-person in their retreat narratives. This doesn't mean, however, that they were entirely able to throw their actual, historical selves into their assignments, but, I believe, most tried to do so. Thus, they created personas they believed relevant to the assignment and audience, but these were personas based heavily and closely upon themselves—actual, historical authors. This is to say, an imagined white audience, perhaps, allowed them—as white students—to construct ethos through portrayals of themselves without having to devise various, complex personas. Most of the white students I spoke with saw the retreat narrative as less than a "serious" academic endeavor, but their feelings of credibility were not compromised by this.

The African-American students, on the other hand, were equally concerned with audience and credibility. However, in their research-oriented essays, they, it seems, tried to efface themselves from the essays entirely. Rarely, if ever, did any of these students employ first-person narration or refer to any personal experiences. The essays they wrote were attempts to appear "neutral" or "objective," that is, the African-American students' assignments were written in such a way that abolished blatant signs of the author's race, class, and gender. In their concern for ethos, each chose the more "traditional" assignment that would boost credibility by allowing them to wear the mask of an unbiased, scientific researcher and writer. Thus, rather an appeal to an imagined white audience, this appears more like an attempt to cover one's head and face entirely—not merely donning a mask.

Up to this point I have speculated about the relationships between student writers and a specific type of place—nature—in order to come to a better understanding of voice, a construction whose various parts function ecologically and balance themselves differently according to the specific rhetorical situation. I would like to close, however, by suggesting that we not only consider the relationships between writing and place but that we examine writing itself as a place, that is, writing *is* a place where certain things happen—a terrain whose topography is constructed by actual authors, ethos, personas, and audiences, as well as the physical or geographic sites in which writers write. However, we must keep in mind that all of these discursive components are shaped by additional factors such as gender, race, class, and other cultural, social, political, economic, and institutional forces. Ecocomposition, then, to speak broadly for a moment, surveys writing and maps its various contours. It attempts to understand the ecological balance that occurs among the various discursive elements I've discussed throughout this essay, components that gives every writing its individual shape and form—or, should I say, scenery or landscape?[5]

NOTES

1. Problems constantly emerge when one defines or uses the word *nature* because of its varied historical, cultural, social, institutional, and economic meanings. For the purpose of this essay I try to resist outlining a definition of "nature" in order to show how students themselves understand and define it. When I make reference to the word *nature*, it should be understood as the realm that students themselves are supposed to construct, identify, and define by making direct contact with what *they* understand as "nature." Thus, responses to the assignment were as diverse as the students themselves.

2. The assignment sheet for this assignment reads as follows: "In 750–1,000 words write one of the following essays: (1) Find a contemporary environmental issue that we have not discussed in class and write an opinion paper about it, that is, summarize the issue at hand providing specific information about this issue. You should also present different sides of the debate surrounding the issue and then offer your own position. Cite where you stand in relation to this issue and why you have these viewpoints and opinions. Relevant personal experiences, of course, are also helpful in providing an account of your position. (2) Write your own narrative of retreat. In this narrative, you should venture into an area that you consider natural or "nature." This may be a park, a forest, a lakeside, or whatever you choose. When writing, keep in mind Thoreau's statement in "Ktaadn": "Talk of mysteries!—Think of our life in nature,—daily to be shown matter, to come in contact with it" (71). This essay is your personal response to nature firsthand: what do you see, feel, understand, like or dislike, and, for instance, what significance do you perceive in this area for your community and your own life? Remember the types of things Thoreau and Dillard discussed, but make sure you don't emulate them directly."

3. It seems that gender would logically play a role in such a scenario. However, in this case it seems to be relatively inconsequential. The class was split pretty evenly along gender lines. Of the sixteen white students, nine of them were women, and of the fourteen African-American students, eight of them were women. Of the two white students who chose not to write a retreat narrative, one was male and the other female.

4. For more on this topic see Randall Roorda's *Dramas of Solitude: Narratives of Retreat in American Nature Writing*, chapter 2, "Going Out, Going In: Narrative Logic in Thoreau's "Ktaadn."

5. I would like to offer a word of gratitude to Roorda whose work in composition theory and pedagogy, nature writing, and retreat narratives in general provided me with initial interest, ideas, and directions for my own class instruction and research. I am also grateful to Sidney I. Dobrin and Cindy Ireen Key for their helpful suggestions and proofreading.

WORKS CITED

Alcorn, Marshall. "Self-Structure as a Rhetorical Device: Modern *Ethos* and the Divisiveness of the Self." *Ethos: New Essays in Rhetorical and Critical Theory.* Eds. James S. Baumlin and Tita French Baumlin. Dallas: Southren Methodist University Press, 1994. 3–35.

Cameron, Sharon. *Writing Nature: Henry Thoreau's Journal.* Oxford and New York: Oxford University Press, 1985.

Dillard, Annie. *Pilgrim at Tinker Creek.* New York: HarperPerennial, 1999.

Elbow, Peter, ed. *Landmark Essays on Voice and Writing.* Ed. Peter Elbow. Mahwah, NJ: Hermagoras Press, 1994.

Elliot, R. C. *The Literary Persona.* Chicago: University of Chicago Press, 1982.

Foucault, Michel. "What Is an Author?" *Language, Counter-Memory, Practice: Selected Essays and Interviews.* Ed. Donald F. Bouchard. Ithaca: Cornell University Press, 1977. 113–38.

Fox, Thomas. "Repositioning the Profession: Teaching Writing to African American Students." *Composition Theory for the Postmodern Classroom.* Eds. Gary A. Olson and Sidney I. Dobrin. Albany: State University of New York Press, 1994.

hooks, bell. "When I Was a Young Soldier for the Revolution: Coming to Voice." *Landmark Essays on Voice and Writing.* Ed. Peter Elbow. Mahwah, NJ: Hermagoras Press, 1994. 51–58.

Manes, Christopher. "Nature and Silence." *The Ecocriticism Reader: Landmarks in Literary Ecology.* Eds. Cheryl Glotfelty and Harold Fromm. Athens: University of Georgia Press, 1996. 15–29.

Mauss, Marcel. "A Category of the Human Mind: The Notion of the Person; The Notion of the Self." *The Category of the Person: Anthropology, Philosophy, History.* Eds. Michael Carrithers, Steven Collins, Steven Lukes. Cambridge: Cambridge University Press, 1985. 1–25.

Park, D. B. "The Meanings of 'Audience.'" *College English* 44 (1982): 247–57.

Roorda, Randall. *Dramas of Solitude: Narratives of Retreat in American Nature Writing.* Albany: State University of New York Press, 1998.

Thoreau, Henry David. "Ktaadn." *The Maine Woods.* Ed. Joseph J. Moldenhauer. Princeton: Princeton University Press, 1972.

Trimble, Stephen, ed. *Words from the Land: Encounters with Natural History Writing.* Expanded ed. Reno: University of Nevada Press, 1995.

White, Evelyn C. "Black Women and the Wilderness." *Literature and the Environment: A Reader on Nature and Culture.* Eds. Lorraine Anderson, Scott Slovic, and John P. O'-Grady. New York: Addison Wesley Longman, 1999. 316–20.

White, Richard. "'Are You an Environmentalist or Do You Work for a Living?': Work and Nature." *Uncommon Ground: Toward Reinventing Nature.* Ed. William Cronon. New York: Norton, 1995. 171–85.

Service Learning and Ecocomposition:

Developing Sustainable Practices through Inter- and Extradisciplinarity

Annie Merrill Ingram
Davidson College
Davidson, North Carolina

The different readings increased my interest in the environment and environmental issues, and therefore, I enjoyed our writing assignments . . . we always seemed to relate the global issues back to our community through community service.
>   —Student's Course Evaluation

Never give children a chance of imagining that anything exists in isolation. Make it plain from the very first that all living is relationship. Show them relationships in the woods, in the fields, in the ponds and streams, in the village and the country around it. Rub it in.
>   —Aldous Huxley, *Island*

Many institutions now offer environment-oriented composition classes, both at the freshman level and for more advanced writers. The variety of environmental readers and anthologies available likewise attests to the progress being made in environmental education. Building on these developments in making the study of environmental issues more widely available, we can further the efficacy of ecocomposition by considering not only *what* we teach but also *how* we teach. One way of taking ecocomposition a step further is to incorporate service learning into the environmental writing class. A service-learning component benefits not only students and teacher—in terms of greater motivation, productivity, and investment in the course—but also the wider community, while broadening the scope and contribution of the class in real, tangible ways.

I regularly teach a section of English 101 (first-year composition) on environmental issues with an environmentally related community service component, and I have found that service learning provides an ideal way of bridging the theory-praxis gap in the ecocomposition classroom. Ecocriticism and composition studies overlap in their emphasis on community interaction, whether it be preserving the biodiversity of an ecosystem, maintaining sustainable practices, encouraging collaborative learning, or building a composition community. These theoretical concepts also contribute powerful metaphors to the ecocomposition classroom experience. Students who work together outside class and in the community develop the trust and interactive skills that enable them to succeed in composition activities such as peer review and substantive revision. An interdisciplinary curriculum linked to extradisciplinary service opportunities likewise gives students a firm knowledge and skills base in environmental issues.

   8:30 A.M., Saturday. Few students are awake at this hour, let alone dressed and ready to go somewhere. A group of students from English 101-G: Environmental Writing gather in a dormitory parking lot and wait for the van to arrive. The weather is overcast, gray, and cold; the conversations focus mostly on last night's parties. Although the students are sleepy, they smile when I greet them with an overly cheerful "Good morning!" and ask if they have enough warm clothes on. Justin drives up in the van; we pile in and head off to the Catawba Lands Conservancy's Wildflower Glen nature preserve, a place where none of us has been before.

GETTING GROUNDED: THEORETICAL CONCEPTS

Ecocriticism, in its focus on both literature relating to environmental topics and critical approaches foregrounding environmental concerns and concepts, provides some useful theoretical principles for the ecocomposition teacher and researcher. While few studies (before this volume) exist on ecocomposition, there is a growing body of material on ecocriticism. In her introductory essay for *The Ecocriticism Reader,* Cheryll Glotfelty gives this definition: "simply put, ecocriticism is the study of the relationship between literature and the physical environment" (xviii). Similarly, one could define ecocomposition as "the relationship between composition and the environment." Such a definition, however, while it fairly represents the field's dual rhetorical and environmental components, fails to convey how ecocomposition's whole is greater than the sum of these two parts. Ecocomposition is as much an ideological practice as a pedagogical one; as I see it, one cannot teach an ecocomposition content divorced from an ecopedagogy—a teaching approach that considers the class' impact on its immediate and larger environments, from the paper and energy resources we use to the relationships and interactions we foster to the activities in which we participate, both during and outside of regular class hours.

The *eco-* in ecocomposition and ecopedagogy foregrounds, again quoting Glotfelty, "relationships between things, in this case, between human beings and the physical world. . . . [It] implies interdependent communities, integrated systems, and strong connections among constituent parts" (xx). In the ecocomposition classroom, students and teacher share in the responsibilities for learning, information dissemination, and progress; interactive exercises such as discussion, workshop, and peer review comprise the majority of classroom activity. Readings, conversations, extracurricular activities, and a variety of writing assignments contribute to the "integrated system" of the course as a whole. While the small size of most composition courses already enables "strong connections among constituent parts," the added commonalities of interest (in the environmental course content) and involvement (in curricular and extracurricular activities) further promote closeness within the group. By keeping ecology's central principle of interrelatedness at the forefront of course design and implementation, the ecocomposition instructor can create courses that not only teach students to write, but that also encourage them to become a more fully aware and active species of student and citizen.

We can offer a more fully integrated ecocomposition experience when we include service learning in the course curriculum. Service learning is a form of experiential education: students learn and develop, both personally and intellectually, through active participation in thoughtfully organized, meaningful community service. Service learning encourages students to learn outside the formal classroom setting; to make connections between their education and their ongoing personal development; and to become responsible, active, committed citizens of their community. A community service component benefits students, instructor, and the community in many ways. As students learn civic responsibility and attain greater awareness of environmental issues and their community, they also become more motivated, interested, and enthusiastic about the course. Ecocomposition students who commit to a service project write better papers, enjoy their assignments more, and develop a greater investment in both the subject matter and their own learning process. Teachers likewise learn more about the local community outside the institutional walls and, if they are already involved in environmental activism, are able to integrate their teaching work and service work. As one who uses service learning in my courses, I too have become more invested in them and more motivated. Doing meaningful and relevant work outside the classroom has enlivened and enriched my teaching of ecocomposition. For the community, the advantages of service learning are obvious: organizations and individuals provide opportunities and expertise, establish relationships with members of the nearby academic community, and participate in a mutual process of teaching and learning.

Ensuring this kind of mutuality is one of the basic principles of service learning. In order to be successful for all concerned, projects should meet community needs, where the target community, not the teacher or student, identifies these needs and initiates the projects. In the classroom, the service activity should be an integral part of the curricular learning, not ancillary to it; by providing regular opportunities for reflection and evaluation of service/learning links, teachers can ensure the relevance of the service-learning experience. Ellen Cushman, in a recent opinion piece for *College English,* argues for the value of service learning not only for students but also for faculty, particularly those who are considered or who consider themselves "public intellectuals": "academics who have grown weary of isolation and specialization and who hope their work might have import for audiences beyond the initiated few" and who "combine their research, teaching, and service efforts in order to address social issues important to community members in under-served neighborhoods" (329). Cushman includes principles of service learning in her description of what activist academics can accomplish:

> When public intellectuals not only reach outside the university, but actually *interact* with the public beyond its walls, they overcome the ivory tower isolation that marks so much current intellectual work. They create knowledge with those whom the knowledge serves. Dovetailing the traditionally separate duties of research, teaching, and service, public intellectuals can use the privilege of their positions to forward the goals of both students and local community members. In doing so, they extend access to the university to a wider community. Academics can reach these goals in two ways: service learning and activist research. (330)

Service learning and activist (or action) research are distinct extradisciplinary approaches, often seen as having distinctly different ideological origins and aims.

To some educators, "service learning" has negative connotations, both for those providing service (students) and for those receiving service (community members)—what Cushman identifies as a "liberal do-gooder stance" (332). Moreover, the word *service* might have religious overtones, remind faculty of dreaded committee work, or imply a hierarchical sense of noblesse oblige. Action research, founded in principles of mutuality, circumvents the server/served dichotomy: "When activist fieldwork is a cornerstone of the course, students and community residents can develop reciprocal and dialogic relations with each other; their relationship is a mutually beneficial give-and-take one" (330). Practitioners and advocates of "service learning" have begun to make the transition to activist research, not just in using the new terminology but in fundamentally redefining the impulses behind, and processes involved in, this form of experiential education. However, activist research is not always as easily incorporated into an ecocomposition course, particularly one for students at the beginning of their college careers. Successful action research projects are initiated by the community, often after a period of mutual acquaintance, asset mapping, and needs assessment with academics. Such projects require a complex variety of skills, including sophisticated (and ethically sound) methods of data collection and data analysis, by students who have either already learned these skills or who are learning them as one of the course's primary goals. For these and for other reasons, action research projects are often better served by students in courses whose main goals involve more than improved composition skills. That said, the ideological principles of activist research can and should be integrated into service-learning projects, enhancing their efficacy and helping to dismantle the implicit hierarchy of any form of "service."

While any course can accommodate service-learning components, those focusing on environmental issues are particularly well-suited for incorporating community-oriented experiential pedagogies. Ecocomposition courses, which generally have an inter- or multidisciplinary content and cover current issues as well as abstract concepts, can easily include service-learning activities focusing on the immediate campus community, the local city or town, or larger, even international, communities. Just as "environment" includes not just wilderness but also urban areas and the classroom, so too does "community" include nonhuman communities. Students in various sections of the service-learning ecocomposition courses I teach have worked on establishing an organic community garden, at a local land conservancy site, with the Sierra Club's Inner City Outings program, in shoreline and highway cleanup activities, for the state Public Interest Research Groups (PIRG), and in tutoring and mentoring programs (focusing on environmental education and activity). They volunteer their time at a nearby raptor rehabilitation and education center, help build drift fences for a reptile and amphibian monitoring and conservation project, and participate in water quality management and shoreline erosion research. On campus, they promote environmental awareness and education by participating in the recycling program, publicizing energy conservation strategies, and suggesting paper-reduction techniques to students, faculty, and staff. For possibilities farther afield, many schools offer "alternative spring break" trips to urban or rural environments, both in the United States and abroad; interested students and their ecocomposition instructor could participate in such a trip. If financial aid is needed to participate, fundraising should be made one of the course's experiential learning activities.

These example activities are grounded in sound pedagogical practices, yet they raise important and controversial theoretical questions. These projects can be viewed as anthropocentric: for example, intervening in raptors' lives by giving them emergency treatment and, if they prove unable to be returned to the wild, using them in education programs for humans. Building and maintaining trails at the Catawba Lands Conservancy directly interferes with the natural ecosystem of the Wildflower Glen site: even though they will be used for education purposes, do the trails ultimately support or undermine the organization's conservation efforts? The Inner City Outings program involves accompanying inner-city youths on outdoor activities such as day hikes and overnight camping trips; however, would these children be better served in programs that teach them to value their inner-city environment and to learn about the species that inhabit urban nature? To paraphrase a question by one of this volume's editors, is saving nature an anthropocentric project?

The question gets at the heart of using service learning in ecocomposition. As ecocritics and teachers, our objectives are primarily ecological, seeing everything as interrelated—yet "saving nature" suggests that humans have positioned themselves in a role superior to the rest of the environment, rather than as an integrated part of that whole. Service learning need not—indeed, should not—replicate the kinds of anthropocentric hubris and domination that have led to the current state of ecological crisis. Service learning, in contrast to service per se, tries to avoid such pitfalls by integrating the extradisciplinary with the curricular: by preparing students intellectually for their extracurricular projects beforehand and engaging them in thoughtful reflection afterward, service learning as a whole encourages students to analyze their attitudes toward the environment. Such analysis may seem to be ultimately anthropocentric, and here is the Archimedean Paradox of ecocriticism, Where do you find a place to stand outside of language itself? Is truly nonanthropocentric ecocriticism even possible? The medium of print and the vehicle of human language are inherently anthropocentric, even when the attitudes expressed therein endeavor not to be. This essay cannot resolve such fundamental contradictions, but I will suggest that at the concrete level, education is one of our primary tools for countering ecologically unfriendly stances and habits.

As an example, we can use education to develop a sense of interconnectedness by promoting the concept of sustainability. Going beyond environmentalism's focus primarily on physical or natural environments, sustainability also takes into account issues of social justice, economic viability, humane practices, and long-term implications and consequences. Sustainable practices—whether in agriculture, economics, politics, development, or pedagogy—consider the impact of humans not only *on* their environment but also *in* their environment. Preserving the rain forests, for example, is short-sighted at best and exclusionary and inhumane at worst if it neglects the economic viability of local rain forest communities. Social ecologists such as Murray Bookchin insist that "only insofar as the ecology movement consciously cultivates an anti-hierarchical and a non-domineering sensibility, structure, and strategy for social change can it retain its very identity as the voice for a new balance between humanity and nature and its goal for a truly ecological society" (60). Pedagogically, sustainability encourages learners (teacher and students) to consider the immediate as well as the long-term effects of issues and their proposed solutions. In the most obvious environment of the classroom, I encourage students to recycle outdated flyers posted around campus by printing their papers (final drafts as well as intermediate ones) on the reverse side. I promote respectful interactions and the use of inclusive language: behavior we should support in any course, but one whose import is underscored within a context of learning about sustainability.

Organizations such as Second Nature and the Center for Respect of Life and Environment (CRLE, a division of the Humane Society of the United States) promote sustainability in education, recognizing the fact that the "greening" of academia involves not only environmental curricula but also sustainable practices throughout education—courses, majors, research opportunities, and specialist faculty; ecologically sound buildings, landscaping, and transportation; an energy-saving ethos; nonoppressive forms of institutional investment; and nonhierarchical pedagogies and forms of governance—in short, a revolution in what currently constitutes most academic cultures. Teachers interested in learning more about educating for sustainability can visit these organizations' websites: Second Nature's www.2 nature.org, and www.starfish.org, CRLE's www.crle.org, and www.ulsf.org (the Association of University Leaders for a Sustainable Future).

Issues of social justice and environmentalism also intersect in the deep ecology and environmental justice movements. Students who read about the issues and policies of these movements learn to consider "environmentalism" within a larger context, one that considers social ecology as well as natural ecology. Giovanna Di Chiro, in considering "the convergence of environment and social justice," states that environmental justice provides a way of "redefining environmentalism" and "reinventing nature" (300, 310). A philosopher Arne Naess, originator of the term *deep ecology,* distinguishes between it and a "shallow ecology" concerned primarily with the immediate causes and solutions of particular environmental problems such as air and water pollution: "ecologically responsible principles are concerned only in part with pollution and resource depletion. There are deeper concerns that touch upon principles of diversity, complexity, autonomy, decentralization, symbiosis, egalitarianism, and classlessness" (95). One result of introducing students to broader definitions of environmentalism can be a wider range of relevant service-learning and action research projects: under this larger rubric, issues such as hunger and homelessness, racism, sexism, workplace safety, and unionization all become issues of environmentalist concern. As Di Chiro writes of a Los Angeles community's fight against the construction of a solid-waste incinerator in their neighborhood; it "also initiated a host of other community actions on issues such as housing, schools, drugs, and neighborhood security. These issues were seen by the activists to be as 'environmental' as those of hazardous waste, air quality, and land use" (299). While the fight against a solid-waste incinerator might be an unusual example of neighborhood environmental activism, the related issues are very familiar. Every community has issues in which environmental and social concerns are conjoined.

10:30 A.M. I stop raking for a moment to look at my watch and am surprised that time has passed so quickly. We arrived at the site over an hour ago and met Robert, one of the conservancy's most active volunteers. He gave a bit of history and then put us to work. Justin and Tom dig postholes at a spot where a small bridge will span a sharp dip in the trail; Sarah and Bethany shovel gravel into a wheelbarrow and transport it down the trail to fill in at the bridge site. Taleshia and Wendy and I grab rakes and begin clearing the trail of the leaves that have fallen during the autumn and winter. The work goes quickly and the students seem remarkably chipper. I can see tangible results of my labor, and I'm glad to be outside, moving, talking with enthusiastic young people.

REACHING OUT: PRACTICAL APPLICATIONS

Ecocomposition courses are by nature interdisciplinary, focusing not just on literary texts but also on works from disciplines such as biology, ecology, economics, political science, ethics, history, and religion. As principles of ecology and sustainability would suggest, the more diverse the (course) components, the richer and more effectively functioning the (classroom) environment. Writings from different disciplines and from interdisciplinary perspectives give students a broad-based introduction to environmental studies and to a variety of rhetorical models to emulate. In an ideal world, I would create my own anthology of essays, the best writing relating most specifically to the topics of my ecocomposition course. In my real world, however, I use ready-made environmental readers. Every major textbook publisher has one; I have used Melissa Walker's *Reading the Environment,* Scott Slovic and Terrell Dixon's *Being in the World,* and Chris Anderson and Lex Runciman's *Forest of Voices.* These anthologies cover a wide range of topics, authors, and essays, and all three contain useful supporting apparatuses.

My ecocomposition syllabi tend to be arranged by topic or theme, rather than by discipline or rhetorical mode. Since most essays combine various rhetorical modes—and since most writing assignments my students encounter will require them to do likewise—a theme-based, multidisciplinary arrangement provides the best coverage and range of examples. I begin with a familiar topic—place—and assign readings focusing on detailed observation and description of particular locales. Their first paper is a personal essay on a place they know well. Subsequent unit topics include wilderness experiences, environmental ethics, other species, environmental activism, and of course, the research paper (see the appendix for the full syllabus). Sequencing of assignments—where each paper builds on skills learned in the previous assignment—determines the order of units, which generally move from the personal, local, and familiar to more abstract, global, and unfamiliar topics. Short research papers develop students' skills in using the library and integrating different sources of information before they embark on the long research paper project, which is often linked, explicitly or implicitly, to their individual service project. Last spring, for example, a student who spent more than forty hours (twice the required amount) during the semester in training and volunteering at a local raptor rehabilitation center wrote a final research paper on the advantages and disadvantages of wild bird rehabilitation. In addition to her library research, she incorporated the wealth of knowledge she had acquired during her service work into the paper—and turned in a vivid, persuasive, and eloquent essay.

Complementing the interdisciplinary content is the extradisciplinary component of service learning. I initially jumped into service learning with little training and less knowledge of local opportunities; I participated in a semester-long faculty workshop on service learning only *after* I had taught my first section of service-linked ecocomposition. But learning by trial and error (and I endured my share of both) can be very effective, if not particularly efficient. Here are some of the guidelines I have learned along the way:

- If possible, advertise the course in advance as having a service-learning component. Students should choose to participate in service learning, not be forced into it. (The same principle holds for the topic-based ecocomposition course, which will run more smoothly if students have chosen to take it because they have some desire to learn about environmental issues.)

- Identify on- and off-campus environmental organizations. If your institution has a Service Coordinator or Service Learning Office, use their resources, too. Avoid reinventing the wheel: try to find out if other colleagues have engaged in service learning or action research, and avoid duplicating their efforts. Do, however, take advantage of other colleagues' experiences with service learning and action research, and learn what proved to be successful and what did not (and why).

- Contact representatives of agencies and organizations with an environmental focus or sustainability component: first by telephone, then follow up with a letter confirming any plans. (If you have a Community Service Office, perhaps one of its staff members could help with this phase of the project.) Ask what their volunteer needs are, What responsibilities are involved? Is training necessary? Find out their scheduling needs: How many hours, what days, flexible or fixed schedules, can start/end dates be accommodated into the academic term calendar? Would they prefer a one-time group effort, or an ongoing, regular, individual commitment?

- If incorporating service learning for the first time, start small: perhaps by including one or two group projects, or one paper based on students' individual service commitments.

- Maintain relationships with appropriate organizations: this reduces the work load of setting up new projects each time you teach the course, enables you to present opportunities to students based on your own familiarity with them, and often results in learning about new projects because the contact organizations will keep you informed.

Several organizations have useful websites for service learning: the American Association of Community Colleges (www.aacc.nche.edu), Florida International University's Volunteer Action Center (www.fiu.edu/~time4chg/ Library/bigdummy.html), Campus Compact (http://140.198.64.46/ academic/compact/index.html), Communications for a Sustainable Future (http://csf.Colorado.EDU/sl/), and the National Society for Experiential Education (www.nsee.org).

Another crucially important step in designing ecocomposition courses with a service-learning component is determining how to integrate group and individual projects into the course curriculum. Omitting the connection between service work and class work significantly diminishes the "learning" aspect. One useful protocol uses a read—do—reflect—write model: students first read about the issues undergirding particular service projects (for example, before the trip to the Catawba Lands Conservancy site, we read essays about land ethics and the conservation-preservation debate); then they participate in the service project; after the project, they reflect on the experience (ideally, both immediately afterward in a group discussion and later on in writing); and finally, they write a paper on a topic designed to incorporate the previous three forms of learning.

Reflection and evaluation should always be included in the service-learning process. Early on, guided reflection (asking students specific questions about their service experience) can give them models for thinking about the experience in terms of their intellectual and personal development; as they become adept at evaluating and reflecting on what they have accomplished, this kind of structured guiding will become unnecessary. A combination of factual and more open-ended questions tends to yield the most insightful responses, for example, What specific activities were you involved in? What skills were required? What new abilities or knowledge did you acquire? What did you talk about or think about as you participated? What do you think you accomplished? Would you do anything differently the next time? What was the value of the experience? What did you learn—about yourself, about other people, about the place, about issues related to the project?

Have students keep a regular service journal: if possible, do so electronically in a format that enables all students to have access to the journal. Formats such as a Notes conference allow students to write individual entries grouped within a specific topic; everything written in the conference remains available for viewing to all of its members. In these journal entries, encourage reflection and analysis as well as narration and description of students' projects; also encourage them to read and respond to each others' entries. The service journal helps to create greater community within the class; once they have spent time together both in class and outside of class, they become more comfortable interacting in written form, too.

In addition to the less formal writing activity of the service journal, assign one or more papers directly related to the student's service project, for example, students can research the background of their organizations or their issues of primary concern, interview and write profiles of other volunteers, and argue for or against controversial aspects of a project. If students become involved in activist research, the project itself will provide a number of paper topics. Set aside time in class every few weeks for students to give progress reports about their projects: for validation, support, and help with any difficulties—and to recognize and acknowledge their efforts. If possible, invite members of organizations or community research teams to speak to the class about these projects, too. Maintain an article file with magazine and newspapers pieces relevant to the course's content and ongoing projects. Encourage students to publicize their efforts by publishing their work in campus and local community newspapers. One student gave this suggestion in the final course evaluation: "a semester-long pictorial scrapbook of the individual service projects would add enthusiasm, incentive, and motivation for the completion of the project"; similarly, students can design their own illustrated, written summaries of their service activity as one course assignment.

12:00 noon. The rakers, trail-levelers, and gravel-haulers have finished working. We gather down the trail to watch Tom, Justin, and Bethany put the final touches on the bridge, a bridge that didn't exist a few hours ago, except in the form of some boards, posts, bolts, nails, and gravel fill. Tom proudly proclaims, "Cool! I've never built anything before in my life!" We're all excited to see that we have accomplished something so real; *when the trail opens again this spring for visitors, they will have a new section of the site to explore, along a path we helped to build and maintain.*

GOING FORTH: RESULTS AND IMPLICATIONS

In their final course evaluations, students have been overwhelmingly enthusiastic about, and supportive of, the course's service-learning focus. Two other well-received aspects of the course are the frequent use of peer review and the variety of assigned readings. All three components are designed to promote interdisciplinarity (readings from many different disciplines, covering a range of topics and issues), extradisciplinarity (work done outside the classroom: the service-learning projects), and sustainability (community-building activities, such as group service projects and in-class peer review). A selection of student responses to the final course evaluation (using standard forms provided by the college, written anonymously, and not available to the instructor until after grades are due) reveals their own assessments of service learning in an ecocomposition class. In answer to the question, "What elements of the course and instruction did you find most helpful to the accomplishment of the course's goals?" students from three different sections provided these comments:

- "A group service project definitely promoted group unity and closeness outside the classroom. Our individual service projects allowed us to pursue our own interests, gain valuable insight and experience into the endeavor at hand, and provide a basis for a term project that was intrinsic to our work and lives."

- "The service component of the course kept me very active outside of the classroom and gave me a lot of interaction with other people who are trying to help the environment."

- "The service portion of the course was the biggest contributor to the close-knit atmosphere, especially the group projects. The individual service was a great way to get close to classmates as well as to become more environmentally aware."

- "We had a class environment that really lent itself to accomplishing the goals of the English 101 course. The general enthusiasm was at first provided by the professor but as the semester continued, the majority of the class became involved. . . . In addition the service component of this course was inseparable from the accomplishment of the course's goals. It was also amazingly rewarding."

- "The service component of the class was helpful, fun, and educational. I loved spending time and getting to know my classmates, donating to the community, and learning through all of the community service I did this semester."

- "The service journals using the Notes conference also helped me learn to better reflect upon my experiences, and to communicate them effectively to others. I enjoyed the variety of works that we read, not only because of the subject, but they also gave a wide range of styles (which I think helps me to expand my own)."

- "The required service component to this course helped me understand more clearly elements of the environment I had not ever focused on. This made it easier to write about the environment."

- "The peer review sessions helped us work together as a class."

- "I loved the service requirement. I got so much out of it and the community we created with our classmates in support of our projects was awesome!"

Ultimately, the results and implications of service learning in ecocomposition are limited only by the imaginations and efforts of those who participate. I would like to think that a combination of ecocomposition and service learning begins a quiet revolution in one group of students' thinking, a process that continues after they finish the course. Murray Bookchin asserts that "as long as domination organizes humanity around a system of elites, the project of dominating nature will continue to exist and inevitably lead our planet to ecological extinction" (60). In its own small way, a service-learning component in an ecocomposition course can help to dismantle these hierarchies—between teacher and student, humans and the natural environment, the "haves" and "have-nots."

Developing ecocomposition courses with a service-learning component might sound like a lot of extra work, and it often is. I have yet to perfect my courses, create the most effective curricular links, or spend significant amounts of time outside the classroom actually participating in service activities (rather than spending my time in setting them up). I am still learning about which types of projects are best suited for the pedagogical, intellectual, and ideological goals of the course. But for all the additional time and energy commitment that service learning entails, it yields even greater rewards. I have become more motivated and more invested in teaching first-year composition. I have learned a tremendous amount— about local and global environmental issues, about the community, and about effective, nonhierarchical, liberating pedagogies. I have also gotten to know my students much better as a result; these relationships tend to last well beyond the semester in which we have English 101 together. Many of these students have gone on to design their own interdisciplinary environmental majors, have stayed involved with environmental organizations and service work, have received grants for environmental research and service, and have assumed leadership positions in campus environmental organizations. The work they begin in an ecocomposition class becomes a gift that keeps on giving.

As teachers of composition, we must instruct our students to communicate clearly and effectively; as ecocritics, we should also guide them to incorporate environmentally sound practices inside and outside of the academic context. Clear and effective communication is, after all, a

sustainable practice: one requiring a sensitivity to audience and environment, an awareness of immediate purpose and long-range consequences,
the ability to identify problems and propose solutions, and the commitment to include and inspire others. Service learning can help to accomplish all of the above.

*1:00 P.M.. Everyone grabs something to carry back down the hill: rakes,
shovels, trash, bags, and one piece of coffee cake left over from the morning
snack break. I get lunch from the van and meet them at the picnic site, a table
and benches set up along one section of the trail. Students share one knife to
spread peanut butter and one knife for strawberry preserves; they joke and
huddle together for warmth; they thank each other for small courtesies. Robert
shows us a few of the early-blooming wildflowers that give this site its name; I
photograph the bloodroot and hypatia. When lunch is over, we gather our
trash, sort the recyclables, thank Robert for his time and expertise, and head
back to campus in the van. The heater is blowing full blast and the students
are glad to be warm again. I walk to my office, where I continue writing this
article. Early this morning, I felt that I really didn't have time to take this di-
version from my work—but now I realize that I didn't have time not to.*

WORKS CITED

Anderson, Chris, and Lex Runciman, eds. *A Forest of Voices: Reading and Writing the Environment.* Mountain View, CA: Mayfield, 1995.

Bookchin, Murray. "Social Ecology." *The Green Reader: Essays toward a Sustainable Society.*
Ed. Andrew Dobson. San Francisco: Mercury House, 1991.

Cushman, Ellen. "Opinion: The Public Intellectual, Service Learning and Activist Research." College English 61:3 (1999): 328–36.

Di Chiro, Giovanna. "Nature as Community: The Convergence of Environment and Social Justice." *Uncommon Ground: Rethinking the Human Place in Nature.* Ed. William
Cronon. New York: Norton, 1996. 298–320.

Glotfelty, Cheryll. "Introduction: Literary Studies in an Age of Environmental Crisis." *The
Ecocriticism Reader: Landmarks in Literary Ecology.* Eds. Cheryll Glotfelty and Harold
Fromm. Athens: University of Georgia Press, 1996. xv–xxxvii.

Huxley, Aldous. *Island.* New York: Harper, 1962.

Naess, Arne. "The Shallow and the Deep, Long-Range Ecology Movement. A Summary."
Inquiry 16 (1973): 95–100.

Slovic, Scott, and Terrell Dixon, eds. *Being in the World:An Environmental Reader for Writers.* New York: Macmillan, 1993.

Walker, Melissa, ed. *Reading the Environment.* New York: Norton, 1994.

Appendix: Course Syllabus

English 101–G: Environmental Writing
TR 2:30–3:45—Chambers 208
Dr. Annie Merrill Ingram—Spring 1999
Office Hours: M 11:30–10:00, Tu 10:30–12:30, Th 4:00–5:30,
F 10:00–noon
Preyer 118—892-2487—aningram@davidson.edu

COURSE DESCRIPTION:

Welcome to English 101-G: Environmental Writing. This course fulfills the first-year composition requirement but also incorporates a specific topic focus—the environment—and an experiential learning component. Service projects, action research, fieldwork, and outdoor learning activities (for example, through Davidson Outdoors) will augment work done in class.

As a first-year composition course, English 101-G introduces you to the critical and analytical writing required of all Davidson College students. Frequent papers and informal writing assignments will keep your composition skills honed and ready. Informed discussion and active classroom participation comprise the majority of class sessions; we will also work together in workshops, peer review, and office-hour conferences.

A mandatory experiential learning component accompanies Environmental Writing. We will participate as a class in one or two group projects, and each student will develop an individual project(s) to work on throughout the semester. Previous students have been involved with the

Davidson College Environmental Action Coalition, Catawba Lands Conservancy, Carolina Raptor Center, and the Sierra Club's Inner City Outings program. Early in the semester, you will learn more about these and other opportunities that will enable you to integrate your academic learning with "real-world" experiences.

Required Texts:	Slovic and Dixon, *Being in the World* [BITW] Fowler and Aaron, *The Little, Brown Handbook,* 7th ed. [LBH] Masumoto, *Epitaph for a Peach*

Grading:	First short paper	5%
	Four additional short papers @10% each	40%
	In-class essay	10%
	Long research paper	20%
	Revision paper	10%
	Service project/Notes conference	7.5%
	Class preparation and participation	7.5%

SYLLABUS

Tu 1/12   Introductions

Getting Situated: The Importance of Place

Th 1/14   BITW: Kumin, "Menial Labor and the Muse" (421); Sanders, "The Singular First Person" (622); Harrigan, "The Secret Life of the Beach" (72); Ehrlich, "On the Pond Again" (301); Zwinger, "Fort Bottom to Turks Head" (264); Houston and Houston, "Manzanar, U. S. A." (539); Sanders, "Cloud Crossing" (359). **Come to class prepared to answer; What do these essays have in common regarding their attention to place?**

LBH: "Critical Thinking, Reading, and Writing" (1–19)

W 1/20   BITW: Welty, "Some Notes on River Country" (457); Abbey, "The Great American Desert" (468); Berry, "A Country of Edges" (477); Williams, "Yucca"

(484); Anzaldua, "El retorno" (492); Least Heat-
Moon, "Atop the Mound" (496)

LBH: "Developing an Essay" (24–61)

F 1/22   **First short paper due at the start of class:** 2–3 pages,
500–800 words. Using techniques of narration and description, write about a PLACE you know well. **In class: workshop
on paper 1.** Two volunteers will make copies of their papers
for each student in the class + me; these copies are due outside
my office by 3:00 P.M. on Thursday, 21 January. Students will
pick up copies of the papers and read them before class.

Going Wild: Explorations of Wilderness Experiences

Tu 1/26   BITW: Hilbert, "Disturbing the Universe" (229); Hopes,
"Crossings" (234); Hogan, "Walking" (246); Abbey,
"Floating" (255); Tallmadge, "In the Mazes of
Quetico" (274); Bass, "The Nantahala" (289); Harris,
"What in the World Am I Doing Out Here?" (296)
          LBH: "Drafting and Revising the Essay" (63–77)
"Avoiding Plagiarism" (578–85). **Do exercise 6 and
turn in at the beginning of class.**

Th 1/28   BITW: Bird, "Letter VII" (309); Muir, "Prayers in High
Mountain Temples" (321); Kerouac, "Gonna Climb
that Mountain" (328); Roberts, "Five Days on
Mount Huntington" (339); Elder, "The Plane on
South Mountain" (425); Eiseley, "The Flow of the
River" (517)
          LBH: "Writing and Revising Paragraphs" (85–123)

Tu 2/2   **Paper 2 due at the start of class:** 3–4 pages,
800–1,000 words. Research another person's wilder-
ness experience and write a paper analyzing its
salient features (location, conditions, preparation,
dangers, surprises, spiritual dimension, etc.).
          LBH: "Giving and Receiving Comments" (80–82)

Th 2/4   **Library Orientation: meet at the reference desk of
the Little Library at 2:20 P.M.**

Environmental Ethics: Responses and Responsibilities

Tu 2/9 BITW: Dillard, "Fecundity" (53); Thoreau, "Walking" (189); Pollan, "Why Mow?" (433); Quammen, "The White Tigers of Cincinnati" (444); Littlebird, "The Hunter" (545); Eiseley, "The Winter of Man" (565); Daniel, "The Impoverishment of Sightseeing" (592)

LBH: Argument (126–43)

Th 2/11 BITW: Momaday, "An American Land Ethic" (605); Kittredge, "Owning It All" (612); Meeker, "Nuclear Time" (619); Williams, "Save the Whales, Screw the Shrimp" (634); Quammen, "Dirty Word, Clean Place" (646)

LBH: Argument, continued (144–60)

** We welcome your attendance and participation in the "Sustainable Campus Design" workshop sponsored by the Associated Colleges of the South and hosted by Davidson, 12–14 February. **

Tu 2/16 **Paper 3 due at the start of class:** 3–4 pages, 900–1,200 words. Write an argument about an environmental ethics issue you find important. Research required.

Encountering the Other: Species, Habits, and Habitats

Th 2/18 BITW: Janovy, "Tigers and Toads" (14); Finch, "Very Like a Whale" (20); Dillard, "Living Like Weasels" (27); Quammen, "The Face of a Spider" (32); Austin, "The Scavengers" (43)

LBH: "Essay Examinations" (738–45)

Tu 2/23 BITW: Thomas, "Death in the Open" (49); Daniel, "Some Mortal Speculations" (84); Carrighar, "Parent Birds" (95); Hoagland, "Dogs, and the Tug of Life" (100); Matthiessen, "The Snow Leopard" (110)

Th 2/25 **In-class essay: bring to class a blue book, two pencils or pens, and a watch or clock.**

2/27–3/7 Spring Break

Tu 3/9   BITW: Sanders, "Listening to Owls" (120); Hubbell, "Becoming Feral" (133); Walker, "Am I Blue?" (137); Hay, "A Season for Swallows" (160)

          LBH: Emphasis, Conciseness, Variety (338–54)

Th 3/11   **Paper 4 due at the start of class:** 2–3 pages, 500–800 words. You may choose to write a comparison/contrast, narration/description, analysis, or argument paper (or some combination). Only restriction on topic is that it must pertain somehow to animals. Research encouraged but not required.

The World We Live In: Thinking Globally and Acting Locally

Tu 3/16   BITW: Henson, "Magnificent Desolation" (5); Raymo, "The Blandishments of Color" (173); Blum, "Plans and Changes" (347); Silko, "Landscape, History, and the Pueblo . . ." (573)

          LBH: Voice (230–32). **Do exercise 10 and turn in at the beginning of class.** "Choosing and Using Words" (454–80)

Th 3/18   BITW: Weiner, "The New Question" (661); Nelson, "Oil and Ethics: Adrift on Troubled Waters" (673); Nichols, "Keep it Simple" (679)

          LBH: "Clear Sentences" (266–95)

Tu 3/23   BITW: Fischhoff, "Report from Poland" (684); Maathai, "Foresters Without Diplomas" (694); DiPerna, "Truth vs. 'Facts'" (699)

          LBH: "Clear Sentences" (continued) and "Effective Sentences" (297–336)

Th 3/25   **Paper 5 due at the start of class:** 4–5 pages, 1,000–1,500 words. *"What if. . . ."* imagine a scenario with local and/or global environmental consequences (e.g., what if everyone in the world woke up one morning and found that all the cars were gone?) Conduct research to learn the necessary information for discussing the implications of your scenario, then write a paper briefly describing the scenario and more fully analyzing its implications and consequences.

Adventures in Research

Tu 3/30   BITW: Wilderness Journals selections: Thoreau, Muir, Teale, Le Guin, and Pyne (371–408)

             LBH: "Beginning a Research Project" (516–46)

Th 4/1   BITW: Gould, "Sex, Drugs, Disaster, and the Extinction of Dinosaurs" (63); Black, "Walking the Cape" (192); Lopez, "The Image of the Unicorn" (204)

             LBH: More on Sources (546–61) and "Working with Sources" (563–77)

Tu 4/6   No class. Easter holiday.

Th 4/8   In-class research paper workshop: bring questions, problems, questions, and success strategies.

             LBH: Developing the Research Paper (585–97)

Tu 4/13   Peer Review for the research paper: bring a copy of your finished paper.

Th 4/15   No class: work on revising your final research paper.

F 4/16   **Long research paper due at 5:00 P.M.: 8–10 pages, 2,000–3,000 words.**

Final Words: *Epitaph for a Peach*

Tu 4/20   *Epitaph for a Peach,* ix–153

Th 4/22   *Epitaph for a Peach,* 157–235

F 4/23   **Shakespeare's B/Earth Day at 722 N. Main**

Tu 4/27   Last class: experiential learning project presentations Conclusions

Tu 5/11   **Revision paper due at 5:00 P.M.**

English 101-G: Assignments and Policies

All work for English 101-G is subject to the Davidson College Honor Code. Please pledge all written work.

Class Participation: This is essential to the success of English 101-G. Your class participation grade includes arriving on time, bringing necessary materials, being fully prepared for class, participating frequently and actively in class discussion, and writing informal assignments as indicated on the syllabus.

Papers: You will be writing six short papers and a longer research paper for this course. Guidelines for specific paper assignments are given in the syllabus; additional details will be forthcoming as necessary. I encourage frequent revision and support your use of the Writing Center. I also welcome you during office hours or appointments to discuss any of your questions, concerns, drafts, and revisions.

Notes Conference: You must have a valid e-mail account in order to participate in the Notes Conference. The Notes Conference has several purposes: (a) As the place for your experiential learning project journals, it provides a forum for discussing your own project and learning about those of your classmates. (b) It enables you to respond to assigned readings, to prepare for class or to continue a discussion begun in class. (c) It gives you the opportunity to create your own discussion topics related to issues, readings, papers, or projects. I will evaluate your Notes Conference entries according to the **quality** of their content (50%), your **promptness** in meeting deadlines (25%), and the **quantity** of both individual notes and total number of entries (25%).

In-Class Essay: Since many of the writing assignments you will have as a Davidson College student will be examination essays, you will learn strategies for writing an effective in-class essay and write one as part of your assignment for the unit on animals. *Please bring a blue book, two pens or pencils, and a watch to class on February 25.*

Research Paper: Comprising eight to ten pages, the research paper is the longest writing assignment you have for this course. *You choose the topic for your research paper: the only limitation is that the subject must be related to some aspect of the environment.* You are welcome and encouraged to choose a topic that is related, directly or indirectly, to your experiential learning project. You will already have written at least three short research papers (nos. 2, 3, and 5) and be familiar with the research resources of the Little Library, based on your participation in the Library Orientation on February 4. **Start thinking about your research paper topic now; the best papers take time to develop!**

The paper is due on Tuesday, April 13. During class, you will exchange papers with a classmate and give one another feedback and suggestions for revision; a portion of your grade will include the quality of peer review you give. On Friday, April 16, the revised final research paper is due; a portion of the grade will also include the extent to which you have followed your peer reviewer's suggestions and carefully revised the paper.

Peer Review, Workshop, Individual Conferences: All three of these interactive techniques will help you to develop and improve as a writer. Because they are such an important part of the writing process, your performance in these activities will also comprise a portion of your grade. Please treat the work you are reviewing with respect and careful attention; remember, your work is being reviewed, too! Early in the semester, we will discuss which kinds of collaborative activity constitute Honor Code violations and which do not.

Attendance: You may have two unexcused absences. Thereafter, each unexcused absence will lower your final grade by two points. I excuse absence only for serious (and documented) personal illness, family emergency, or authorized college activity (e.g., athletic competition).

Late Work: Work turned in after the due date and time will be penalized by one letter grade (ten points) for every twenty-four hours the work is late, including weekends, breaks, and holidays, for example, a paper due at 2:30 on Thursday and turned in at 2:50 on Thursday is already a day late.

Please note that technological malfunction is NOT a valid excuse for late work. I will grant extensions for serious extenuating circumstances, but you must pursue this option as early as possible. I grant no extensions on or after the due date.

Restoring Bioregions Through Applied Composition

Paul Lindholdt
Eastern Washington University
Cheney, Washington

From twin perspectives—as an environmental organizer and a university professor—I present this essay. As an organizer I lead the 1,200-member Upper Columbia River Group of the Sierra Club, regional affiliate of the world's largest environmental organization, an organization stigmatized for being bureaucratic, mainstream, even staid. The club plays upon the place-based attachments of its membership, enhancing those attachments through educational outdoor excursions. Our members are conservative in the sense of *conservation*—resistant to the changes that cause the destruction of beloved wild places. As a professor I practice service learning and some environmental education, which is under increasing scrutiny by right-wing think tanks, by foundations, and by Congress. My research makes me ever mindful of the politicization of the humanities and sciences alike. Indeed, many recriminations of higher education (e.g., that it is a last bastion of Marxism and a haven for "tenured radicals") focus on the study of English language and literature.

The need I see for an applied composition emerges from a different critique of the profession. The distinction between exoteric and esoteric culture can help to set up boundaries for my critique. If exoteric culture encompasses those arts and entertainments suitable for communication to the general public, then the esoteric arts are recondite, capable of being comprehended only by the select few, the inner circle, by those who have mastered specialized forms of knowledge.

Too much of what is written about the language arts demeans good writing. It accords primacy to theory over praxis, carrying those theoretical dimensions far beyond a healthy balance, and thereby diminishing the honest promises of succinct communication. The subject matter of such a theory is, as Hamlet objected, "Words, words, words" and little more.

Words that belie the scrupulous claims of those who compose them; which complicate the problems of race, class, and gender they seek to alleviate; which do nothing to offset the imbalances of power that typify techno-industrial society. Elitism masquerading as egalitarianism. If scholarly fascination with theory and abstraction contradicts the needs of those less fortunate species and people we champion, cruel ironies ensue. What is said in jest is largely true—while the deconstructionists were seizing the English departments, Ronald Reagan was seizing the world. Who fell asleep at the watch? Carl Safina has noted of graduate study in the sciences, "Oddly, much of my academic training discouraged meaningful involvement in the public arena. Professors taught graduate students to purge from research proposals any taint of the 'applied' " (A80). Safina's observation rings true, too, for the pursuit of advanced degrees in the language arts. Discourse communities have their own lexicon, and yet the syntax and diction, the styles by which certain professors of language arts try to map routes toward an improved society, all too often frame an "official style," in Richard A. Lanham's phrase (56–80)—arrogant, specialized, void of particularities, estranged and estranging, even to a majority of colleagues in languages, communications, and literatures. I propose that we loosen the grasp of official styles, and shrug off careerist pretexts "to sound learned and scientific—disinterested, impersonal, factual" (60). Let's begin instead to legitimize the profession through innovative research and validate personal experience in our work and classrooms.

Language study as skills only, for instructors and students alike, can stultify. It is meaningless in a moral sense, "academic" in the pejorative, to compose essays or study culture when that work is detached from consequences. Consequentiality can arise, though, from place-based or bioregional study as it couples with more personal modes of communication and the affective domain. Leaders of the environmental movement know this lesson well. And so it is essential for us educators to activate ourselves, cultivate place-based attachments and sympathies, explore more personal modes of discourse in our own research and in our classes, and instill a renewed sense of consequentiality to make language study more meaningful to students. Civic participation need not take radical forms, nor does it have to toe the line of political correctness along green parameters. Praxis in the language classroom only needs to restore the *action* in that word's meaning. If compelled to adopt denominations, I would favor the term *applied composition*. In my own classes it takes the form of letters or editorials to regional, local, or national periodicals; petitions to leaders of industry, business, or government; public performances of polemics or exhortatory discourse; appeals to members of environmental organizations;

and excursions into participatory democracy of all sorts, beginning by examining the policies and practices of the college or university itself and extending from physical plant to language habits. In our composition classrooms a skeptical regard for theory—which is as subject to planned obsolescence as our technology—might invite us to excavate cast-off practices. What, for instance, did we lose when we marginalized the personal narrative? And if belles lettres were ousted, as writing teachers turned from written product toward process and now toward "postprocess," maybe we should revive literary modeling and stylistic emulation. More to the point, any plan for restoring bioregions through composition will mean integrating more exigency-based discourse forms and more disparate disciplines. In a spirit of interdisciplinarity in the following section, I review the humanist tradition show how it erects barriers between our species and nature, draw upon some research from environmental educators, and examine the case of a research-activist who routinely incorporates critical and rhetorical tools in his work. In so doing I recommend ways in which my colleagues can restore a sense of consequentiality to their writing classes by encouraging a vital sense of place.

THE SHOW WE DROVE FROM TOWN

A sense of place, with an emphasis on natural space, has become all but lost to most of us today. If we gain it as a child, we often lose our sense of place in nature once we become adults and responsibilities begin to press upon us. We do not take the time, as a rule, to learn the features of our bioregions. In our work as scholars and teachers, we rarely study nature unless we teach the sciences. Humanists, we teach theoretical "humanities." Our built environments, more comfortable all the time thanks to technology, enclose and cushion us, embargo nature, and allow us to forget that we depend upon the natural world for food, water, air, and even for spiritual balance. Deborah Tall tells the striking story of a friend who, visiting his mother, got lost in the suburbs among streets indistinguishable in name and appearance: "all the houses an identical rosy beige, he drove around desperately in [his mother's] car, pressing the garage-door opener, waiting to see which door would open. . . ." (104–5). Few anecdotes capture the loss of place-connectedness as well. Our planetary population, six billion this year, curbs meaningful opportunities to escape the bustle and hum that accompany civilization and urbanization. But more than populations and circumstances divide us from empirical wisdom of watersheds and ecotones, biologic economies and growing seasons, erosion rates, and

rainfall inches. Our separation from the lands and waters of our home-
lands stems also from complex cultural shifts that are tied up with historical humanism and its dependence on technology.

Humanist assumptions underlie our family dynamics and consumer
habits, tastes in arts and entertainments, and our educations and the
classes we teach. When R. F. Kennedy Jr. addressed an auditorium full of
people at my university, he ended his fine speech on "Our Environmental
Destiny" with a set of humanist appeals: Because so many American arts,
belles lettres, and government tenets are based on nature, we should save
natural spaces as a natural archive of our culture. Not for their own sake,
not because nature is alive and life has been accorded legal rights, but because saving nature saves our heritage. "Humanism," as I use it here, is a
philosophical orientation or paradigm that privileges the human; it depends heavily upon science, upon verifiable experience and rationality; it
valorizes philosophy, technology, and the arts; and it distrusts supernatu-
ralism, religious ritual, and emotional exuberance as a rule. Highly judg-
mental in his views, David Ehrenfeld provocatively defines humanism in
his essay as "the religion of humanism: a supreme faith in human reason—
its ability to confront and solve the many problems that humans face, its
ability to rearrange both the world of Nature and the affairs of men and
women so that human life will prosper" (5). Emphasizing reason and rationality in particular, humanism has erected cognitive barriers between us
and the natural world, according to Ehrenfeld. It has also, I allege, contributed to overspecialization in the academy, whereby the only professionals with legitimate claim to study nature are scientists. Thanks to the
excesses of rationalism and humanism, too, professors of English no
longer speak a lingua franca, so disparate are our discourse communities.
Richard A. Lanham has written, on style in our profession, "At its worst,
academic prose makes us laugh by describing ordinary reality in extraordi-
nary language" (4). The fascination with theory that often besets language
studies is an unexamined outgrowth of humanism.

Overspecialization is a related problem in American society at large
and in the academic "disciplines" in particular. Alfred North Whitehead,
writing in 1929, decried " 'The mediocrity of the learned world,' " which
he traced to its "exclusive association of learning with book-learning' "
(Orr 1996, 19). Instead he endorsed " 'first-hand knowledge,' " that is,
knowledge gained through empirical experience rather than second-hand,
thus discounting knowledge gained vicariously (19). Crippled by the vic-
ariousness of our work, many of us language professors traffic in abstraction and theory. Rarely, though, are we called on to demonstrate the veri-
fiability of our concepts and claims. Hence we vex ourselves to develop

rationalistic vehicles of assessment for the writing classroom to try to gauge the success of student writers. Such quantification is apt to be incompatible with ecocomposition, insofar as it cannot assess analogy-making, passion, or spiritual growth. We render lip service to interdisciplinarity in the form of "writing across the curriculum," but we implement it only rarely. Compartmentalized thinking in general is one source of our present environmental crisis. Science, for instance, often gets overlooked in the formation of public policy. Due to specialization, similarly, science is becoming increasingly politicized (Wilkinson and Ehrlich and Ehrlich), while some language theorists wrongly adopt the language of the social sciences. On the other hand, journalists like Todd Wilkinson, science correspondent for the *Christian Science Monitor,* are required to write proficiently in areas outside their preparation. They practice interdisciplinarity and apply critical thinking daily to concrete features of the world. Peer review in the world of journalism is rigorous and constant; a journalist's clients, his readers, get to critique their service provider in guest editorials, commentaries, and letters to editors.

The show we drove from town, when we educators embraced humanism and strove to become theoreticians, is nature as a site of inspiration and wonder, a route to the truth. It is not rational, hence not humanistic, to regard nature as a route to human improvement. The seventeenth-century Puritan poet and rhetorician John Milton, admired as a jewel in the crown of English Renaissance humanism, revealed the apparent incompatibility of humanism and nature. In his paradigm, nature (Satan in the snake's shape) occasioned Adam and Eve's tragic fall from grace. In his poetic hymn "On the Morning of Christ's Nativity," news of the newborn God-in-man drives pagan deities from the sacred groves, at the same time driving nature outside the reach of human reverence. Those nature deities in Milton's devotional poem grow superfluous, shamefaced, tawdry, and frail beside humanity's resplendent savior-to-be, Jesus Christ; "Nature in awe to him / Had doffed her gaudy trim," which is to say that abject nature deferred to Christ's greater qualifications and glory (2. 32–33). Significantly enough, nature throughout the poem is female, while Christ is male. She seeks "To hide her guilty front with innocent snow" (1. 38); that is, she mantles herself in December whiteness to feign innocence and purity. Similarly Shakespeare's King Lear, in his distress on the heath imagining a "simpering dame," raves about the "riotous appetite" she disguises, especially in that risky space below the waist, whose domain 'is all the fiends'; there's hell, there's darkness, / There's the sulphurous pit, burning, scalding, / Stench, consumption" (4.6.114, 123–25). Nature, in the humanist equation, is female. Accordingly she is dissembling, sexually charged, and thus dire and deadly.

Vestiges of such attitudes remain today. Depraved men and savage creatures abide in nature, women are sullied, and children drown or suffer attacks by beasts. Humans must be vigilant, wary of the wild, and zealous enough to effect "regeneration though violence" when necessary (Nash and Slotkin). Does this sound like dangerous ground for students of English language studies? One common response to the antihumanistic leanings of environmental educators is that we "degrade" people.

Milton's humanistic poem depicts nature, revealed in the light of Christ, as the grotesque source of humanity's unfortunate fall from grace. Genius loci is involved in that fall. The origin of our species' sorrow, nature, is "Pollute[d] with sinful blame" and blasted with "foul deformities" (2. 41, 44) for its complicity. Likewise the sun, understood today as the daily progenitor of life on Earth, "hid his head for shame / As his inferior flame / The new-enlightened world no more should need. . . ." (2. 80–82). Here Milton exercises great artistic license in depicting a sun overshadowed by the infant man-god. Here is the quintessence of humanism: that our species does not need the sun, so great is humanity and the human god. Such a theocentric fancy belies our biocentric knowledge that death begets life. Spiritual life originates in heaven, while "the old dragon under ground," Satan, outgrowth of the planet's bowels, "wroth to see his kingdom fail, / Swings the scaly horror of his folded tail" (2. 168, 171–72). Planetary powers appear evil in Milton's worldview, and thus it falls on humans to overthrow that evil—through rationality, technology, and faith. The most telling instance of humanism's supremacy over nature occurs in Milton's poem with the revealing expulsion of animated nature when the Christ-child arrives. Then, from "haunted spring and dale," the "parting Genius is with sighing sent. . . ." (2. 183, 185). A protector or guardian deity in classical antiquity, the "Genius" typically pertained to a particular place, as in the Latin genius loci, a distinctive character or atmosphere of a place with respect to the impression it makes on the mind. Peculiarly enough, as if aware that intolerance of paganism flaws Milton, the editors of The Norton Anthology of English Literature furnish this disclaimer: "With the coming of Christ all these picturesque local deities are dismissed, and the poet clearly regrets their departure" (Abrams et al. 1440n.). "Regrets"? The editors furnish no instances of the poet's regret, nor is that regret evident; moreover, the editorial "picturesque" is irretrievably condescending. In a second apparent attempt to rescue Milton from unregenerate humanism, the editors comment in another footnote, "Like ghosts at sunrise, the pagan gods, geniuses, and fays (fairies) are all bound to disappear at the rising of the Christian sun" (1442n). Neither Milton nor his editors deserve more blame than other writers of modern times, but they do furnish canonical examples both of humanism's sway over indigenous place and of our curricular alienation from nature.

Without directly attributing this alienation to humanism, many other nature writers and environmentalists have lamented what we lost when we tossed out our erstwhile reverence for natural places. If compositionists were to reintegrate literature into their classrooms, the ends of ecocomposition would be enhanced. In particular Annie Dillard, 1974 Pulitzer Prize-winner for nonfiction, deplores our species' resolute silencing of nature. Writing as a Christian herself, she indicts the Judeo-Christian tradition for teaching us a lesson we have taken too hard to heart. That lesson is "the muteness of the human stance in relation to all that is not human" (92). Outside of some "granolas" and scientists, such muteness seems routine. In her gentle jeremiad Dillard sadly notes, "It is difficult to undo our own damage, and to recall to our presence that which we have asked to leave. It is hard to desecrate a grove and change your mind" (88). The damage, culturally speaking, has been done. Applying composition courses toward the tough job of restoring those desecrated groves is something we can do, a challenge worthy of the stakes. Observe closely, Dillard recommends; attend as if attention were an epistemology, for until the show we drove from town returns, "until the pagan gods slip back to their hilltop groves, all we can do with the whole inhuman array is watch it" (90). Watching so closely would involve a mystical process that is alien to theoretical humanists; it requires "sacrifice, the suppression of self-consciousness, and a certain precise tilt of the will, so that the will becomes transparent and hollow, a channel for the work" (88). It is hard for me to imagine composition straying so far from its comfort zones unless it were to embrace the emerging ecoconsciousness, unless it were to effect a merger with environmental education. Corroborating Dillard, Deborah Tall contends that "Judaism is the religion that by and large defused the religion of sacred place" (106). Tall tackles this tender subject with the insight of one raised in the Jewish faith: "The pagan gods the early Jews set out to overthrow were the numerous place-defined, local nature deities" (106), as we see in Milton and in others who shaped Judeo-Christian humanism.

REGAINING A SENSE OF PLACE

Environmental educators agree on the need to foster sensitivity to place both inside and outside the classroom. By doing so we begin to unyoke ourselves from a dependence on theoretical humanism for our identities.

Students gain an empirical grasp of the fact that we are animals first, mammals who share 98 percent of our genetic material with chimpanzees, and humans only second. Particularly in entry-level classes, most particularly in primary grades, students who are encouraged through composition to explore and develop connections to nature inside their personal lives appear from the extant research to be more apt to thrive as scholars and postgraduate professionals. Wisdom derived from experiences, emotions, memory, and personal history can cultivate greater interdisciplinary sophistication; it can also counterweight the faulty warnings toward objectivity that unbalance the scales of so many disciplinary forms of knowledge. It can encourage a virtual reinterpretation of the world. On a most intimate level, place-based attachments to the past can empower citizens to shape the future.

That future might appear increasingly global and mobile, but this need not dissuade language arts teachers from urging students to restore a sense of place. David W. Orr asserts that much contemporary angst and disaffection can be remedied by helping to develop "a deep concept of place as a repository of meaning, history, livelihood, healing, recreation, and sacred memory and as a source of materials, energy, food, and collective action" (1994, 163). Failure to do so will perpetuate the trend toward becoming not merely " 'dis-placed' people who are physically removed from their homes," but indeed " 'de-placed' people, mental refugees, homeless wherever we are" (163)—a threat that is worth exploring for the benefit of the criminals and homeless in America today. Here, again, Tall's chilling story of the garage-door opener comes to mind. Lost in a human-centered world, we lose our topographic bearings and perhaps some of ourselves. Teachers of literature and rhetoric can begin to establish a place-based awareness among students by assigning them to read writers who explored deeply the genius loci of beloved places and sometimes worked to preserve them—Sarah Orne Jewett (on late nineteenth-century Maine); John Muir (on Yosemite and the Sierra-Nevada); Sigurd Olson (on Minnesota, Wisconsin, and the Great Lakes); Edward Abbey (on the desert Southwest); and Linda Hasselstrom (on South Dakota). Such writers can model the healthy desire to affiliate oneself with a region—named or unnamed, small or large, cultivated or wild, lush or dry. To affiliate is "to bring or to receive into close connection as a member or a branch," "to connect or associate oneself." The root word is Latin *filius,* meaning "son," which suggests (when the concept is applied to place relations) actual genetic connections to one's district of desire. Closely related emotionally if not etymologically are the Greek suffixes -*philia,* meaning "friendship," and -*philos,* translated as "relatedness." This Greek suffix has picked up some unfortunate connotations of pathology, as in necrophilia or pedophilia, thus partially eclipsing the more healthy denotations of intimacy and attraction that inform "biophilia" and "philosophy." For the ends of ecocomposition, these Latin derivations demonstrate that what we affiliate with is yoked to where we've lived.

A Harvard biologist E. O. Wilson (1984) has rejuvenated the roots of the word *biophilia*, which appears in none of the standard dictionaries but first was used by the psychoanalyst Erich Fromm. Wilson's biophilia hypothesis holds that " 'the connections that humans unconsciously seek with the rest of life' " are innate (Orr (1994, 46). To whatever degree life remains tied to the land—through air, water, animals, or plants for food—biophilia can broadly suggest a connectedness and an affiliation with specific places as well. *Locophilia* (place-relatedness), to coin a term too cumbersome to catch on, would be nice to induce, to engender in students if indeed it is too late for most of them to remember place-affiliation in a collective unconscious. As Orr laments, however, reflecting upon education today, "Locality has no standing in the modern curriculum" (1994, 129). In literary studies, for instance, the closest focal point is sectionalism or regionalism—usually referred to, somewhat pejoratively, as "local color"—a subspecies of literature characterized by slang and vernacular speech patterns, "quaint" folkways and folklore, and rural characters or "rustics." Scholars and critics still rarely condescend to treat local-color literature and characters as anything more than antiques or curios. Decrying the lack of serious locality studies in higher education today, Orr created another neologism, *biophobia*, which he defined as "the culturally acquired urge to affiliate with technology, human artifacts, and solely with human interests regarding the natural world" (1994, 131). More and more studies of literature and culture are coming to acknowledge the negative consequences of technology on people and the environment (e.g., Glendinning and Lindholdt).

If biophobia is antithetical to the purposes of environmental education, biophilia is essential—not that students can be taught to love life, only given the opportunity and shown the ropes and rewards through the study of place. Although environmental education is a relatively new field, most practitioners seem to agree with Orr;

> If by some fairly young age . . . nature has not been experienced as a friendly place of adventure and excitement, biophilia will not take hold as it might have.
>
> An opportunity will have passed, and thereafter the mind will lack some critical dimension of perception and imagination. (1994, 143)

Perception and imagination, perhaps the most pertinent words in this passage, lead to the practice of using place as the basis for prompting critical thinking in courses. Adult learners can be taught to bring their perceptions and imaginations to bear on the place-based materials of history, religion, public policy, psychology, and personal memory in ways that younger students perhaps cannot. If youthful opportunities often pass too fast to establish the strongest bioregional affiliations, the greater range of older students' experiences and interests can serve nonetheless as a forceful surrogate. The more sophisticated passions and ambitions of adult learners have their own compensations and might lend themselves more fully to restoring bioregions through applied study.

The desire to affiliate, whether intellectually or emotionally, can reverberate with power for students of the language arts. The interests of compositionists and environmental educators can come together. Mitchell Thomashow, in his provocative study *Ecological Identity,* draws from related forms of identity politics and argues that developing a profound sense of oneself in relation to natural ecosystems supplies a necessary foundation for the labor of environmental advocacy. Thomashow calls this development of oneself "ecological identity work" (5). Adapting psychological and spiritual models, Thomashow argues that "ecological identity describes how we extend our sense of self in relation to nature, and that the degree of and objects of identification must be resolved individually" (3). Analyzing oneself as an outgrowth of place becomes a challenge to be met by studying—inevitably through writing—the particulars of one's ecological origins. Just as "family of origin" studies have proven fertile approaches to counseling psychology, Thomashow's ecological identity practice shows a twin promise, both for maturing in adult learners those affiliations that have been shortchanged in youth, and for helping to vanquish youthful disaffiliations with family and place. Ecological identity work also could help to restore some of the lost consequentiality of language classes. The tantalizing possibility exists for teachers of rhetoric and composition that ecological identity work can reintegrate an estranged citizenry and help restore degraded ecosystems if applied in writing courses.

Underlying Thomashow's compelling study is the belief that "It is the personal introspection that drives one's commitment to environmentalism" (5). Far from the Protestant model of self-examination, as practiced by the American Puritans especially, ecological identity work does not seek to dwell on sins and commitments, lapses and leaps of faith, but rather on the social and biophysical particularities of one's place of origin. William Wordsworth, himself a powerful advocate for the particularities of nature in the Lake District of eighteenth- and nineteenth-century

England, recommended drawing on "emotions recollected in tranquillity" to recapture the emotional fluxes of childhood (148). And Wordsworth's poetry is vividly place-based. Yet recollecting emotions in tranquillity today not only is not part of the current college curricula, it is tacitly discouraged by the pace of cinematic entertainments, the blitz of television imagery to which we all fall susceptible, and by incessant print and audio persuasions to participate in pop-culture trends and fads. Reflection is rare.

Thomashow finds adult learners very interested, when asked to recount their most memorable environmental experiences, in exploring "childhood memories of special places, perceptions of disturbed places, and contemplations of wild places" (7). This narrow range of recollected emotions, all locked into perceptions of place, implies a dialectic or process to be worked through before synthesis can be attained. If memories of special places and wild places are devoutly to be wished for and affiliated with in our curricula, then disturbed places naturally will be regretted and despised. The eye despises what repels the heart and mind. The urgent introspection of ecological identity work, like the solitude nature writers often undergo, "is not framed as alienation and atomism but refigured as affinity and integration. . . ." (Roorda 404). The upshot in composition students might be imaginative projection toward a more restorative time, or a new or renewed commitment to community service or activism.

APPLYING ECOCOMPOSITION ON THE GROUND

Efforts to restore damaged bioregions through applied composition need not reinvent the proverbial wheel. A growing body of research in integrative studies, and in rhetoric and composition, analyzes some ways in which teachers can legitimately incorporate service learning in their courses. (Defined variously as paid or unpaid action taken to enhance the community, service learning typically complements one's major field.) If teachers combined service learning with curricular opportunities to allow students to affiliate with nearby bioregions, indeed if ecocomposition courses were designed dynamically to acquaint students with local issues and to build on affiliations, the emotional growth of those students could prove to be a powerful stimulus for their writing and imbue composition with that missing consequentiality. Terrell Dixon and Lee Smith, working with disaffiliated students in urban Houston, Texas, have explored some forms of service learning that they claim have reactivated composition:

Students work together in teams to read, analyze, and write essays on urban environments and ecology. In addition, they work with environmental groups and agencies in the community, such as the Galveston Bay Foundation, an inner-city park, an arboretum, and the Local Emergency Planning Commission, and write documents specifically for these groups, like reports, trail guides, press releases, and educational brochures. Students also keep journals in which they reflect on their service learning experiences. (A3)

In the model Dixon and Lee practice, students begin by augmenting analytical and collaborative skills; next students discover organizations that can benefit from those skills, and they then apply those skills on behalf of the organization, all while they are exercising a common form of metacognition—writing a reflective journal—that seems to be a first step toward Thomashow's more ambitious and more deeply spiritual ecological-identity work. Dixon and Lee refer to their experiment as an "innovative blend of service learning and ecocomposition with an urban focus," one that proves challenging and rewarding because it "immerses students in a public discourse with its particular rhetorical demands, preparing them more effectively to write in the workplace" (A3). This model, then, is one aimed pragmatically toward the demands of professional communication. Working collaboratively, the Houston students learn to develop communities at the same time they develop their cooperative skills.

SAMPLE PRAXIS

For my own classes I have created a three-stage process to enhance critical thinking about place. This process is aimed toward self-actualization, exploration, and enlargement of affiliations. My students' intimacy with places begins with their choosing some place out-of-doors where they compose journal entries for the class. The stipulation to write outdoors can become burdensome in winter, but during other seasons most students enjoy having an excuse to get out, get away, if only for a half an hour. Some travel the eight miles to Turnbull National Wildlife Refuge to gather inspiration, while others just step outside the dormitory and crouch beneath a juniper to fulfill this requirement for the class. Later in the quarter we take a field trip to that wildlife refuge, and students are offered the chance to spend some quiet time reflecting and writing there. The three stages toward critical thinking about a place involve imagination, analysis, and evaluation.

Day 1: Imagination: Try to imagine your particular place from the perspective of someone other than yourself. Project yourself, for instance, into the mind of an animal, bird, or tree you have seen; a character, narrator, or author you have read; or a farmer, rancher, or logger you have met. Write freely about your place using the voice of this entity as you imaginatively conceive it to be. Take chances. Let your imagination flow.

Day 2: Synthesis: From the perspective of the same entity you used in Day 1, analyze your geographic place by separating it into some of its components: for instance, air, water, soil, and the varieties of lives these components maintain. Or alternatively, study how the parts of this place seem to fit together. How do they rely upon each other, integrate? Try to narrow your analysis to some particular human presence or impact. How do cars affect your place? How about cattle? Farming? Hikers? Paddlers?

Day 3: Evaluation: Judge the value of your place according to one principle, for example, what value has your place as a bird or animal habitat? As a source of beauty? As human recreation? How about services, like filtering water to the aquifer?

Once such thinking beyond the self becomes familiar to student writers, once they learn how to connect this way with place, they have the option to be "placed" people wherever they are. If we as teachers can think of our most significant work as less ideological than practical, and more spiritual than quantifiable, then maybe ecocomposition as a theoretical field of study can move beyond abstractions and into the affective domain where consequentiality and activism can be taken seriously.

THE EXAMPLE OF ERIK RYBERG

Erik Ryberg embodies this concept of applied composition. An environmental activist now by professional bent, he studied for two years toward his Ph.D. in English language and literature at the University of Virginia before dropping out to try his hand at saving the planet. He spent some months in jail for civil disobedience. A native of Oregon, he now works full time to restore at-risk ecosystems and bioregions in the abundant public lands of the West. He tramps across those lands, bearing witness firsthand to the damage inflicted by timber-industry clear-cuts and Forest Service logging roads, private ranchers grazing cattle, and off-road vehicle enthusiasts pursuing combustion-fueled sports. To expose that damage, he publishes an illustrated and well-written newsletter entitled *The Stump*, a punning title that squints down two paths—toward the ugly remnants of industrial logging, and toward that place from which declamatory notices issue. Interested especially in forest ecology, Ryberg has worked for several "ad hoc citizens advocate groups" and as a researcher in Montana, Idaho, and in Washington for the Missoula-based Ecology Center. Currently living in Seattle, he agreed to a telephone interview. In particular I was curious to learn from him how he believes his work connects with place, and is inspired by place. Frankly I wanted to learn how, as both a professor and a Sierra Club leader, to use the tools of ecocomposition to entice my students and volunteers to become front-line researchers like Ryberg. My ultimate purpose would be to encourage spiritual connections to place and to translate those connections into ecological consequentiality.

On the matter of place, he chastened me as a teacher for believing that I could ever presume to choose a place to which my students truly would be apt to attach. Erik is pessimistic about the prospect of common field trips instilling place-based affiliations. He is certain that

> those sorts of things never worked for me. Having somebody take me somewhere never really worked. It always ended up being their place. I got most involved with a place when chance arose from doing my own research. One of the best ways to get somebody fired up about a place, and this trick was pulled on me a long time ago, is to find people who are already interested in forest conservation and give them an EA [environmental assessment] to read. Then let them know that if they want to do anything about the timber sale that's about to destroy that place, they should consider commenting on the projects and writing an appeal because nobody else is going to do it.

"Nobody else is going to do it." There's a sense of consequentiality. How many of us English educators can say the same for the latest article, textbook, or theory we are advancing? And even if we can say with all honesty that nobody else is going to do the work we are undertaking, who among us could say that that work would be consequential or tangible in any fashion comparable to preserving a forest ecosystem? The work Ryberg so often is undertaking, the work of scrutinizing agency-written documents known as "environmental assessments" or "impact statements," has immediate significance. It furnishes bases on which to write appeals, and writing appeals saves forests. Ryberg concluded on place by observing, "there's a kind of responsibility that you have, and you also have the power if you choose to exercise it." He was talking about responsibility, democracy and citizenship, and the power of artful writing and speech, to effect change in the face of sciences that are compromised and politicized. Composition teachers bear a related responsibility to teach consequential writing well.

REFLECTING ON THE EXAMPLE OF ERIK RYBERG

The process by which Ryberg reads, writes appeals, and halts timber sales and grazing allotments warrants attention in the context of ecocomposition, but first some background on the relevant political processes. Agencies like the Bureau of Land Management and the Forest Service justify themselves by selling products (e.g., grass for grazing and pine and fir trees for timber) to ranchers, loggers, and other resource-dependent interests. Because the lands those agencies administer are public, held in the public trust, the products yielded by those lands are sold at subsidized rates. Until recently no one cared if a rancher, for example, grazed a cow-calf pair on federal lands for $1.35/month. As environmental awareness has risen in recent decades, however, so have competing claims for the best use of those lands. Nor do campers like to sleep among cow-pies nor fishing enthusiasts see the banks of trout streams eroded by Hereford hooves. Using language, activists like Ryberg can "aim" their love for wild places toward grazing allotments and timber sales that they question in writing.

Analytical and evaluative skills developed by studying rhetoric, literature, technical writing, or literary criticism come in handy, as one might imagine, for reading between the proverbial lines of bureaucratic documents that offer lush acres of our native birthright for sale or lease. Writer researchers like Ryberg who love the land can wield their skills to restore degraded bioregions or prevent the initial degradation. They engage by firsthand knowledge with "the real world." Working for modest salaries or wages, they make "service" a livelihood; they enact the principles of democracy and practice citizenship in ways we hope service learning will; "We call it activism, but it's really just part of being a citizen; it shouldn't have such a grand name." By any other name, "activism is a very fertile ground" for applying writing skills. And "It is probably the duty of a rhetoric professor," he lectured me, "to show examples of what to do with those skills if you want to." If ecocomposition is listing toward professional communication, at least as we see it in the work of Dixon and Lee, it can justifiably list as well toward enrichment in the liberal arts. Students, Ryberg notes, "shouldn't be made to learn critical thinking and writing skills just to use them in the service of Microsoft or other corporations.

Students should be taught that they can use them however they want." And "however they want" I take to mean that students should not have to toe the line of political correctness along green parameters; nor should they have to practice critical thinking necessarily in the service of the writing teacher's environmental bent.

How does Ryberg apply his writing skills? "There's a lot of writing associated with my job, and so it helps to be able to write clearly." He composes "appeals, legal briefs when we sue, information requests, propaganda pieces, letters to the editor, columns, and so forth." His candor is refreshing. Specifically I was interested in learning how he goes about the appeals process. He looks at government documents, he says, for "tensions, and then you try to find or try to suppose what those tensions are about, what might be going on behind the lines and behind the text." Such presuppositions about agency dishonesty arise from his belief that "a bureaucracy like the Forest Service uses language to make reality as irrelevant as it can." Language for agency writers, Ryberg believes, is intended "to cover up or shade over what's actually happening on the landscape. And the job of an activist is to plow through that language and find out what's really happening." Here Ryberg sounds like a poststructuralist literary critic, an inquisitive reader who applies the pressure of a hermeneutics of suspicion to every text he or she reads. The difference is that such suspicious regard is arguably more warranted, more justifiable, in the case of documents whose writers have so very much to gain by enacting subterfuge. Literary artists are "creating something that provides an immense amount of joy, while writers of EAs are doing it wholly for themselves." Sounding like a disciple of Jacques Derrida, Ryberg recommends that "You have to take what they're telling you, and you have to find where the tension is and where the absences are. You have to learn to read the text as if it's concealing something." Such telltale signs are difficult to discern and more difficult to describe, but they are "the equivalent of watching body language when someone is talking." Unlike many a practicing poststructuralist critic or composition theorist, Ryberg is performing a discernible service to his immediate community and to future generations. His work is consequential.

CONCLUSION

To gain greater consequentiality, the principles of rhetoric and composition need to be applied. Students yearn to discern results in their work, to see outcomes beyond well-crafted sentences and convincing persuasive discourse, payoffs that can be assigned no precise value in the marketplace. Trends in literary, composition, and language studies of recent decades— away from symbols, themes, and morals and toward race, class, and gender—constitute gestures in the right direction. But they remain chiefly gestures due to an alienating reliance on theory and abstraction, on ingenuity, on overly specialized language, and on invention for invention's sake. Symbolic and largely inconsequential, such trends remain humanistic, anthropocentric, even "speciesist," as some of us have begun to say. The emerging ecocomposition will demand that writing teachers selectively integrate principles of environmental education, which is a field of study that is gaining more maturity and sophistication. Ecocomposition likewise will require us to expand our spheres of sympathy to include other species and bioregions, and to extend our ethical regard to nature and nature's rights. There is a hopeful future for all life on this planet, and writing and teachers can help to shape it.

WORKS CITED

Abrams, M. H. et al., eds. *The Norton Anthology of English Literature.* 6th ed. Vol. 1. New York: Norton, 1993.

Dillard, Annie. "Teaching a Stone to Talk." *Teaching a Stone to Talk: Expeditions and Encounters.* New York: Harper Perennial, 1982.

Dixon, Terrell, and Lee Smith. "Service Learning and Environmental Writing." *MLA Newsletter* 30.2 (Summer 1998): A3–A4.

Ehrenfeld, David. *The Arrogance of Humanism.* New York: Oxford University Press, 1978.

Ehrlich, Paul R., and Anne H. Ehrlich. *Betrayal of Science and Reason. How Anti-Environmental Rhetoric Threatens Our Future.* Washington, DC: Island, 1996.

Glendinning, Chellis. *When Technology Wounds: The Human Consequences of Progress.* New York: Morrow, 1990.

Kennedy, Robert F. Jr. "Our Environmental Destiny." *Horizons Speakers Series.* Eastern Washington University. 10 February, 1999.

Lanham, Richard A. *Revising Prose.* 1979. 3rd ed. Boston: Allyn, 1992.

Lindholdt, Paul. "Rage Against the Machine: Edward Abbey and Neo-Luddite Thought." *Coyote in the Maze: Tracking Edward Abbey in a World of Words.* Salt Lake City: University of Utah Press, 1998. 106–18.

Nash, Roderick. *Wilderness and the American Mind.* New Haven: Yale University Press, 1967.

Orr, David W. *Earth in Mind: On Education, Environment, and the Human Prospect.* Washington, DC: Island, 1994.

————. "Reinventing Higher Education." *Greening the College Curriculum: A Guide to Environmental Teaching in the Liberal Arts.* Eds. Jonathan Collett and Stephen Karakashian. Washington, DC: Island, 1996. 8–23.

Roorda, Randall. (1997). "Sites and Senses of Writing in Nature." *College English* 59 (1997): 385–407.

Ryberg, Erik. Telephone interview. 26 January 1999.

Safina, Carl. "To Save the Earth, Scientists Should Join Policy Debates." *Chronicle of Higher Education.* 6 November, 1998, A80.

Slotkin, Richard. *Regeneration Through Violence: The Mythology of the American Frontier, 1600–1860.* Middletown, CT: Wesleyan University Press, 1973.

Tall, Deborah. *From Where We Stand: Recovering a Sense of Place.* Baltimore: Johns Hopkins University Press, 1993.

Thomashow, Mitchell. *Ecological Identity: Becoming a Reflective Environmentalist.* Cambridge: Massachusetts Institute of Technology, 1995.

Wilkinson, Todd. *Science Under Siege: The Politicians' War on Nature and Truth.* Boulder, CO: Johnson, 1998.

Wilson, Edward O. *Biophilia: The Human Bond With Other Species.* Cambridge: Harvard University Press, 1984.

Wordsworth, William. "Preface to *Lyrical Ballads* (1800)." *The Prose Works of William Wordsworth.* Vol. 1. Eds. W. J. B. Owen and Jane Worthington Smyser. Oxford: Clarendon, 1974. 116–58.

"Written In Its Own Season":

Nature as Ground in the Postmodern World

Edward Lotto
Lehigh University
Bethlehem, Pennsylvania

The postmodern world seems to delight in pulling the rug out from under us, in calling into question any ground we might try to stand on. From the tricky fictions of DeLillo and David Foster Wallace to the trickier architecture of Peter Eisenman, from Jean-Francois Lyotard's warnings about grand narratives to the proliferation of cable channels that bring us every amateur guitar player in the local coffeehouse, the old solid ground we used to share and stand on is dissolving beneath our feet. As Lester Faigley notes, the key assumption behind the postmodern critique "is that there is nothing outside contingent discourses to which a discourse of values can be grounded—no eternal truths, no universal human experience, no universal human rights, no overriding narrative of human progress"(8). In calling into questions the old grounds of belief, the postmodern critique has done much good work in seeing through the naturalization of privilege in Western culture, work that has helped free many human beings. But along with this freeing power, postmodern thought also brings problems. Faigley refers to these problems as the "impasse of postmodern theory," and he uses an essay by Patricia Bizzell to discuss this impasse.

Bizzell's essay reviews a series of responses to E. D. Hirsch's cultural literacy proposal, and Bizzell notes that none of these responses offers a way to "regain a national public discourse," as Faigley puts it. Bizzell goes on to argue, "To take the next step, we will have to be more forthright about the ideologies we support as well as those we attack, and we will have to articulate a positive program legitimated by an authority that is nevertheless nonfoundational"(671). Faigley notes that the problem here is finding an authority that is nonfoundational. He asks, "How is such a program to be constructed? Is it possible to develop a 'positive program legitimated by authority' without reference to some sort of metanarrative?

What conception of the subject will this program offer"(20)? In this essay, I want to argue that the concept of nature can serve as this sort of non-foundational authority. A careful use of it can indeed work as a ground for thought and action both in the classroom and in the world. It can serve as a powerful authority in a world that has at least the glimmerings of an eco-logical ethic, and it can used in a nonfoundational way if we use if prop-erly. Much of value can be done in our classrooms if we avoid both the po-sition of natural realism, which claims that nature is somehow outside human intellectual constructs, and the extreme postmodern position, which insists on telling us over and over that any belief in the value of na-ture only reinforces the power of the ruling ideology.

In order to make this argument, I must imply two seemingly contra-dictory things: first, that, to some degree, any position we take to nature is one that culture has constructed, and, second, that nature can serve as a useful and pragmatic ground in a postmodern world that seems to deny us any place to stand. The reason these two beliefs are contradictory is that grounds usually are solid and unchanging, at least the grounds with which we feel most secure. To take as a ground a position constructed by culture demands that we both give up any belief in the uniqueness of the ground as well as any hope that it will remain solid forever. It demands that we be mobile and ready to change and grow. In fact, it demands that we rethink our whole sense of what a ground is. None of these things is easy, and I suspect that there is something in human nature that resists them.

In order to avoid the contingent nature of this ground, nature writing, like realism, a genre that most people now believe is constructed in the same way the postmodern novels of John Barth are constructed, likes to present itself as close to the real, natural world out there. In some ways, the claim is that good nature writing takes us out to the woods around Walden Pond or the Blackfoot River of Montana so that we can experi-ence what Thoreau or Norman McLean have experienced, so that we can "be" in the wild even though our physical bodies are sitting in a dull office in the city. There is something so seemingly solid and unchanging about the natural world. In part Thoreau and McLean earn the right to their books by having been there, by being authentically in nature in a way that allows them to present nature whole, in a way that makes the window of language disappear so that we join them in watching the waves on the pond or river. Thoreau acknowledges the strength of this belief when he writes about a new project in his journals, "A Book of the seasons—each page of which should be written in its own season & out of doors or in its own locality wherever it may be"(Buell, 131).

Of course, any reader with the slightest bit of sophistication has to question both what the experience was "really" like for the authentic writer about nature and also how language has shaped this experience. In its most extreme form, a social-constructionist with a postmodern sensibility would say that the actual experience out in nature is totally inaccessible both to the reader and probably to the person out there having the experience. Our categories are so shaped by culture and so powerful that everything we see is filtered through them. This extreme social-constructionist would see as naive the belief that in reading about nature we are somehow getting at what it is "really" like. On the other hand, many people who read about nature and who do spend a lot of time "out there" would see the postmodern position as being "unnatural"—how hard it is to avoid using the very words under contention—and somehow overly civilized and counterproductive.

Let me return to my seemingly self-contradictory position—that our place in nature is, in part at least, constructed yet can serve as a ground for action—and take up the major objections to it. One is what might be called the "matter-of-fact position," or, in short, the "natural position." This position can be summarized in the words of a reader of an anthology I did with Richard Jenseth. As the reader said of the title, *Constructing Nature,* nature simply is not constructed. It simply is out there, a fact of nature as it were, a fact that we can't argue with. Common to this position, although not necessarily so, is the belief that nature offers some sort of solace or power of regeneration. We have been torn out of nature by our civilization and have lost track of our true selves, the selves that are in harmony with the natural rhythms of the world. For a person who believes these ideas, the idea of thinking about nature as constructed even in part by culture seems just wrong-headed. The whole problem is culture, the ways in which it destroys us and our happiness, so to discuss nature in terms of culture is to destroy all that is of value in nature. Let me call a nature course that is invested in these ideas a "romantic nature course." Such a course should help students understand what they have lost in becoming civilized and should help them get back in touch with nature itself. The course should teach students to read nature writing in a way that makes language a clear window on the world. When students read *Walden* they should experience the power of the long contemplative hours Thoreau spent looking at the pond, and when they read *A River Runs Through It,* they should feel the ache in the arm when a big fish is pulling you into the deepest part of the rushing river. In an ideal world, part of the course would actually be taught outside, with students being in nature while they read and talk about it. In fact, this is just the sort of course Randall Roorda describes in the opening anecdote of his recent excellent article on the sites of nature writing.

This sort of course is very appealing, and I find a lot of strengths in it. For many students, it is just what they want. In a writing course I often teach with nature as the theme, the students who enroll love to read works that try to place them in nature or that argue in some way for the value of nature. They love A *River Runs Through It* and "Landscape, History, and the Pueblo Imagination" by Leslie Manmon Silko. In assigning these works, and others, I was encouraging them in their ecocentric beliefs. Although at times I pushed them to read a bit more complexly, often I was satisfied with this straightforward reading. As we read and discussed, there was a growing sense in the class that nature has value in and of itself, that we need to respect it, even though there were always students who questioned how much we need to keep nature intact. I suspect that this is true of a lot of courses on nature, that many of them function to take students out of themselves and encourage them to act in ways that will help preserve our planet. And I think this was a valuable part of the course. But I wanted to do more than that; I wanted to help my students see that the way in which we make decisions about nature is shaped by our culture and by an intersecting set of related beliefs, and that these beliefs are themselves shaped by very powerful forces in our culture.

I wanted to do this for at least two reasons. The first is that I wanted to make a place in my course for students who have doubts about the value of nature. Although I don't agree with much of what these students believe, I do think that every class has to allow students to bring to bear their experience and beliefs in as nonthreatening an atmosphere as possible. The second reason I wanted to push my students to think about cultural forces is that it is important to show students that there are a variety of reasonable responses to almost any issue and that the relationship between humans and nature is never a pure one, never a matter of being totally in agreement with the needs of humans or with nature. I want my students to avoid the position of one of the people Michael Pollan mentions in "The Idea of a Garden," an essay that appears in his collection, *Second Nature.* In that essay, Pollan's town has to decide what to do with a stand of pine trees that has been blown down by a tornado. Some people want to clean up the fallen trees and plant new ones and others want to let the trees decompose naturally on the spot where nature took them down. In the course of the discussion, one purist, as Pollan calls him, says, "If you're going to clean it up, . . . you might as well put up condos"(211).

I wanted to avoid this kind of either/or thinking, this sense that if we can't have nature in a perfectly pure state, we can get nothing from nature.

It seems to me that this kind of thinking leads to extremism of the worst sort, an extremism that demands its own way in the face of a vast variety of perspectives. In addition, this kind of thinking can be an excuse for doing nothing. I remember talking with my class about a colleague who bikes to work every day. The students asked what he does when he has to move his furniture, and I said he had to hire a u-haul like the rest of us. Some students took this as a betrayal of my colleague's environmental principals. The argument ran something like this: "See, he has to use gasoline for some things, so we are justified in using as much gas as we like." This is the kind of thinking I wanted to avoid. As Hillary Putnam puts it in an epigraph Lawrence Buell uses, "That everything we say is false because everything we say falls short of being everything that could be said is an adolescent sort of error"(83). Students who want to use this sort of absolutist argument have to learn its problems, and those environmentally conscious students who can sense there is something wrong with it should also learn the problems with an all-or-nothing position so they are not taken in by it. Because of these goals, I was not happy with a course that advocated simply the natural position and had no place for considering seriously other perspectives.

In fact, part of my goal in a writing class with nature as the topic is to teach students about how they are shaped by cultural forces, how their subjectivities are part of other forces within the culture. This goal is one that is shared by many versions of cultural studies. Jim Berlin describes two such courses he has taught in his book, *Rhetorics, Poetics, and Cultures*. In one of the courses, Codes and Critiques, students learn how popular culture positions them, and in the other, The Discourse of Revolution, students learn how their understanding of what is typically called "Romantic British Literature" has been shaped by culture. All such courses try to teach students how language shapes us in league with ideologies. And this is also part of my goal in a writing about nature course, but in addition, I hope to help students see the value of using a provisional ecocentric view to act in the world. I want my students to see that culture has shaped their view of nature and that nonetheless their actions can demonstrate how valuable nature is. I suspect that all cultural studies courses ground their work in some provisional ground, some bedrock value, but not all acknowledge it, for example, it seems to me that most of Berlin's work is grounded in his belief that we must work to divide the resources of the earth more fairly. For a nature course, this provisional ground is a belief in the value of nature beyond the use that can be made of it by human beings.

This goal means that in the classroom I use many of the heuristic techniques that Berlin outlines in his book. To give a sense of the larger structure of the course, let me describe a classroom activity I have seen a colleague use effectively. In a section of the course on wolves, he first had students read an old nature course favorite, *Never Cry Wolf*. The students loved the book and talked about how much they had learned about wolves and how they must be protected. Many of them had read the book before, or had at least seen the movie, and for them it was often an important factor in their interest in nature. The book also made them feel close to wolves since it anthropomorphizes them so strongly. If any book helps us see through the eyes of a wolf, this book seems to be the one that does so. After discussing and writing about Mowat's book, the teacher then turned to *The Company of Wolves* by Peter Steinhart. In this book Steinhart describes the response of wildlife biologists to Mowat, citing one as saying he should be called "Hardly Knowit"(60). Steinhart points out that Mowat in part at least falsified his account of life among the wolves. The students were at first outraged at Mowat's seeming lies. It seemed as if the ground upon which they had staked their empathy for nature was being cut out from under them. But this shaking up of the students' certainty enabled the teacher to encourage the students to resee their commitment to nature and to understand that what Mowat did may have been necessary given the world in which he lived. This sort of work can help students both understand the complexity of thinking and writing about nature as well as the pragmatic reasons for taking a stand on what might seem shaky ground.

In addition to these pedagogical concerns, I also have serious doubts about the efficacy of returning to the romantic natural position. That position is too easily co-opted by the strong temptations our postmodern culture offers. For many students, and other citizens, being environmentally conscious is a matter of recycling when convenient, using "green products" that appeal to the whim of the moment, and going outside to parks or beaches when the weather is beautiful. Our culture is very good at dividing our subjectivities, at making us believe that the place we inhabit now is the right one, even when in the next minute we can be something entirely different. We can recycle our few sheets of scrap paper and then hop into our gas-guzzling, four wheel drive vehicle and go out for Chinese with all its attendant boxes and wrappings for the landfill. I certainly feel these pressures on me—although I don't have a four-wheel drive vehicle, yet—and my students did too. They would complain about the confusion they felt and how different settings brought out different impulses. I had a student who had grown up in Poland and visited her grandparents there often. While in Poland she used her own string bag for shopping, but here she uses the endless plastic bags we all get at whatever store we go to. Of course, one answer to these problems is the natural one, the one that says we need to act consistently and in concert with nature's needs at all times and it is a matter of education to help people see this. But without a culture that reinforces those beliefs, I fear that this attempt will prove to be fruitless. Instead we need to teach our students to understand the forces that work on them and provide a local ground in nature that will help them act progressively in whatever ways are possible.

The other major criticism of my position comes from the postmodern left. This is the critique analogous to the critique of realism, that it is a constructed genre that tries to hide its ideological work behind an appeal to the way things are when the way things are serves to benefit certain classes of people and to oppress other classes. There is a great deal of truth in this criticism. Raymond Williams, a writer I admire enormously, criticizes British pastoralists for leaving out the labor of those who cared for the fields, and it certainly is true that a lot of nature writing idealizes a rural life that often is filled with poverty, disease, and very hard work. Nature becomes a kind of playground for the privileged. Some people have even accused Edward Abbey of this sin since he seems to want to keep natural places away from anyone who doesn't have his proper respect for them. He is the author who writes in *The Monkey Wrench Gang* of destroying road-building machines with glee and gets positively joyous at the thought of blowing up a dam. Of course, Abbey writes not from the perspective of the privileged but from that of one who really appreciates the simplicity and power of nature untouched by human beings. But sometimes it is hard to know when that appreciation turns to the kind of elitism that keeps out all but those who are as pure of soul as Abbey himself. We can see the same problems today in the question of traffic in Yosemite. During the summer, the experience of the park is something akin to rush hour on the Long Island Expressway. But how to keep people out of the park that is theirs?

The problem with this postmodern response is that it sees through everything. It is very good at seeing the interests at play, and at uncovering seemingly realist assumptions, but it provides no place from which to justify any action. In its most extreme form, it gives rise to that endless play that Derrida is perhaps unfairly critiqued for advocating or to the playground of America in Jean Baudrillard's work: Disneyland and Las Vegas as the great American triumphs of the twentieth century. Of course, every leftist who advocates action has some ground for that action, whether it be the question of class for Williams or justice for Berlin, but they all seem to be somewhat uncomfortable with these grounds. I want to suggest that nature provides a ground for progressive action in our world.

To put it another way, in laying out these positions in this way—the *postmodern* versus the *naive natural one,* to use terms I hope nobody will take pejoratively—I have left open for myself the approved postpostmodern position of rejecting binary oppositions and going for both/and kinds of thought. And in part I want to do that. After all, I am a creature of the academy. But I also want to suggest something a bit different too. I want to suggest that writing about nature provides a kind of ground for our thought and the thought of our students that can be used to help them and us think critically and to become better citizens of the natural world and of the social world. In a way I want my students to think in both/and ways, but I also want to preserve for them the ground for action in the world. This is the problem that, it seems to me, both/and thinking has trouble with. We can think that nature is both a place constructed by culture and also a primary experience that all human beings need, but where does that leave us when it comes time to decide whether or not to build the Hetch-Hetchy dam. Yes, we need both the joys our soul can get from the Hetch-Hetchy valley and the water we can get from the dammed river, but should we build that dam or not? Well, as most of us know, the dam was built, the valley is gone, submerged beneath the rising river, and Los Angeles has its water. Was this the right decision? I don't know, but it seems to me that both/and thinking is of no help in important problems like this. In some ways, the turn to both/and thinking is a turn to a form of idealism, a philosophy that is seductive because of the answers it offers, but always disappointing and inadequate in its manifestations in the world as we live it.

Nature has many advantages as a ground for this kind of work, even though I know it is unfashionable to talk about grounds of any sort in the postmodern world. I want to suggest two of the advantages of nature as a ground using the works of Lawrence Buell, and Barbara Ehrenrich and Janet McIntosh. Buell has written a wonderful book on writing about nature called *The Environmental Imagination: Thoreau, Nature Writing, and the Formation of American Culture.* To do justice to the riches of this book is beyond the limits of this essay. But one of his major points in the book is that there is a value in writing about nature that helps to draw us out of our own concerns and begin to consider the value of nature itself. In some way it is like Leopold's call for a land ethic, an ethic that he defines succinctly as "the extension of the social conscious from people to the land"(209). Leopold is careful not to say that the land has the last say in our actions, but he does say we need to consider its value and place in our world and that we need to preserve some of it in a wild state. Buell goes a step further and argues that the facticity of much nature writing draws us out of our own perspectives and encourages us to consider the value of nature in and of itself. Or, to put it more precisely, the facticity of nature writing draws us out of our own concerns and makes us consider the fact of others, the complexity of the world outside us. As Buell puts it, inserting the appropriate caveat in his statement, "But the more fundamental point is that the ethos—betrayed though it may eventually be—of basing art on disciplined extrospection is in the first instance an affirmation of environment over self, over appropriative homocentric desire"(104). Using the example of the poetry of Whitman and the writings of the naturalist, John Janovy, Buell claims that "Both affirm that the caddis fly is just as real as we are, has just as much right as you and I do to be taken as the center of the universe around which everything else shall revolve"(107).

Buell does note that it is certainly possible to shape our work with nature to meet the oppressive ends of some group or other, but he claims that this possibility is even more likely in a postmodern world where there is nothing to check the play of language. As he says,

> Whatever the conscious politics of the reader who espouses a philosophical antireferentialism in the domain of literary theory, that stance underrepresents the claims of the environment on humanity by banishing it from the realms of discourse except as something absent. It forbids discourse the project of evoking the natural world through verbal surrogates and thereby attempting to bond the reader to the world as well as to discourse: it forbids enabling the reader to see as a seal might see. From this standpoint, not mimesis but antireferentialism looks like the police (102).

Although I am a little skeptical about the possibility of seeing like a seal, I think that much of what Buell says rings true. Buell asks us, implicitly at least, to allow some space in our work for the claims of the natural world. On a very practical level we tend to lose sight of the degree to which our existence is grounded in the natural world. Thus, nature can serve as a tentative ground for our work, not in the metanarrative sense, as a framework that can explain all of our experiences, but rather as a kind of cognitive map in Jameson's sense, a set of landmarks that help us get around in the space we inhabit.

The other reason why I would suggest that nature can serve as a ground for us is hinted at in a recent essay by Ehrenreich and McIntosh called "The New Creationism: Biology Under Attack." This essay argues that extreme social constructionists are the new creationists because, just like the old creationists who oppose the ideas of Darwin, they believe that biology has no role in understanding human actions and society. This form of postmodernism is creationist because it suggests that unlike every other living thing on earth, we humans are not subject to biology. As Ehrenreich and McIntosh put it, "Like their fundamentalist Christian counterparts, the most extreme antibiologists suggest that humans occupy a status utterly different from and clearly 'above' that of all other living beings"(12). The authors go on to argue that "This aversion to biological or, as they are often branded, 'reductionist' explanations commonly operates as an informal ethos limiting what can be said at seminars, asked at lectures or incorporated into social theory"(12). The purpose of the essay is to argue for a nuanced inclusion of biology in our understanding of human nature. It claims that we have gone "from what began as a healthy skepticism about the misuses of biology to a new form of dogma"(13) a dogma that has become a straightjacket. The way out of this straightjacket is to work toward a synthesis. Ehrenreich and McIntosh use the work of Phoebe Ellsworth to make this point: " 'There is no biology that is not culturally mediated.' But giving biology its due while taking cultural mediation into account requires inclusive and complex thinking—as Phoebe Ellsworth puts it: 'You need a high tolerance of ambiguity to believe both that culture shapes things and that we have a lot in common' "(15). So maybe we are back to a kind of both/and thinking, but, I would argue, with a difference, the difference suggested by Buell's emphasis on facticity. Reading nature writing, if done carefully, can help take us out of ourselves and can be part of a cognitive map, a kind of ground, which helps us wriggle loose of the straightjacket that the new creationism has surreptitiously, and probably unknowingly, wrapped around us.

Both the work of Buell and that of Ehrenreich and McIntosh help us understand the problems with an extreme social constructionist position. Ehrenreich and McIntosh remind us that human beings do have a natural body, a biologic one, which connects us to all the rest of the environment. Although this body and the thinking it does have been strongly shaped by the culture human beings have created, to say that nature has no hand in shaping us is to deny the obvious. The work of Buell helps us see that grounding our ideas in a concern for the environment does not necessarily lead us to a denial of the rights and to the needs of other human beings. Ecocentrism is no more likely to lead us to ignore the claims of others than is antireferentialism, and it is perhaps less so. Antireferentialism of the sort practiced by Baudrillard is likely to blind us both to the demands of the environment as well as to those of other human beings.

Ecocentrism can, in its extreme forms, lead us to believe that the needs of human beings have no more importance than the needs of the smallest part of creation, that there is no way to decide between killing a wolf and killing a human being. But any belief, in its extreme forms, can lead to fanaticism, and ecocentrism is perhaps less like to go that far for the reasons that Buell lays out. In the work we put into understanding how the world looks through the eyes of a seal we also come to see how the world looks through the eyes of other human beings. Perhaps more dangerous are the sorts of problems raised by Raymond Williams, the tendency to use an idyllic version of nature to cover over class interests. To combat this tendency, we need once more to keep in mind the need to see the world through the eyes of other living beings, including all the human beings who interact with the environment.

Although both of these positions can be seen as supporting a nature course of the sort I described at the beginning of this essay, the romantic nature course that turns its back on the creations of culture, I believe that they are more fruitfully seen as arguing for the sort of course I advocate. In this course students would learn that our connections to the environment are strong, although partial, and that we need to see through the eyes of nature, but also through the eyes of other human beings who are as much a part of nature as any wolf. They will develop the tolerance of ambiguity that will help them understand that "culture shapes things and we have a lot in common." As part of this understanding, they will come to see their beliefs are shaped by culture, and that these beliefs are situated in a web of cultural forces. And, if all goes well in the course, many of the students will leave it with an ability to negotiate in a complex world where the demands of the environment are strong yet always in conflict with other powerful, and often important, forces. They will be able to act within the complex world that surrounds us already and that promises to become only more complex and divisive in the future. And in this future world, they will be mindful of both the history of the human race as it is embedded in the environment and of our continuing dependence on the world around us to sustain our lives.

WORKS CITED

Abbey, Edward. *The Monkey Wrench Gang.* New York: Avon, 1975.

Baudrillard, Jean. *America.* Trans. Chris Turner. London: Verso, 1988.

Berlin, James. *Rhetorics, Poetics, and Cultures: Refiguring College English Studies.* Urbana: NCTE, 1996.

Bizzell, Patricia. "Beyond Anti-Foundationalism to Rhetorical Authority: Problems Defining 'Cultural Literacy.'" *College English* 52 (1990): 661–75.

Buell, Lawrence. *The Environmental Imagination: Thoreau, Nature Writing, and the Formation of American Culture.* Cambridge: Harvard University Press, 1995.

Ehrenreich, Barbara, and Janet McIntosh. "The New Creationism: Biology Under Attack." *The Nation,* 9 June 1997. 12–15.

Faigley, Lester. *Fragments of Rationality: Postmodernity and the Subject of Composition.* Pittsburgh: University of Pittsburgh Press, 1992.

Jameson, Fredric. *Postmodernism: Or the Cultural Logic of Late Capitalism.* Durham, NC: Duke University Press, 1991.

Jenseth, Richard, and Edward Lotto, eds. *Constructing Nature: Readings from the American Experience.* Upper Saddle River, NJ: Prentice-Hall, 1996.

Leopold, Aldo. *A Sand County Almanac: And Sketches Here and There.* Oxford: Oxford University Press, 1949.

Mowat, Farley. *Never Cry Wolf.* New York: Bantam, 1963.

Pollan, Michael. *Second Nature: A Gardener's Education.* New York: Dell, 1991.

Roorda, Randall. "Sites and Senses of Writing in Nature." *College English* 59 (1997): 385–407.

Steinhart, Peter. *The Company of Wolves.* New York: Vintage, 1995.

Don't Forget to Argue:

Problems, Possibilities, and Ecocomposition

David Thomas Sumner
University of Oregon
Eugene, Oregon

The Association for the Study of Literature and the Environment (ASLE) recently published a collection of syllabi on their Web site (Blakemore and Christensen). The variety of syllabi is quite remarkable and includes courses in ecocriticism, nature writing, creative writing, and environmental studies. Here at the University of Oregon, two of my colleagues were asked to edit the collection and, because of the size of the project, they asked me to help edit the composition section. I was eager, of course, to help with such a great project that included a wide variety of innovative syllabi.

In the syllabi that were submitted, I found many interesting classes— classes I would like to take—taught by committed, bright people with whom I share environmental commitments. The classes often read texts by some my favorite writers: Annie Dillard, Edward Abbey, Terry Tempest Williams, Wendell Berry, Barry Lopez, Mary Austin, and John Muir. The instructors often asked the students to participate in creative, interesting, and worthwhile activities—interviewing an expert about some environmental issue, for example. However, I also became concerned. I was concerned because of the title under which these classes were taught: composition. Composition implies a certain focus that was not always clear in these courses. After editing these syllabi, it became apparent to me that before embarking on a project we call ecocomposition, we first need to discuss, argue about, and explore what we mean when we use the term *composition* and the role we see composition playing at the university. The ASLE collection makes it clear that as we begin to define the field of ecocomposition, we need to emphasize not only our commitment to the more-than-human world, but, if we expect to be taken seriously, we also need to be aware of how that commitment fits into contemporary rhetoric and composition theory and practice.

Indeed, composition occupies a unique place within the curriculum of most colleges and universities. It is one of a select group of courses—often the only course—which every student on campus is required to take. There are always a number of liberal education requirements that must be met, but these requirements can usually be filled by a variety of courses from a variety of departments, for example, there may be a science requirement that can be met by either a "Wildlife Biology" class or by an "Introduction to Chemistry" class. There may be a humanities requirement that can be met by "Introduction to Fiction" or "Classical Civilizations." Yet we often require every student to take the same writing requirement.

My point is to ask the following: How do we justify the unique place that composition courses have in the college curriculum? What makes a writing class so important that, in an atmosphere of finite resources and limited time, it takes precedence over other important courses?

Outside English departments, the teaching of writing is often seen as a remedial activity—as a last attempt to teach students the grammar and punctuation skills they missed in high school. I think that most of us who actually teach writing would agree that the role of composition is greater than this characterization. In fact, I would argue that the teaching of writing lays the foundation for a liberal education. More than any other class a writing class introduces students to the intellectual tools of inquiry and reason that allow them to participate in the various discourse communities of the college or university. In support of this thesis, James Crosswhite writes:

> The teaching of writing is nothing less than the teaching of reasoning. To help students to learn to write is a Socratic endeavor in the best and deepest sense. It is an attempt not to transmit received knowledge, but to engage and guide students in discovering and clarifying ideas in the context of written communication. It is an attempt to draw out of students their best ideas, in their most convincing form. It is an attempt to develop and strengthen the abilities of individual people to imagine, to reason, and to judge in the medium of writing. (4)

If composition's purpose is to help our students to imagine, reason, and judge in the medium of writing—if its goal is to introduce our students to the project of academic inquiry—I submit that we must design the courses that we call "ecocomposition" according this stated purpose first. In fact, the very reason why composition enjoys its unique role as a general requirement in the curriculum of so many colleges and universities is be-cause of composition's commitment to the critical skills of inquiry. Fur-thermore, if our ecocomposition courses do not focus primarily on written reasoning, it is difficult to justify them as a general requirement. This is precisely the reason why we must reexamine our assumptions about eco-composition, which brings me back to the syllabi collection.[1] I must admit here that it is often difficult to decipher from a syllabus exactly what is occurring in the classroom, and my discussion of the syllabi submitted to ASLE is not meant to be specific criticism of how these teachers con-duct their courses. I do believe, however, that these syllabi provide a unique window into current conceptions of ecocomposition which, in turn, gives us a starting point for our discussion.

The syllabi that were submitted, with one exception,[2] can be roughly di-vided into three categories: environmental studies courses with a strong writing component, environmental literature courses with an emphasis on the skills necessary to write about literature, and composition courses with environmental readings that employ a "mode" theory of composition.

All of these courses look like great courses. The courses I have classi-fied as "environmental studies" are particularly interesting. They are well designed and include some very creative and useful reading and writing components. The most commonly used text for these courses is Terrell F. Dixon and Scott H. Slovic's *Being in the World: An Environmental Reader for Writers*—a collection which, to quote the editor's introduction, focuses on "many examples of the best American nature writing since Thoreau" (vi). The courses in this category that did not use *Being in the World* used texts in a similar vein, including Farley Mowat's *Ordeal by Ice,* Edward Abbey's *One Life at a Time Please,* and John Wesley Powell's *Exploration of the Colorado River and Its Canyons.*

Along with interesting readings, these environmental studies courses have many interesting writing assignments. One of the more creative and intriguing assignments I encountered is a Natural History of Place. This assignment has several components. First, the student is asked to write an empirical history of a specific place. She is asked to record the different plants, animal, and insects that she encounters. She is asked to record the weather, the light, and the difference that time of day makes. She is then asked to record a personal response to that place, in narrative form, which involves an exploration of the human relationship with the more-than-human world. After all this preparation, the student then goes to the li-brary to do research on the place—learning about its geology, geography, climate, average temperature, precipitation, fossil record, and human history. Through this assignment, the student not only develops an intimate relationship with a specific geography, but she also sharpens her writing skills through the use of personal narrative and empirical description and learns how to do library research.

Yet, despite the valuable readings and the well-conceived writing assignments such as the one just described, these environmental studies courses run into problems when labeled as "composition courses." Although these courses look very useful and meet valuable pedagogical goals by addressing many of my own environmental concerns, I am not convinced that they concentrate heavily enough on the rhetorical skills of written reasoning to fulfill the more general goals of composition. Environmental studies is the main focus in these courses, with the assumption that the skills of written reasoning will be developed along the way as they would in a class entitled The Natural History of Place taught in a biology department. No doubt many students improve their written reasoning skills in such classes. However, if written reasoning becomes secondary to ecology, we run into two distinct problems. The first is the problem of writing itself. Without a more explicit focus on written reasoning, students will have fewer opportunities to develop the writing skills necessary to succeed at the university. The second related problem is one of justification. If the primary focus of composition strays from written reasoning, it will be difficult to justify composition as a general requirement in the curriculum, a justification I believe we have a responsibility to make. The fact that composition is often the only class required of all students rests on the assumption that the skills a student learns in composition are foundational to the rest of his education. [3]

Before I expand on my second listed concern, I want to emphasize that I do find these "environmental studies" courses to be excellent; in an ideal world, I would like to see every student at the university take such courses. After all, the environmental crisis we face must be addressed more directly and creatively if we are to negotiate a way to survive. But I can envision other classes addressing equally valuable issues that do not enjoy general requirement status—courses on world hunger, gender, racism, domestic abuse, poverty, political oppression, or on nuclear proliferation, to name a few. These are all examples of issues that have a claim on our students' attention equal to environmental degradation. Therefore, despite the importance of ecology, if ecocomposition is to be taken seriously and to fulfill the important role of composition in a college education, I would argue that the primary focus must be on written reasoning.

This problem of privileging subject matter over written reasoning in a composition courses based on environmental studies also exists in the second group of syllabi that I have surveyed and that might be classified as "writing about environmental literature." As James A. Berlin notes, since World War II, many universities and colleges have taught freshman writing classes in which literature is the focus (107–15), and in many ways it seems to be a natural fit. First, the task of teaching writing usually falls to English departments, and the majority of English faculty are trained in literature. It seems logical for these teachers to teach what they know and love best. Second, it is assumed, sometimes correctly and sometimes not, that because the members of the English faculty study writing (even if it is a specific type of writing) they will know how to teach composition. Third, it can be argued that the skills developed while writing about literature can be translated for use in a history class or a political science or business class, or anywhere else that the students are required to write while at the university. If this is the case it seems to be just as useful, and perfectly justifiable, to focus on environmental literature as to focus on any other genre.

Yet, doesn't this idea of literature-based ecocomposition run into some of the same problems as the environmental studies approach? Although learning to write about literature is useful, and although these skills can be translated to other courses, can we defend the practice to the university as a whole? Why couldn't the Political Science Department teach a course where students learn to write about topics in that discipline, or why couldn't Anthropology or any other department do the same? In other words, other than the fact that composition is often taught by literature scholars from the English Department, how do we defend a literature-based composition as a university-wide requirement?

In addition, I have a further concern regarding literature-based composition. As George Kennedy notes in his history of rhetoric, there is always a tendency to move from what he calls "primary forms" to "secondary forms" of rhetoric. He argues that the shift is from a civic to personal context, calling this shift "letteraturizazione" (5). My concern is that an ecocomposition course that is literature-based could easily make the shift that Kennedy describes and become less about the student's attempts to learn how to write meaningful arguments that function for them as primary rhetoric and more about the very specific experience of literature. This is not to say that literature cannot play a role in informing primary rhetoric, but it is easy for a literature-based composition to be about the literature rather than about how students can write in a meaningful and important way. James Crosswhite, in his *Rhetoric of Reason,* cites similar reasons for being suspect of a literature literature-based composition and draws a similar conclusion: "I do not believe that [literature] has a great claim on the required writing courses that make up such an important part of the general education curricula of most colleges and universities" (277). Composition, in fact, seems to maintain its claim on general education curricula only when it focuses on primary rhetoric. I am therefore uncomfortable with the environmental literature approach for reasons similar to those I outlined regarding the environmental studies approach. If we are to serve our students well as teachers of composition, ecocomposition must be about something more than environmental literature.

The third type of ecocomposition syllabus I encountered is for writing courses that use a modes-based pedagogy in which environmental texts, and often personal outdoor experience, are used to generate writing assignments. These syllabi usually divide the paper assignments into some of the following "rhetorical modes": personal narrative, definition, description, compare-and-contrast, textual analysis, collaboration, expository writing, summary, and synthesis, research. Most syllabi also usually include argument as a distinct mode. These courses do not run into the same justification problems as the other two categories. Because they focus specifically on writing, they are more easily defended as composition. In other words, if someone from the Philosophy Department were to ask why a class focusing on environmental texts is a general requirement and a class focusing on the history of philosophy is not, it could be argued that the class' main focus is not on environmental texts; rather, the class is discretely focusing on writing and using the environmental texts to generate essays. In short, this class could be defended as a writing class that gives the students important writing skills. The fact that the readings for the course are environmentally oriented is only secondary to the writing that is the course's main focus. My quibble with the approach of these courses is not on a level of focus or of curriculum justification; rather it is on the level of pedagogy. My concern regarding these courses rests with modes as a method for teaching writing.

The use of a modes-based pedagogy in composition started in the nineteenth century (Connors 444–47), but, within the circles of rhetoric and composition theory, it has largely died out. However, as evidenced by the ASLE collection, the use of a modes method in the writing classroom seems to still be very much alive. I am not sure why the modes method still persists, but the reason modes as a method of teaching has fallen out of favor with compositionists is that, to quote Robert Connors, modes "ignore the way writing is actually done" (455). The problem with the modes approach is that it highlights the form instead of the rhetorical situation. As Crosswhite states, a modes approach objectifies "the techniques and strategies of writing" independent "of any consideration of their communicative and pragmatic context" (279). As Albert R. Kitzhaber notes in *Rhetoric in American Colleges, 1850–1900,* "[Modes] turn the attention of both student and teacher toward an academic exercise instead of toward a meaningful act of communication in a social context . . . they substitute mechanical for organic conceptions and therefore distort the real nature of writing" (139).

I can think of no real writing situation in which the formal decisions are not determined by purpose and audience rather than by selecting a preexisting form from a stockpile of possibilities. Even when writing a journal writing, where the writer will be the only reader, the form is determined by the writer's purpose in keeping the journal and by her own expectations as audience. To focus our students' attention on form rather than on the rhetorical situation is to teach them how to write without discussing with them why they write. As John Gage notes, when using a modes method "the actual intention of the writing is to practice using a paradigm, rather than to earn a conclusion that needs earning" (Enthymeme 43). The modes method focuses on a formal practice without an understanding of the purpose for the practice. It emphasizes the act of writing divorced from any real reason to write.

Moreover, if one of the purposes of composition is to teach a set of skills that will translate to a student's other writing assignments[4] and to rhetorical situations outside the academy, we must have a more flexible and adaptable method of composition. It is conceivable that, after taking the writing requirement at the university, a student could be sitting in her sociology course and receive a writing assignment and say to herself, "Hmmm, this assignment is a textual analysis," or, "This assignment is a comparison contrast paper." And, conceivably, the student could be right and could write a paper that fulfilled the expectations of that specific writing situation. This student would be more likely to be successful, however, if she were able to assess the rhetorical situation. What if the assignment did not clearly fit one of the defined modes she was taught in freshman composition? Would it not be better if the student were able to ask questions such as, Who is my audience? What is their expectation? What is at issue here? What are some possible theses? In an essay arguing that thesis, what must be done? What might be done?[5]

My last objection to a modes pedagogy is how it defines argument. Partitioning off *argument* as one mode of writing often leads to a mischaracterization of the term. It leads people to believe that the purpose of argument is to persuade rather than to inquire. The distinction between argument as persuasion and argument as inquiry is an important one. As the editors of *Argument Revisited; Argument Redefined* note, argument is often seen incorrectly as a "power play" rather than an attempt to negotiate truth (Emmel, Resch, and Tenney xii). And John Gage, in that same volume, notes the dangers of this erroneous perception: "Students who believe that they are being taught to argue to prevail over opponents in situations of conflict may believe in consequence that this end justifies any rhetorical practice that leads to winning over or silencing another" (Reasoned 5). Instead, if we teach that the object of argument is to discover the best available reasons, argument is no longer about winning; it is instead about learning. Barbara Emmel, Paula Resch, Deborah Tenney, and Gage all suggest that focusing on argument as inquiry rather than as persuasion is the more useful and ultimately the more ethical approach. By focusing on argument as inquiry, Gage writes, "perhaps . . . we can focus attention on the need to teach argumentative writing as part of an education that foregrounds respect and consideration of the ideas of others" (Reasoned 5).

Furthermore, all of these other "modes" of writing are types of arguments. They may be specific types of arguments, but they are arguments nonetheless. A personal narrative is not a formal argument, but it is using different appeals to make certain points. Any good textual analysis is making an argument for how a text should be read. Even a summary, when done well, will be arguing for what textual details are important. So to give our students a narrow, modal view of argument is to do them a disservice. If they are to become better critical readers and thinkers, they must be able to recognize and evaluate argument in its many forms—in the advertisements they see, in the novels they read, in the news that they encounter.

If we agree that the environmental studies and environmental literature approaches to ecocomposition encounter problems of focus on writing and curriculum justification, and if we agree that a modes approach to ecocomposition, or to composition in general, is inadequate, then how should we proceed? My proposed solution is an argument-based ecocomposition. My use of the term *argument* carries with it the particular assumptions that I just outlined. A course based on argument as inquiry should focus on reasoning and critical thinking rather than on specific persuasive techniques. The goal of such a pedagogy is to assist students in creating arguments that are relevant to them and to their audience. In particular, the goal of such a course is to engage the students in primary rhetoric—to engage them as rhetors, requiring them to create arguments about issues that matter to them. The challenge of such a goal is to design a course that requires the student to actually "create" arguments rather that to merely plug into and reproduce preexisting ones. This is a particularly difficult challenge for an endeavor such as ecocomposition that comes to composition with a specifically foregrounded ideology, for which many of the arguments are ready-made and easily accessed within our culture.

However, before addressing the challenges of an argument-based pedagogy, I want to first describe how it would function in relation to the general education requirements of a college or university and sketch out my vision for an argument-based ecocomposition course. I am working from the assumption that a well-conceived and well-executed argument-based composition course will accomplish two things. First, the students will see how critical thinking and argument can be important to them as members of an inquiring community. Second, the skills that the students develop will translate to other rhetorical situations, both written and oral, in and out of the academy. In short, a well-designed argument pedagogy should help the students develop the essential rhetorical skills that, as Kenneth Burke puts it, help us "maneuver through life" (Foss, Foss, and Trapp 177).

To deal with first things first, the best way to get students to see themselves as writers and as part of an inquiring community is not to impose paper topics upon them, but rather to engage them in the rhetorical situation from which topics arise. As scholars and teachers, how are the ideas generated for our writing? We are part of a larger scholarly community, and our writing and scholarship is done in relation to that community. I am writing this essay now in response to differing ideas about how to best construct an ecocomposition course. This same process needs to be taken into our composition classrooms. We need to create a community of thinkers and writers who are not just fulfilling abstract assignments, but who are generating primarily important questions-at-issue—and I mean important to the students—within a community of inquirers.

It is obvious that teachers must play a guiding role in this process. There must be a subject about which to inquire. If a teacher is interested in ecology, for example, the human relationship to the more-than-human world is as suitable a subject as any. In fact, with the current state of our relationship to nature, it is arguably one of the most important subjects about which to inquire. It is also a subject about which our students often care deeply. What is difficult when teaching ecocomposition is to provide the types of readings that are going to produce real inquiry because inquiry depends on productive disagreement within the discourse community. It is easy for a course that is about such an important issue as the environment to draw like-minded people together and become a cheering section for environmental awareness; but again, this type of class will not accomplish the goals of composition. It is more difficult, but ultimately more productive, to find ways to push past shared assumptions so that new knowledge can be created and new solutions can be invented. To attain this goal, we need to challenge our student's confidence in their own positions and help them examine their own assumptions.

One way to accomplish this is to employ stasis theory. Stasis theory has been credited to Hermagoras of Temnos who wrote around 150 B.C.E. Thomas Conley in *Rhetoric in the European Tradition* tells us that "stasis, in Greek, may be translated either as 'strife' or as 'immobility,' as in the English static" (32). Stasis theory works in the classroom as a way to arrive at real questions-at-issue for the inquiring community. Prompted by readings, the class uses discussion as a way of exploring issues. A major component of exploration should be an attempt to find real points of stasis—points that lie beyond common assumptions. This means that the points of stasis cannot be determined ahead of time. Different groups of students will disagree at different points. Once a point of stasis is reached, a question is truly at-issue because there are members of the community who would answer the question differently. As a result, the students become invested in their arguments because the arguments truly belong to the students. They are no longer participating in abstract exercises; rather they are involved in inquiry about issues that matter to them in their lives.

Let me provide an example from my own classroom. I live and teach in Eugene, Oregon, where environmental consciousness runs high and environmental issues are often debated in the local press. Eugene was at one time a "timber town." The economy here has since diversified, but the issues of if, when, and what to cut are still hotly debated. Civil disobedience in response to timber sales is common. For my composition class, I assembled a group of readings that would consider the role of civil disobedience in a democracy faced with environmental issues. The readings included a selection from Plato's *Crito*, Henry David Thoreau's "Resistance to Civil Government," Martin Luther King Jr.'s "Letter from Birmingham Jail," Jack Turner's "The Abstract Wild," and finally Judi Bari's "Feminization of Earth First!"

In the discussion that followed, what was at issue for my students was not the existence of an environmental crisis, but rather the degree to which such a crisis exists and the best way to respond. Many of my students were native to Oregon and, because of a parent, relative, or neighbor's loss of employment, had been directly affected by the decline of the timber industry. I even had a logging contractor back in school on a government retraining grant. While in the same class I had another student who had been politically active in fighting some of the recent timber sales. As the discussion progressed, we began to reach stasis over the role of civil disobedience in relation to environmental issues.

We agreed as a class that nonviolent civil disobedience had a limited but vital role in a democracy when the democracy was failing to respond to the needs of certain groups. However, here is where the stasis emerged. There were those in the class who felt civil disobedience must be reserved for issues such as civil rights and that protecting "trees" should be done from within the system—through the courts, through petitioning legislative bodies, and through the ballot box. Others felt the traditional avenues took too long and, if they waited for the courts and legislatures, all of the forests would be cut; they argued that environmental protection was just as important as civil rights, and therefore, civil disobedience was justified as a way to protect Oregon's forests.

Although I did select the readings and I did guide the discussion by keeping it on track, these points of stasis were reached by my students through their own inquiry. As a result, real questions-at-issue were raised—questions that they truly cared about. Those questions included: What is the role of civil disobedience in a democracy? Is civil disobedience in response to environmental issues justified? How do environmental issues differ from those of civil rights? How are they similar? The papers they produced were arguments written by active learners. These students were invested in their writing because their theses had come from real discussion and were in response to an issue they cared about.

From a pedagogical view, all points of stasis are not equally effective, however. One of the difficulties faced when using a stasis approach is in finding points that require the students to generate their own arguments about particular issues. In my example, just cited, the questions-at-issue that arose out of stasis required the students to generate their own arguments by synthesizing the readings and the class discussion with their own ideas. Yet, when discussing such a publicly debated issue as the environment, it is easy for students to identify existing arguments and merely plug into them and not benefit from the experience of fashioning an argument that is in some way their own, for example, during the last election cycle here in Oregon there was a ballot initiative which, if passed, would have severely restricted logging on public and private land. The initiative (Measure 64) was discussed at length on the radio, in the papers, and on local television. I had a very environmentally aware student who wanted to write a paper on Measure 64. There was definitely stasis over this issue in our classroom community. There were many students who had expressed opposition to the measure and many others who felt the measure was an important move toward forest health. The problem with this issue and issues like it, however, is that instead of synthesizing ideas from the readings and thinking through the problem for herself, a student may avoid that rhetorical task by simply following a familiar line of reasoning devised from arguments that already exist and simply arranging them into a paper that supports her thesis.

In the first example, most of my students had never seriously considered the role of civil disobedience in a democracy, nor had they ever considered if, when, and why civil disobedience may be necessary. Thus, when the specific question of civil disobedience in relation to environmental causes arose, they did not know of a place to go where people had already resolved the issue for them with a long list of convincing reasons; instead, they had to negotiate their own position. In the case of Measure 64, however, a student could easily go to the voter's pamphlet and lift the arguments he found there. I am not saying that he would not cite his sources, but he would not benefit from creating his own argument in response to a specific issue that arose in a specific inquiring community. This student would not benefit from the learning process that occurs when generating an argument in response to an issue that he is thinking through independently.

With an ideologically based composition such as ecocomposition, good papers can be difficult to generate. It takes skill to design and execute a syllabus that addresses the human relationship with the more-than-human world, while at the same time raising genuine questions-at-issue from points of stasis reached by the students—a skill at which I am continually working. Moreover, we do not do justice to our role as teachers if our composition classrooms merely turn into cheering sections for pet causes, environmental or other. Such classes may generate converts, or even enemies, but they will not provide students with the necessary critical writing and thinking skills to address the complexity of issues they will face in the academy and in life. But if we use stasis theory well, we will be able to help students generate essays that do address real issues that arise from real rhetorical situations, and we can also guide our classes' inquiries into the important issues of the human relationship with the natural world.

Let me address an additional concern by asking a challenging question. Although most of us would be comfortable with a class called "ecocomposition" or "feminist composition" or even "Marxist composition," we would be less comfortable with a class called "Christian composition"; but what are the true differences between these approaches? How can we justify teaching a composition that highlights our environmental commitments and feel that a composition that highlights Christian or Muslim or Buddhist commitments is less legitimate? Is not the teacher of a Christian composition course equally committed to her ideology? My answer to this is that any course that is committed to an ideology—environmental or other—must first be committed to an ideology of rational inquiry—something I believe an argument-based ecocomposition can accomplish, but only at the expense of orthodoxy.

Now, I can already feel my readers bristling and objecting that it is the overemphasis on rational inquiry that has gotten us into this environmental mess in the first place. They will point to Descartes, Bacon, and other rationalists as the cause of our separation from nature. They will also point out that I am merely substituting one ideology for another and that all ideologies are loaded. And my answer to these objections is yes, yes, and yes.

But the key here is in how I am defining rational inquiry. In my definition, I want to emphasize the idea of a self-critical system. Martha Nussbaum points to this feature of rational inquiry in *Cultivating Humanity*. Here she writes that a student who is going to be part of a democracy and ultimately be a world citizen should have "the capacity for critical examination of [herself] and [her] tradition" (9).[6] In other words, rational inquiry should involve the ability of a community to do more than just make claims and counterclaims; it should provide a way for a community to reason together that means all members of the community must be prepared to try on other arguments and change their minds when presented with good reasons. One of the primary pitfalls of teaching a course with a foregrounded ideology is the ease with which such a foregrounding can create areas that are off limits to inquiry. If we are to teach ecocomposition well, we must facilitate all types of reasonable arguments. Orthodoxy is overcome only by one's willingness to consider all sides—all reasons—and to decide what to believe based on such reasons, that is, to be willing to entertain the possibility of changing one's mind.

Lastly, a system of rational inquiry must not ignore an appeal to pathos. A common criticism of Descartes and of other Enlightenment thinkers is their narrow definition of what qualifies as reason. If, in our composition classes, we are truly exploring ways in which we can establish a more ethical relationship with the more-than-human, world we must not follow the enlightenment tendency to discount pathos. When discussing environmental issues, pathos can often help us sympathize with the more-than-human world in productive ways.

Finally, the reason why my commitment to ecocomposition is only secondary to my commitment to a composition based on argument and rational inquiry is that I have arrived at my own environmental commitments through this process. I believe that if we participate in honest inquiry, we cannot help but discover that this world is under threat. I also believe that our greatest hope in saving this world is to learn to argue well, and by this I mean to argue honestly. I also believe that we do the greatest service to our students and to the environment by teaching them to do likewise. If we do our jobs well as ecocompositionists, our students will not only be able to reason together and address environmental concerns, they may also be able to fulfill the ecological hopes of the dialectician in Kenneth Burke's "Dialectician's Hymn":

> If the soil is carried off by flood,
> May we help the soil to say so.
> If our ways of living
> Violate the needs of nerve and muscle,
> May we find speech from nerve and muscle,
> To frame objections
> Whereat we, listening,
> Can remake our habits. (56)

If we teach composition well, I have hope that we, along with our students, can speak for the soil, and for nerve and muscle, and that such speech is the best prospect for, as Burke put it, remaking the habits of our nature as a symbol-using, symbol-abusing species.

NOTES

1. After presenting a preliminary draft of this paper at CCCCs in Atlanta, both Sid Dobrin and Randall Roorda noted that one of the problems with the ASLE collection is that it was solicited by the Association for the Study of Literature and the Environment. An association with such an emphasis on literature, they noted, could only be expected to attract the types of syllabi I discuss here. They suggested that if the organization's name were changed to the Association for the Study of Language and the Environment, or to some other more inclusive term, some of the problems I point out here might be avoided.

2. The syllabus of Michael McDowell, who teaches at Portland Community College, was the exception. Of all the syllabi submitted, his course is unique in the collection because it is an argument-based course in ecocomposition.

3. The need to justify the role of composition to the university and larger community is now more evident than ever following the 1990 controversy at the University of Texas at Austin. For more detail about the controversy and the series of misunderstandings occurred, see Linda Brodkey's article "Making a Federal Case out of Difference: The Politics of Pedagogy, Publicity, and Postponement," in *Writing Theory and Critical Theory* edited by John Clifford and John Schilb. In addition, see Ben W. McClelland, Mark

Andrew Clark, and Patricia Harkin's articles in response to Brodkey in the same volume.

4. I am not arguing that composition transmits a discrete set of skills that is easily mastered and then the student simply moves on to his or her real work. Instead, composition should be an introduction to written reasoning, but, as James Crosswhite notes; "Written reasoning is infinitely perfectible, and needs to be strengthened and transformed, learned anew, at each new level of intellectual endeavor, in each new domain of intellectual work" (5).

5. See John Gage's "Reasoned Thesis" (14).

6. I do think that one of the major flaws in Nussbaum's argument is that she doesn't define the idea of world citizen broadly enough. She wants to draw the line at the edge of humanity. However, we could just as easily use her logic to extend the idea of world citizen to the ecosystems of which human beings are inextricably part.

WORKS CITED

Berlin, James A. *Rhetoric and Reality: Writing Instruction in American Colleges, 1900–1985.* Carbondale: Southern Illinois University Press, 1987.

Blakemore, Peter, and Laird Christensen, eds. ASLE Syllabi Collection. Online. http://www.asle.umn.edu/pubs/collect/collect.html.

Burke, Kenneth. *Language as Symbolic Action: Essays on Life and Method.* Berkeley: University of California Press, 1966.

Conley, Thomas. *Rhetoric in the European Tradition.* Chicago: University of Chicago Press, 1953.

Connors, Robert. "The Rise and Fall of the Modes of Discourse." *College Composition and Communication* 32(1981): 444–63.

Clifford, John, and John Schilb eds. *Writing Theory and Critical Theory.* New York, Modern Language Association of America, 1994.

Crosswhite, James. *The Rhetoric of Reason: Writing and the Attraction of Arguments.* Madison: University of Wisconsin Press, 1996.

Dixon, Terrell F., and Scott H. Slovic. *Being in the World: An Environmental Reader for Writers.*

Emmel, Barbara, Paula Resch, and Deborah Tenney, eds. *Argument Revisited; Argument Redefined.* Thousand Oaks, CA: SAGE Publications, 1996.

Foss, Sonja K., Karen A. Foss, and Robert Trapp. *Contemporary Perspectives on Rhetoric.* 2nd ed. Prospect Heights, IL: Waveland Press, 1991.

Gage, John. "The Reasoned Thesis." *Argument Revisited; Argument Redefined.* Eds. Barbara Emmel, Paula Resch, and Deborah Tenney. Thousand Oaks, CA: SAGE Publications, 1996.

———. "Teaching the Enthymeme: Invention and Arrangement." *Rhetoric Review* 1(1983): 38–50.

Kennedy, George. *Classical Rhetoric and Its Christian and Secular Traditions From Ancient to Modern Times.* Chapel Hill: University of North Carolina Press, 1980.

Kitzhaber, Albert R. *Rhetoric in American Colleges, 1850–1900.* Dallas: Southern Methodist University Press, 1990.

Nussbaum, Martha. *Cultivating Humanity: A Classical Defense of Reform in Liberal Education.* Cambridge, Harvard University Press, 1997.

Writing Home:

Composition, Campus Ecology, and Webbed Environments

Bradley John Monsma
Woodbury University
Burbank, California

Thinking about ecocomposition has been a little like walking through California's coastal chaparral intending to learn the spring flowers only to be distracted by birds and from birds by butterflies. Seeming distractions hone insight, and the best stories reside in the relationships. Sometimes, in giving up the clear pursuit one is granted a glimpse of how things might fit together. What follows, therefore, combines description of an ecocomposition course design with reflection upon experiencing it. Here are the elements whose relationships are crucial to both practice and theory.

First, the university campus, a borderland between urban and open space, provided an ecologically interesting space for inquiry. On one side, it is situated a couple hundred yards from Interstate 5, the main thoroughfare running between Mexico and Canada. Across the freeway toward the cemented Los Angeles River sit the television and film studios. Climb into the Verdugo Hills behind campus and you can see Mickey's silhouette stuck to the side of a Disney high rise. But these same hills are the home of deer, coyotes, ravens, and even the occasional mountain lion. If it rains in winter, the meadows and trailsides spring monkey flowers, tomcat clovers, lupines, prickly phlox, sages, and phacelias. Students regularly see deer grazing on the soccer field and hear the coyotes at night. The ravens fly over the quad toward their easy lunches in town.

For many of my students, this borderland is wild. They've lived their whole lives in intensely urban environments, experiencing little of what most middle-class Americans would consider the wilderness or nature. From diverse cultures and continents, overburdened with school, work, and family responsibilities and "geared" toward their prospective professions, they tend to experience natural environments as being on the other side of the window of their lives. They see just enough to notice the estrangement. My experiments with ecocomposition began with the expectation that writing could become a way for students to seek awareness and to demonstrate knowledge of the local environment. I wondered whether these first-year students would become the grassroots that would bring the environment to the attention of a budget-strapped, overworked university community that always seemed to have more pressing concerns.

Second, I wished to find a way to use an ecology-based course content to lessen the typical artificiality of the composition exercise. Too often, no genuine audience for student writing exists outside the class, and the purpose for writing is most often defined in rhetorical terms only. Students seem to enter classes expecting to defend positions they do not hold. Belief matters less than artifice. They learn to distrust the language they speak and hear, to substitute big words for small ones, abstract words for those tied to the senses and to things. They learn to do this for grades that seem to be arbitrary and they file returned papers where they can be sure never to see them again. Despite the process models that dominate college writing instruction, students learn early that "academic discourse" is most unnatural. A requirement for this course, therefore, was to find a natural, responsive audience for my students' writing.

Third, it so happened that as I designed the ecocomposition course, the university began a program in which all incoming freshmen were to have notebook computers. I was strongly encouraged to revise my writing course to foreground the use of the computers and that magic pill—the internet. So while I needed to find opportunities to make appropriate use of the technology, I also hoped to introduce a counterdiscourse. Was it Max Frisch who warned that "Technology is the knack of so arranging the world that we don't have to experience it?" I wanted to make sure my students could consider the experiential and epistemological consequences of their new tools. I wanted to balance, or at least contrast, their experience of the instantaneous, global characteristics of on-line information with local knowledge of ecological interdependencies that often become apparent only through patient attention to a particular place.

The fourth piece of the puzzle involved questions of how to represent the knowledge gleaned through the research project at the heart of the course. In my own reading and research in ecocriticism I continually confront questions about cultural representations of nature and relationships between the linguistic constructions and their material reality. At one level I wished to build a course and a research project that asked students to pay careful attention to the nature of an urban place and to use language to begin to articulate not only their own relationships to that place but also those of the entire ecological community. Yet, I also hoped to find ways for students not only to write about nature but also to consider the forms, conventions, and consequences of their representations. The foregrounding of computers in the course added a layer of complexity to these questions.

In designing the research project that would structure the course, I found inspiration in the work of the nature writer and natural historian Barry Lopez. In the essay, "The Passing Wisdom of Birds," Lopez calls for contemporary American culture to reexamine our experience in the New World and to consider adopting a "fundamentally different way of thinking" (198) about nature. To do this, he suggests that we protect and contemplate intact ecosystems. But he also emphasizes the need to nurture cultural wisdom: "We need to immerse ourselves thoughtfully in what is being written and produced on tape and film, so that we become able to distinguish again between truthful expression and mere entertainment" (203). He offers a practical first step in combining these two modes of inquiry: that each university in the country might create the position of "university naturalist." This position would be responsible for "establishing and maintaining a natural history of the campus, would confer with architects and grounds keepers, escort guests, and otherwise look out for the nonhuman elements of the campus, their relationships to human beings, and the preservation of this knowledge" (205). Lopez's suggestion recognizes the university campus as an excellent site for acknowledging and cultivating interdependencies between nature and culture. The "university naturalist" position, however, seemed like too great a task for one college student. Therefore, I put a whole class to work at compiling a natural history of our campus in a pursuit of wisdom appropriate to our place on the border between the Verdugo Hills and urban Los Angeles. The vision of the project would be both ecological and cultural. Ultimately, it would try to articulate community. The word *ecology*, after all, comes from the Greek *oikos*—"home" and "dwelling place," and *logos*—"talking," "logic," and "legend."[1] The project, therefore, sought the home legend, the story and logic of our place.

To begin the project and to consider the direction of inquiry, students walked the twenty-two acre campus "reviewing" what they were accustomed to seeing, considering the place through their nonvisual senses, and analyzing the possible effects on their perceptions of their choice of time of day, weather conditions, season, and the like. After writing of their experiences, each person selected a topic from within the range of possibilities they discovered: water use, specific flora and fauna, landscape design, pesticide and herbicide use, waste disposal and recycling, the energy efficiency of buildings, and so forth. Class members then set about investigating their chosen topics, learning textual, hypertextual, and interpersonal research methods, and conducting continued "fieldwork" and observation. Throughout these interim steps, students were writing and revising the strands that would gradually form their final documents. They were learning what students do in typical composition classes: how to organize, develop paragraphs, and argumentation strategies; how to estimate audiences and meet their expectations; how to control tone; and so forth.

As the students worked, the goals of the project gradually coalesced as the ecological relationships within the students' inquiry became manifest. The further each person delved into a particular subject matter, the more he or she began to understand its ecological context and conferring with other researchers. As Phong investigated nonnative plants used in landscaping, she found herself consulting Jaime who was researching herbicides and Tim and Shana who were studying campus water use and the history of water in southern California. The relationships between researchers were not imposed artificially, but grew organically as students found the need for them. The class began to act as a cooperative community of researchers, and as this notion became self-conscious, they were always reminded that their connections were rooted in their place and subject matter; they learned to think beyond humans in defining community.

As the research progressed, the class was faced with the question of how the final form of their writing might represent the relationships between researchers and between subject matters. I asked students to consider the extent to which the "traditional research paper" would resegment the connections and complexities of which they were becoming aware. There is a hint of irony in the fact that the administrative push toward technology provided a tentative answer to our problem of representation. Instead of writing individual research papers, students contributed to a web page and began to think of it both practically and metaphorically. Instead of separating researchers and research, the web page allowed students' writings to be linked to each other where the subject matter warranted and to internet research materials. The final document thus became a metaphoric demonstration of the ecological web linking human and nonhuman elements of the campus community and the surrounding area. The on-line, interlinked documents also became available to a real and potentially responsive audience. Students who became committed to their information and knowledge, who came to advocate positions and actions, learned that their words could have an affect on their own community. Or not. It all depended upon their presentation, the persuasiveness of their arguments, the quality of their research, and in some cases, the practicality and cost-effectiveness of their solutions to problems. The internet became crucial to creating a genuine, meaningful context for students' writing. On the one side, the research project extended the idea of the university community to nonhuman members. On another, the writing provided a bridge between students and people on campus with whom they otherwise would have little contact. In highlighting the ways in which classroom practice defines and enacts community, the project's ethical significance became apparent.

In his recent examination of the ethics of internetworked writing, James E. Porter uses compelling geographic metaphors to describe the effect of computers on the writing classroom: "When the writing classroom employs internetworked communication, classroom borders are opened and new parties admitted to the rhetorical and social mix" (3). Well-established ethical conventions are disturbed in "a new geographic region where our old trustworthy borders (classroom vs. workplace, speech vs. writing, industry vs. academy) are no longer viable" (5). Internetworked writing invites the outside in. It is important to note, however, that Porter's geographic metaphors are metaphors only. The soil has been shaken from their roots; the social relationships they point to extend only to humans. This absence is crucial to ecocompositionists who work with computers, especially considering that the computer "influences the consciousness of the writer and shapes both the production and reception of the writing, enabling (and constraining) certain writing practices" (9). Yet such anthropocentrism mirrors previous ethical inquiry into composition instruction. Porter's excellent review of studies in ethics and composition reveals the expected ethical foci involving the flow of power in the classroom, race and ethnicity, feminism, economics, and the politics of technology. Porter and others have recognized how computers add an additional layer of complexity to questions of compositional ethics. Cynthia L. Selfe and Richard J. Selfe Jr., for example, suggest that even computer interfaces assert the cultural values of segments of society that produce them. They see interfaces as the "linguistic contact zones" that Mary Louise Pratt describes as "social spaces where cultures meet, clash, and grapple with each other, often in contexts of highly asymmetrical relations of power, such as colonialism, slavery, or their aftermaths as lived out in many parts of the world today" (Selfe and Selfe 482). Like Porter, Selfe and Selfe use metaphors of terrain to orient and segment their study, though they do not delve into ecological matters. Their headings read, "Computers as Learning Environments," "Mapping the Interface of Computers as Educational Space," and "Interfaces as Maps of Capitalism and Class Privilege." It must be the task of ecocomposition to remind us that material environmental conditions also affect the social spaces that

come to bear upon discursive acts and the types of consciousness they encourage.

If approaches to compositional ethics imply definitions of community, the practice and theory of ecocomposition ought to reintroduce the
other-than-human into ethical considerations of writing communities.
We ought to ask whether internetworked writing might be used and
thought of in ways that expand and demonstrate our notions of difference,
connection, and integrity. Why should not Aldo Leopold's "Land Ethic"
provide a foundation for an ethics of rhetoric and technology? "A thing is
right when it tends to preserve the integrity, stability, and beauty of the biotic community. It is wrong when it tends otherwise" (262).

Like too many dreams of environmentalists and writing professors,
the practical effects of my course's research project were somewhat disappointing. The students' writing clearly improved over the course of the semester, as did their research and web-authoring skills. However, I had
overestimated the level of computer education and support the students
would be receiving outside the class. I wondered whether anxiety about
the technology had occasionally transferred to anxiety about writing and
impeded students' development. I also regretted the amount of class time
spent dealing with computer questions rather than those more directly related to writing. I had to struggle to keep the class focused on writing. In
part because of these concerns, I will in the future be teaching this course
as a first-year, second-semester critical thinking course rather than as an
introductory composition class.

Still, the students in the class seemed to regard the resulting web page
with a certain amount of pride and satisfaction initially. It indeed represented their work as individuals and as a group. Links between papers represented ecological, economic, and practical relationships. However, the
web site began to disintegrate during the following semester. Since students had posted their work to free, off-campus web sites, to which I had
linked the main course page, they could delete their work at their own dis-
cretion. I had encouraged this method at the beginning of the semester in
response to student concerns about their work being publicly available in
perpetuity. Some students removed their projects as they recognized how
much effort would be required after the course to produce fully convincing research and highly polished documents. Not everyone, after all, received *As* at the end of the course. Even those whose work was excellent
continued to develop their writing and research skills in other courses, and
it was not long before they saw their projects as failing to represent their
current abilities and standards. Furthermore, some students continued to
think about their topics after grades had been turned in, and as their

thinking developed they felt compelled to update their work or to delete it. In retrospect, it seems that many students internalized processual modes of thinking and writing while the product, for all its potential flexibility as a webbed document, was static without continual attention.

The effect of the course on the ecology of the campus was minimal. Lawns were still overwatered, the air conditioning still ran too cold, the campus was "beautified" with little thought to ecological ramifications, and a large portion of the hills behind campus was bulldozed for a housing development. Even where students produced persuasive analyses and plans for improvement, staff and administration responded coolly. Those who read the student work said, essentially, "that's nice, I've got to get back to work." The proposals, after all, were coming from first-year students, among the least powerful members of the human campus community. Moreover, our university curriculum, like most with its many disconnected courses in different disciplines, does not promote long-term development of ideas or the following through of ideas toward practical results. Instead, we tend to create artificial exercises that simulate the real work we pretend occurs only after graduation. To maintain the status quo and avoid challenging ideas emerging from course work, those challenged must simply wait for students and professors to move onto the next round of classes. A possible solution to this may be to teach composition classes based on campus ecology regularly, every term if possible. The publication of student work on-line could allow successive classes to develop, expand, and possibly replace the work of previous classes. Eventually, a critical mass of informed advocates might provide a consistent voice for change that would be heard and taken seriously by those who have the power to act.

Ultimately, the success of this project may rest in its least tangible or quantifiable aspect—the potential changes in the consciousness of students, in their way of thinking about and experiencing language and place.

To begin to understand this change, one might consider the social nature of language and how place and language combine in the formation of the self. Social theories of language have encouraged practitioners of composition and rhetoric to see writers as more than autonomous, independent intellects. Linda Flower, a leading proponent of social discursive theories, argues that we ought to understand writing as an interactive social and cognitive process. Students, according to this view, negotiate tensions between competing forces for making meaning. "Social," however, has typically been understood in exclusively human terms. This is despite the fact that the Russian psychologist Lev Vygotsky, whose social theories of language have influenced composition studies, used weather metaphors to suggest that the self is permeable and fluid, that the self does not stop at one's skin (Zebroski 152). This notion is similar to that more recently expressed by David Abram who points out that "the boundaries of a living body are open and indeterminate; more like membranes than barriers, they define a surface of metamorphosis and exchange" (46). Or in the words of Paul Shepard; "The epidermis of the skin is ecologically like a pond surface or forest soil, not as a shell so much as a delicate interpenetration. It reveals the self as ennobled and extended . . . as part of the landscape and ecosystem" (quoted in Bowers 204). If we understand the body not as a protective shell but as the means by which we meet that which is other than human, then we can also understand embodied language as one of our links to the environment in which we breath, speak, and write. It was crucial, therefore, for my students to begin their projects outside, walking the grounds, as well as in the library and on-line; this is to say they began phenomenologically as well as intellectually. The idea was for students to come to understand the body and language as means of exchange with the earth. They were to give local, earthy, nonanthropocentric habitation to the oft-quoted line by the Russian philosopher M. M. Bakhtin: "language, for the individual consciousness, is on the border between oneself and the other" (239). A key idea of ecocomposition is that the "other" can be conceived of as "other-than-human." Ecocomposition might encourage understanding of the role of ecosystems and environments in the dialogic relationships that form ourselves and our words.

Indeed, for Abram and for those who participate in oral languages in particular places, thought and language emerge from the breathing body as from the earth. Abram explains with reference to the phenomenologist Merleau-Ponty that "the sensuous, perceptual world . . . is relational and weblike in character, and hence that the organic, interconnected structure of any language is an extension or echo of the deeply interconnected matrix of sensorial reality itself" (84). The image of words as web may be familiar to readers of Native American literatures in which contemporary authors write within the context of oral traditions, as does Leslie Marmon Silko in the novel, *Ceremony:*

> The word he chose to express "fragile" was filled with the intricacies of a continuing process, and with a strength inherent in spider webs woven across paths through sand hills where in the morning the sun becomes entangled in each filament of web. It took a long time to explain the fragility and intricacy because no

word exists alone, and the reason for choosing each word had to be explained with a story about why it must be said this certain way. That was the responsibility that went with being human, old Ku'oosh said, the story behind each word must be told so there could be no mistake in the meaning of what had been said; and this demanded great patience and love. (35–36)

I don't pretend that an internetworked, ecologically based student research project can begin to mimic the rootedness of oral storytelling, or that it can recover what has been lost in textual and technological culture's estrangement from the world. However, it may be a start. As an enacted technological metaphor, "webbed" writing might reinvest language with flexibility and impermanence. It might encourage writers to respond readily to other writing and to changes in the world. It may encourage participation to accompany analysis, conversation, and storytelling to accompany isolated thinking. Though webbed words can never become real community, we might choose to use the technology in ways that remind us of the relationships that sustain us.

NOTES

1. See Tom Jay's essay, "Familiar Music," for a wonderful gloss on the word *ecology.*

WORKS CITED

Abram, David. *The Spell of the Sensuous: Perception and Language in a More-than-Human World.* New York: Vintage, 1996.

Bakhtin, M. M. *The Dialogic Imagination: Tour Essays by M. M. Bakhtin.* Ed. Michael Holquist. Trans. Caryl Emerson and Michael Holquist. Austin: University of Texas Press, 1981.

Bowers, C. A. *Education, Cultural Myths, and the Ecological Crisis: Toward Deep Changes.* Albany: State University of New York Press, 1993.

Flower, Linda. *The Construction of Negotiated Meaning: A Social Cognitive Theory of Writing.* Carbondale: Southern Illinois University Press, 1994.

Jay, Tom. "Familiar Music." *Orion* 15.4 (Autumn 1996): 52–56.

Leopold, Aldo. *A Sand County Almanac.* San Francisco: Sierra Club/Ballantine, 1970.

Lopez, Barry. "The Passing Wisdom of Birds." *Crossing Open Ground.* 1988. New York: Vintage, 1989.

Porter, James E. *Rhetorical Ethics and Internetworked Writing.* Greenwich, CT: Ablex, 1998.

Selfe, Cynthia L., and Richard J. Selfe Jr. "The Politics of the Interface: Power and Its Exercise in Electronic Contact Zones." *College Composition and Communication* 45 (1994): 480–504.

Silko, Leslie Marmon. *Ceremony.* 1977. New York: Penguin, 1986.

Zebroski, James Thomas. "The Social Construction of Self in the Work of Lev Vygotsky." *The Writing Instructor* 8 (1989): 149–56.

Contributors

Anis Bawarshi is an Assistant Professor of English at the University of Washington, where he teaches courses in rhetoric and composition. His research interests involve the concept of genre and its relationship to rhetorical situation, invention, and the writer. Currently, he is collaborating on a textbook that uses genre to help students better understand and navigate various rhetorical situations, and is completing a book on genre and the role of the writer. He has published articles and interviews in *JAC: A Journal of Composition Theory, The Writing Center Journal, Writing on the Edge, Issues in Writing,* and *Kansas English;* recently his article, "The Genre Function," appeared in *College English.*

Stephen G. Brown is an Assistant Professor of English and Director of the First-Year Writing Program at the University of Tampa. His articles have appeared in *JAC, Review of Education,* and *College Literature.* He's written a book, *Words in the Wilderness: Critical Literacy in the Borderlands.* He is currently working on a second book, which draws on his experiences teaching in Hawaii, and that similarly foregrounds issues affecting the acquisition of literacy across cultures.

Colleen Connolly teaches courses in composition, composition theory, contemporary literatures, women's literature, and popular culture at the University of South Florida. Her current research interests include feminist theory, contemporary rhetorical theory, and critical theory. Her articles and reviews have appeared in *JAC, Rhetoric Society Quarterly, Teaching English in the Two Year College,* and *Composition Forum.*

Sid Dobrin is an Associate Professor of English and Director of Writing programs at the University of Florida. He also serves on the faculty for the university's College of Natural Resources and Environmental Studies. He is the author, coauthor, editor, and coeditor of several books and collections including *Natural Discourse: Toward Ecocomposition* (with Christian Weisser), *Constructing Knowledges: The Politics of Theory-Building and Pedagogy in Composition,* and *Saving Place: An Ecoreader.* His first book on fishing, *Distance Casting,* explores relationships between writing and fishing. An avid fisherman, diver, and all-around blue water bum, he spends most of his time in, on, or under the water, and like Paul in the movie version of *A River Runs Through It,* only needs another three years until he can think like a fish.

Julie Drew is an Assistant Professor of English at the University of Akron where she teaches composition and cultural studies. She is currently coauthoring a rhetorical and political history of the Cuyahoga Valley National Recreation Area in northeast Ohio. She is also a displaced Floridian, whose love of sunshine, saltwater, and bare feet is somehow enhanced by a newly acquired appreciation of thermal underwear.

Greta Gaard is the author of *Ecological Politics: Ecofeminists and the Greens,* editor of *Ecofeminism: Women, Animals, Nature,* and, with Patrick D. Murphy, has edited *Ecofeminist Literary Criticism: Theory, Interpretation, Pedagogy.* She is an Associate Professor of Humanities at Western Washington University's Fairhaven College. Currently, she is writing a volume of ecofeminist creative nonfiction essays.

Annie Merrill Ingram is an Assistant Professor of English at Davidson College. She regularly teaches courses in ecocomposition and environmental literature with service-learning components. Her current research interests include the practical and theoretical intersections of ecopedagogy and ecocriticism. In addition to her work on environmental topics, she specializes in nineteenth-century American literature and culture, especially gender studies, and has written articles on various women writers.

Christopher J. Keller teaches composition, nature writing, and British literature at the University of Florida. He has written several reviews and articles about nature, myth, composition, and discourse theory, and he is currently coauthoring (with Sidney I. Dobrin) a book of interviews with nature writers, entitled *The Nature of Writing.*

M. Jimmie Killingsworth is a Professor and Director of Graduate Studies in English at Texas A&M University. He has taught at five universities and is the author of five books and over fifty articles in American literature, rhetoric and composition, and technical communication, including *Ecospeak: Rhetoric and Environmental Politics in America* (coauthored with Jacqueline S. Palmer), which won the 1992 NCTE Award for Best Book in Technical and Scientific Communication.

John Krajicek is a teacher and doctoral student in discourse studies at Texas A&M University. He is currently doing research on the rhetoric of nature writing and the pedagogy of ecocomposition.

Paul Lindholt is a Professor at Eastern Washington University, in the Columbia Plateau bioregion where he spent much time as a child and where he teaches English and Integrative Studies. He has published articles on Edward Abbey, colonial natural histories, and the politics of the antienvironmental backlash known as "wise-use."

Mark C. Long is an Assistant Professor of English and American studies at Keene State College, where he teaches courses in expository writing, twentieth-century literature, Americans studies, literature in the environment, and critical theory. He has published essays on writing program administration, theories of reading in this study of American literature, the earlier writing of William Carlos Williams, and the poetics of Denise Levertov. He is currently at work on a book on William Carlos Williams and the tradition of American poetry.

Edward Lotto teaches at Lehigh University, where he directed the writing program for eight years and has run the Writing Center for fifteen. He teaches undergraduate and graduate courses in writing, and occasionally courses on writing about nature and American Romanticism. He has edited a nature anthology with Richard Jenseth called *Constructing Nature: Readings from the American Experience* and has published articles in *College English* and *The Writing Center Journal*. He is a past editor of *The Writing Center Journal*. As a child, he wanted to be a forest ranger, but his guidance counselor talked him out of it.

Brad Monsma is an Associate Professor of English at Woodbury University in Burbank, California, in what's left of the Los Angeles River watershed. An avid whitewater kayaker and backpacker, he has published articles on Native American literature and cross-cultural literary theory, most recently in *SAIL: Studies in American Indian Literatures* and *Modern Language Studies*. He is currently teaching an interdisciplinary course in California natural history and nature writing and is active in efforts to restore steelhead habitat in southern California.

Derek Owens teaches in the English Department and directs the Writing Center at St. John's University in Queens, New York. He lives on Long Island with his wife Teresa and son Ryan. His book *Survival and Sustainability: Composition's Role in the New Curriculum* is under contract at NCTE Press as part of their Refiguring English Studies series.

Arlene Plevin has been involved with environmental issues as a teacher, writer, and activist. She studied at the University of Iowa Writer's Workshop, receiving an MFA in poetry, and she has taught composition and journalism courses at Clemson University, Indiana State University, and Georgetown University. Plevin has worked as a writer/editor for the National Wildlife Federation and as Director of Publications for the League of American Bicyclists. Her work has been published in *Technical Communication, Deliberative Discourse, and Environmental Rhetoric Connections and Directions; The Literature of Nature An International Sourcebook,* and *Bicycling* magazine. Her books include one for the National Education Association and one on bicycling for *Fodor's Sports,* and she has bicycled throughout the world. Currently, she is finishing her PhD in English at the University of Washington.

Randall Roorda, an English professor and Writing Program Administrator at the University of Missouri-Kansas City, founded and coordinates activities for ASLE-CCCC, a special interest group in ecology and composition affiliated with the Association for the Study of Literature and Environment. The author of *Dramas of Solitude: Narratives of Retreat in American Nature Writing,* he is currently at work on a study of genres of participation in nature.

David Sumner is a doctoral candidate and teaching fellow at the University of Oregon. He has taught courses in composition, American literature, and environmental literature. He has also taught experiential summer courses in both nature writing and fly fishing and literature. When he is not teaching or writing, he roams the Cascades with his wife, his children, and his fly rod. He just defended his dissertation, "Speaking a Word for Nature: Rhetoric, Ethics and American Nature Writing."

Christian Weisser is an Assistant Professor of English at the University of Hawaii (Hilo). He is coauthor of *Natural Discourse: Toward Ecocomposition* (with Sidney I. Dobrin) as well as several other articles dealing with ecocomposition, public writing, and public intellectualism. His work has appeared in *The Writing Instructor, Composition Forum, Teaching English in the Two Year College,* and other journals. Christian comes to ecocomposition through his interests in discourse, education, and coastal and marine environments. He is an active member in The Surfrider Foundation, The Cousteau Society, and the Reef Environmental Education Foundation.

Index